# THE HISTORY OF THE NORTH HARRIS MONTGOMERY COMMUNITY COLLEGE DISTRICT

## A Silver Anniversary Commemorative

Edited by

Theresa Kurk McGinley

ISBN: 0-9654999-7-9

Library of Congress Catalog Card Number: 98-66105

*Editor:*   Theresa Kurk McGinley
*Publisher:*   Ron Lammert
*Designer:*   Charles A. Newton, III

### Photo Sources

Allied Spring Bank
Elizabeth Battle, Aldine Independent School District
Elmer Beckendorf
W.E. Crozier
Drew Hazzlerigg
Houston Chronicle
Houston Metropolitan Research Center, Houston Public Library
The Humble Museum
Klein, Texas Historical Foundation
Marilyn Theiss Kron
North Harris College
NHMCCD, District Office
John M. Robinson
Tim Sadlon/TGS Photo
T.C. and Irene Stallones
Rebecca Tautenhahn Strack Stone
W. W. Thorne
Lessie Upchurch

# CONTENTS

*This book is made possible*
*by the generous contributions*
*of the following sponsors:*

**Mitchell Energy & Development Corporation
and The Woodlands Operating Company, LP**

**Mr. and Mrs. Michael C. Riddle
Riddle & Brazil, L.L.P., Attorneys at Law**

**Houston Lighting & Power Company**

# LETTER FROM THE CHANCELLOR

"Nothing happens unless first a dream."
- *Carl Sandburg*

## DREAMS ENVISIONED, DREAMS REALIZED

Imagine what north Houston was like in the 1950s — mostly rural farm land with very little commercial interest. Many of the farmers wanted to send their children to college so they could improve their livelihood and better their lives, but a university education was expensive and remote, and extra hands were needed to work the land. The dream of building a community college for the families of those farmers was born then, but it was only a dream.

In the 1970s, when the area began to boom, community leaders realized that education was central to their community's competitive success, and the voters agreed. The dream took flight and North Harris County College was born.

When the college opened its doors in fall 1973, founding President W.W. Thorne and his 15-member staff welcomed 613 students to the first classes, held at Aldine High School.

As we celebrate our 25th year, the dream has become a reality to nearly 290,000 students. Countless careers, families, businesses and lives have been improved through education. The achievements of our students prove that dreams come true.

North Harris Montgomery Community College District has grown into an 1,100-square-mile college district that serves 1.2 million north Houston residents. We are now the sixth-largest community college district in Texas with four colleges, five off-campus sites, nearly 22,000 credit students each semester, an additional 12,000 non-credit students, and The University Center — surpassing the founders' dreams many times.

But our mission today is the same as it was 25 years ago: NHMCCD is committed to delivering quality education close to home — where students can easily find credit and non-credit courses, quality faculty, career training, flexible schedules, academic advising and financial aid.

And a place to fulfill their dreams.

Cindy is a single mother of three who dropped out of high school when she got pregnant with her first child. She enrolled in a GED class and eventually earned an associate's degree. She is currently working on her bachelor's degree in computer technology. She has a great job. She owns her own home.

Carla's children were all grown, and she wanted to complete the education she began 20 years ago. She was intimidated about everything from trying to remember algebra to feeling odd about being the oldest student in class. With persistence, Carla has "aced" most of her classes and is now making plans to attend The University Center. Her children are most proud.

Rick joined the U.S. Marines right out of high school. He thought college was beyond his reach academically and financially. When his service was over, he signed on with North Harris College. He then received a full scholarship to the prestigious Baylor College of Medicine/Rice University Honors Pre-med Academy. He's now attending Texas A&M with his sights set on becoming a doctor.

These students never imagined what their dreams and an education would bring to their lives. NHMCCD takes people from where they now are to where they have never been before.

This Commemorative History is a celebration of our first 25 years. You will learn about the historical background of north Harris and Montgomery Counties, as well as the institutional history of each of our colleges. You'll meet our founders — dreamers who longed for a complete and thriving community. And you'll read about The University Center, a partnership that brings together all the opportunities higher education has to offer.

Although the first 25 years has come to an end, the community college dream hasn't dimmed because, like dreams, education is an ever-evolving, continuous, lifelong journey. And our commitment, like that of our founders, will continue to reflect George Bernard Shaw's immortal words: "Some men look at things the way they are and say, 'Why?' I dream of things that never were and say 'Why not?'"

**Dr. John E. Pickelman, Chancellor**

# FOREWORD

STATE OF TEXAS
OFFICE OF THE GOVERNOR

## by **Governor George W. Bush**

### *COMMUNITY COLLEGES: THE OIL OF THE 21ST CENTURY*

I like to think of community colleges as the oil of the 21st century. If they are tapped properly, they are a tremendous resource to Texans of all ages and backgrounds. There are a number of reasons why.

For one, community colleges serve a diverse population, from high school students not ready for college, to corporate executives trying to improve their knowledge of accounting. They offer degrees for those that need them, job training for those who want to learn a skill, and classes for those who just want to learn something new about art or Texas history.

Community colleges also are accessible, affordable, and available. They have earned their name by staying close to the community. There are numerous community college campuses that make education easy for those who want it.

Texas community colleges also offer one of the best educational bargains in the country, with tuition and fees well below the national average. And our community colleges have made themselves accessible by offering night classes for those with day jobs and day care for those with young children. In short, community colleges are helping people help themselves.

Another major reason community colleges are the oil of the 21st century is because they provide a market driven education. They have the flexibility to design educational programs which meet the needs of a particular industry or community. As technology changes, market change. Texas community colleges are helping ensure that our workers aren't left behind.

I support the special role of our community colleges. I urge all Texans to be lifelong learners. Reading is an important way to expand knowledge, explore ideas and enrich your life. Attending community college classes can help Texans gain a new skill or expand their appreciation for history and art.

I am a strong supporter of our community colleges, and encourage my fellow Texans to use the many resources they provide. Congratulations on the 25th Anniversary of North Harris Montgomery Community College District, and best wishes for continual success in providing educational excellence and service to the community.

*George W. Bush*

# ACKNOWLEDGMENTS

There are many individuals responsible for the production of the NHMCCD Commemorative History. I would like from the onset to thank all involved for their courtesy and assistance. The support received from the Chancellor, Dr. John E. Pickelman, and Dr. Sanford C. Shugart, the president of North Harris College, was most appreciated. The decision to start a Commemorative History Project of the college district, and provide sufficient time and support in order to conduct the necessary research and write the book, came exclusively from these two individuals. Their interest in the overall project fueled the desire to get it done in a relatively short period of time. Special thanks go to Dr. Roy Lazenby, President and CEO of the NHMCCD Foundation to secure sponsorship for the publication of this book, and to establish a 25th Anniversary Scholarship Fund with proceeds from the sale of the book for students to continue in their educational journey.

Words of appreciation extend to Governor George W. Bush of the State of Texas for his unwavering support of education, and his contribution of the Foreword.

The oral histories collected in interviews with North Harris County Junior College founder, W.W. Thorne; the original Board members—E.M. Wells, M.M. "Rusty" Morris, W.E. Crozier; charter administrators including first Chancellor, Dr. Joe Airola; charter faculty and staff members, provide important insight into the history and formation of the college district. These individuals generously donated their time and effort, several traveling long distance, to be part of this Commemorative History Project. Many contributed personal photographs, letters, and other historical records. The stories collected on the oral history tapes will preserve the history of the institution for future scholarship.

Thanks go to the independent school districts of Aldine, Spring, and Klein for allowing access into the archives, and providing information on local history. Elizabeth Battle of Aldine ISD was consulted on the history of the Aldine area. Dr. Diana Severance, chief historian of the Klein Historical Foundation, was generous with information on the Klein/Spring area, and provided several historical photographs of the local German community for inclusion in the book. Norma Wheat and Karen Parker of the public relations department of Spring ISD made available the archival collection on local history. Joan Link, former executive secretary to the late John Winship, provided information on the Spring superintendent who envisioned a community college for this area.

For local history, area descendants provided a wealth of information. John M. Robinson, of the founding family of Old Town Spring, was most generous in contributing firsthand information through personal interview, and sharing of historical photographs on Spring and Klein from his extensive personal collection. Rebecca Tautenhahn Strack Stone, of the pioneering family of Westfield, shared her family's long history through interview, documents and assorted historic photographs of the area. Lessie Upchurch, Tomball historian, donated historic photographs from her collection, and contributed to the local history for the Tomball chapter through personal interview.

Several area descendants were found at North Harris College. Theiss family members, including Marilyn Theiss Kron, Marvin and Aileen, gave an informative walking history tour of their father's land which is now North Harris College campus grounds. The Carl Theiss homestead, once a family truck farm, is located on Aldine-Westfield Road. Arlene Schultz, of the Schultz and Baumgartner family, provided much information on the Baumgartner farm located on Turkey Creek across Aldine-Westfield, as well as local history of the surrounding area. Gary Clark, of the pioneer Lemm family, enthusiastically shared familial history as well as natural descriptions of the local area.

Judy Crocker, vice president of Alamo Title Agency of Houston, graciously donated the title search for the first fifty years of the North Harris College land deed. In researching the county archives, Jim Yarbray, Deputy Clerk of the Harris County Clerk's Office in Houston, assisted this author in tracing portions of the college deed back one hundred years further, as well as locating town plats for the surrounding communities of Westfield, Spring, and Aldine. Carol Riggs and M. Johnson of the Texas Forestry Museum in Lufkin, assisted in providing research information on the local sawmills of the area.

In preparation for the writing of an institutional history, the archives of North Harris College's Learning Resource Center (LRC) and the Administrative District Office were openly made available for research. Cindy Seale Dial and Judy Stubblefield at the District Office were most helpful in researching the voluminous Board minutes. Charles Jones, former Director of the LRC at North Harris College, assisted in providing archival material and early photographs of the college. Drew Hazzlerigg, Media Supervisor of the LRC, photographed college grounds, area landmarks, and directed the many photo reproductions. Anne Douglass, and the reference librarians of the Texas Room, Houston Metropolitan Research Center of the Houston Public Library, assisted in locating archival information on the area, including the invaluable Schleuter collection of historic photographs depicting northern Harris County at the turn of the century.

In the course of my work, I have received the encouragement and counsel of many colleagues and friends. I am grateful to Marilyn D. Rhinehart, Division Head of Social Sciences at NHC when the project began, for her review of the entire manuscript, and initial recommendation that I take on the enormous task of Project Director, as well as historian. I am also grateful for the support of my family, which took an active interest in the overall research project and the production of this history.

Lastly, I would like to particularly thank all of the NHMCCD Commemorative History Team writers: Kathie S. Fulgham, Rebecca Tate, Nellie Thorogood, Geraldine Gallagher, Bill Law, Doug Boyd, Link Hullar, and Dean Wolfe. These talented authors willingly assumed the challenge of preparing a history of their own individual colleges, provided valuable suggestions, and were able to meet tight deadlines, enabling publication in time for the 25th Anniversary of the college district.

**T. McGinley**
Houston, Texas

# INTRODUCTION

The publication of this NHMCCD Commemorative History Book marks the twenty-fifth anniversary of the establishment of the first college district to serve residents in northern Harris County. North Harris County Junior College was created by the citizens of Aldine, Spring, and Humble school districts through an election held on October 7, 1972. This election was the result of a long campaign led by area school superintendents, board members, steering committee members, and local civic leaders who had envisioned the establishment of an institute of higher education north of Buffalo Bayou.

Although community colleges have been in existence since the turn of the century, their popularity as an institution of higher education is a modern phenomena, beginning at the conclusion of World War II. Similar to other urban centers, the movement to create a community college outside the city of Houston had begun in the postwar period. Millions of returning veterans, sponsored by the federal G.I. Bill, flooded university and college campuses, creating a real problem in the shortage of classrooms and instructors. The immediate advantages of a community college movement, supported by U.S. President Harry S. Truman, were that they would rectify an overloaded educational system and provide a myriad of opportunities for all citizens. The drive to establish North Harris College followed this national pattern. The founding fathers discussed the possibility of a community college in the postwar 1950s, at a time when the northern part of the county was still fairly rural with little commercial base. In the 1960s, there were actually several attempts begun by different groups to start a college in the area, but the first serious effort emanated from downtown Houston. This attempt was to consolidate the Greater Houston area by establishing an extensive thirteen-district Harris County system of community colleges. Based on the Dallas County Community College model, this early attempt surprisingly failed at the urban ballot box. Houston considered the outlying areas as too far away and too remote from the inner core. It is interesting to note that in the failed attempt, northern Harris County voters from Aldine, Spring, Klein, and Humble, overwhelmingly showed support for the establishment of a local college to serve their communities.

Once the momentum began to establish a community college in the northern part of the county, it was difficult to ignore. At civic meetings, and PTA meetings, the issue of establishing a community college was continually raised. Houstonians scoffed at the idea, considering northern Harris County as large tracts of undeveloped land, consisting of either farmland or forest, with little history. To the contrary, the surrounding communities of Aldine, Spring, Klein, Tomball, and Humble, have had a long and remarkable history revealing several periods of boom and bust, coinciding with changes in the economy and technology. The railroad connection, the timber industry, and the impact of oil, dramatically affected all four local communities. Further changes incurred during the land boom of the 1960s and early 1970s period, forever altered the original rural landscapes. One of the major prerogatives of the NHMCCD Commemorative History Book was to include a brief history of the local communities to provide background information on the areas that the college district serves. The inclusion of local history places the college district in a more thorough historical context. NHMCCD's several college campuses and satellite outreach centers provide an important reflection of the community and its needs.

The book begins with a history of North Harris College, the original and largest campus of the district. Founded in October 1972 via local election, the first college classes were temporarily held in area high schools beginning in 1973. Over 600 students enrolled for the first college courses at Aldine High School. The permanent new college campus, nestled in the woods of a 185 acre site, opened its doors in 1976. As the population of northern Harris County continued to rapidly grow, North Harris College likewise expanded. Several new campuses were added, creating an extensive multi-campus college district. In less than one decade's time, Kingwood College was established to serve students in bordering Montgomery County in the east, followed closely by Tomball College in the west.

The original three independent school districts of Aldine, Spring, and Humble, which had unified to establish the North Harris College system in 1972, were subsequently joined by five other districts including Tomball, New Caney, Conroe, Willis, and Splendora. Currently, the school districts are equally represented with four from northern Harris County and four from southern Montgomery County, reflected by the modern district title North Harris Montgomery Community College District. The newest college campus in the district is Montgomery College, located in The Woodlands master-planned community. Montgomery College opened in August of 1995, with a dedication by Governor George W. Bush. The premiere facility, The University Center, also located in The Woodlands, officially opened in January 1998. The University Center links the community college district with several senior level universities, such as Texas A&M. Students are provided with the opportunity to complete advanced degrees close to home.

Each college campus has a separate chapter in the book, written by its own representatives, contributing to the overall district history. A biographical chapter is included on the key founders of North Harris County Junior College. For simplicity's sake, the modern name, North Harris College, will be used throughout the book in reference to the original campus. The founders responsible for the establishment of the college were visionaries, educators and community leaders who recognized the need for an institution of higher learning to serve students in northern Harris County. Little did they anticipate the extensive multi-campus institution that North Harris was to become. Today, NHMCCD ranks as the sixth largest community college district in the state of Texas, encompassing an area of over 1,000 square miles. The district consists of four individual colleges serving northern Harris and Montgomery Counties, The University Center, several satellite centers such as Carver and Parkway, and an administrative center.

With the establishment of the district in 1972, North Harris College became the first community college to serve students in the rapidly growing suburban areas of northern Harris County. The permanent new campus site, located in the Aldine district, was selected in 1973. The campus was centered at approximately an hour's distance in either direction to the nearest senior universities, and particularly situated between the three adjoining school districts of Aldine, Spring, and Humble. At the time of purchase, the college site was heavily timbered in parts, with Turkey Creek running through the eastern boundary. Pine forest, prairie, or pastureland were dominant area features. This began to change as northern Houston experienced a land boom in the late 1960s-1970s period due in large part to the construction of a new Intercontinental Airport. The impact of Houston's Intercontinental Airport (today called George Bush Intercontinental) on the local economy was enormous, affecting local real estate and boosting commercial land development. The population swelled, as relocating families were attracted to the wooded northern areas of Harris County. Many new suburbs began, including the master-planned communities of Kingwood and The Woodlands. The first college president, W.W. Thorne, and the original Board members, aptly recognized the need for the expansion of the district in several different directions in order to better serve the increasing numbers of new students. The success of the college district, as revealed by its rapid growth, can be particularly credited to its sensitivity to both the communities and student needs. The multitude of programs offered in academic, technological fields, and enrichment courses, provide area residents and youth with unlimited opportunities for advancement.

The NHMCCD Commemorative History project was developed to document the formation of the college through the examination and preservation of historical record, which included the collection of oral or "living" histories. The founders of the college, including W.W. Thorne, Steering Committee members, the original Board of Trustees, charter administrators and faculty members, former students, were contacted for interviews. Although not all of the collected information appears in this book, the oral history tapes will be stored in the historical archives of North Harris College and available for future scholarship. The time restraints posed in the production of a commemorative history book, as well as the sheer number of individuals responsible for the college's success, prevented the writer's team from interviewing everyone involved in the formation of the college. Countless individuals have served to make the institution a success. The excitement of the early years is obvious in talking with select faculty and administrators. Charter members particularly recall being part of "one large family" working toward a common goal. The students felt it too, despite the fact that for the first few years North Harris College classes were held in area high schools while the permanent campus was built. The many sacrifices, the lack of space and privacy, the temporary facilities, did not deter the enthusiasm of the original group. Charter lists appear at the end of each individual college chapter identifying original members. The chapter on North Harris College will also include a list of students of the first graduating class.

The NHMCCD Commemorative History project began in earnest in the spring semester of 1996, upon approval from the Chancellor, Dr. John E. Pickelman, and the NHMCCD Board of Trustees. At that time, a research plan was drawn up, and individual writers were nominated, many by college presidents. Each of the writers was responsible for the production of a separate manuscript on the history of their individual colleges. These college histories provide background on the formation of the institution as well as a history of the community that it serves. The outlying northern areas of Aldine, Spring, Humble, Tomball, and The Woodlands of southern Montgomery County have fascinating histories of their own, typically and unfortunately overshadowed by the history of downtown Houston. Many readers will find the local histories quite interesting and informative. Longtime residents will appreciate the collection of lore, while new residents to the area will learn the history of the areas in which they now live. Several interviews were held with descendants of the area's founding families.

Twenty-five years ago, northern Harris County looked much different from the way it does today. The area was still rural in many respects, with vast patches of woods or pastureland located on either side of the narrow freeway. The products of truck and dairy farmers supplied the urban center of Houston. Corn, sweet potatoes, cabbage, and figs, were just some of the

local area crops. Today, few notice the old pecan groves located in the area. Fewer still remember the magnolia figs and orange groves that dotted Aldine. Modernity has erased many of these traces of the past. Greenspoint Mall and the surrounding business complexes were built on what was once pastureland. Grazing cows and horses could be seen from the freeway. Houston's Intercontinental Airport, located near Farm to Market Road (F.M.)1960, opened in 1969. Residents recall the airport area as marshland, and full of grain. Charter North Harris College board member, M.M. Morris, remembered that, "it rather amazed me when they decided to build an airport there. You could ride a horse and in some places bog the horse down to his belly..I didn't think you could pour enough concrete to support a big jet airplane."[1] Nonetheless, the construction of an international airport attracted a multitude of businesses and land developers to the area. Subdivisions grew in row after row along F.M. 1960 and elsewhere in response to relocating businessmen, particularly those involved in the oil industry. Oil is the foundation of Houston's wealth, with oil wells struck early in the century in nearby Humble, and then in Tomball. It is important to recall that by 1966, ten major natural gas companies maintained headquarters in Houston.[2] Natural gas storage fields and transcontinental pipelines were located within a one hundred mile radius of downtown Houston, with much of the oil rich land found in a corridor of northern Harris County. Many older area residents found their first jobs working on the pipeline. Even today, it is not uncommon to see cattle grazing near oil and gas storage tanks or gauges.

The land boom and subsequent population increase in northern Harris County directly affected the local school districts. The construction of new schools could not keep pace with the growing population. Not surprisingly, the drive for the establishment of a community college originated from two local area school superintendents, John Winship of the Spring independent school district, and W.W. Thorne of the larger district in Aldine. These two superintendents had early on recognized the need for a local institution of higher learning for the benefit of their high school graduates, as well as the local community. With the population growth incurred during the early 1970s, and with the public interest stirred from the failed earlier attempt, the time seemed right to organize a movement for the establishment of a community college. With the leadership and perseverance of particularly Aldine superintendent, W.W. Thorne, a community college drive was organized and brought to the determinate ballot box.

North Harris County College was long awaited by area residents. Despite the boom and bust cycles of the northern communities, citizens had expressed continual interest and support in the establishment of a community college. To many area residents, the University of Houston and Sam Houston State in Huntsville were located too far away, and the expense involved in both tuition and room and board, posed financial obstacles.

The formation of a college at the hands of the community in a truly grass roots movement, is an interesting success story. The drive to form a distinctly "people's" college was a response to a national trend in higher education that occurred after the war and especially promoted by U.S. president, Harry S. Truman. A farmer's son, Truman was denied the opportunity to complete his college education due to the lack of financial resources. This personal experience would shape his future domestic policy as it applied to education. In a report known as the Truman's Commission on Higher Education, community colleges were regarded foremost as "democratic" institutions, open to all students, and with a mission to serve a variety of needs from liberal arts to vocational training. Immediately after World War II, higher education was particularly affected by the passage of federal legislation providing veteran soldiers with the opportunity to complete their education. Many veterans, such as

founder W.W. Thorne, and several founding Board members, were recipients of this important benefit. The postwar G.I. Bill continues to be regarded as a landmark piece of legislation in the promotion of higher education. American military personnel, many who could not afford to continue their education past high school, were now encouraged to go back to school and train for new fields and hence opportunities in re-entering a changed workplace.

The latter part of the 1960s witnessed the greatest growth of community colleges nationwide. At that time, individual State Coordinating Boards of Higher Education were established in virtually every state of the union. The establishment of North Harris County College via the election of October 1972, was part of this overall national trend. As the population of northern Harris County continued to grow, the need for a community college became apparent to serve area needs. Students would be able to gain full college credit close to home, eliminating the expense of housing and tuition costs at senior level institutions.

The success of NHMCCD, as marked by a quarter century of service to the residents of northern Harris County and Montgomery County, is captured in the contents of this book. Reflecting on the past serves as a springboard for the future. As the latter chapters on "future stars" and The University Center reveal, the history of NHMCCD is far from complete, and a story far from over. The groundbreaking for the innovative University Center, the first in the state of Texas, ushers in an exciting new era for community colleges. One might correctly say, that today is just the beginning....

**Theresa McGinley**
Project Director and Editor

---

# NOTES

[1] M.M. Morris, Interview with author, 1996.

[2] David G. McComb, *Houston: A History* (Austin: University of Texas Press, 1969, 1981), p.129.

# THE FOUNDERS

### by Theresa Kurk McGinley

North Harris County College was created by the citizens of the Aldine, Spring, and Humble school districts on October 7, 1972, the date of a successful election that affirmed the need to provide accessible and affordable higher education to the residents of northern Harris County. The voters of these three areas, coordinated in their efforts by the leadership of Aldine superintendent, W.W. Thorne, had publicly expressed their support to create a junior college for the area. The election established the North Harris County Junior College District, and governance by the first seven members of the College Board of Trustees. A bond issue was passed allowing for the purchase of land, and the construction of a new college campus. North Harris College, an institution anticipated for nearly twenty years, became the first college of the new district to serve area residents.

With the passage of the election, the college scheduled classes almost immediately in local high schools while a permanent campus site was selected and built. In the interim, Aldine High School

*John A. Winship, superintendent of Spring Independent School District, promoted the movement to establish a community college in the area.*

served as the college's temporary home. The new campus of North Harris College opened its doors to the community in 1976. The 185-acre heavily wooded site was situated in an optimal location at the approximate geographic center of the three local school districts. Although October 7, 1972 marks the anniversary of the formation of the college district, the vision for a community college in the area occurred much earlier in the aftermath of World War II. The domestic changes incurred by the war, such as the increasing movement of the population into the suburbs, had permanently altered the rural nature of the surrounding landscape. The founders of the college were members of a generation affected to large degree by the impact of the war and the changes made to their own communities.

The founding of a college requires broad based community interest and support, involving countless people who sacrificed both time and effort to see their vision become a reality. The area's school superintendents and board members, many of whom served at the helm of the college's preparatory Steering Committee, local PTA members, community leaders and friends, all deserve recognition as being instrumental in the founding of North Harris College. In keeping with the overall philosophy of community colleges, North Harris College began as a people's college, serving the needs of area residents and youth.

Two school district superintendents deserve special recognition for their vision and leadership in the founding of an institute of higher education in northern Harris County. Both were dedicated educators who recognized the needs and concerns of their own students, and the local community. John A. Winship, superintendent of the Spring school district, was responsible for spearheading the campaign to establish a local community college. W.W. Thorne, superintendent of the Aldine school district, was the builder of the vision, and the key force behind the college drive. Thorne is held in high regard as the founder and first president of North Harris College, responsible for, amongst the myriad of administrative and political duties concerning the start up of a college, the detail work needed in the organization and construction of a permanent campus. In future planning, Thorne was also responsible for ushering in the multi-campus concept as the student population in the surrounding areas, such as Kingwood, continued to rapidly grow.

The initial drive to establish a community college in northern Harris County occurred during the 1950s. John Winship, superintendent of the Spring Independent School District, repeatedly expressed the need to establish an institution of higher learning to serve local students. Winship was reacting to the conditions of the postwar period in north Houston and elsewhere, and the disturbing statistics which revealed that a large percentage of the nation's high school students did not, or were unable to, continue their education past the secondary level. Several important factors, such as the lack of funding and accessibility, prevented particularly small town students from attending college. Postwar conditions were such that overcrowding in the existing universities and colleges meant rejection for new students who applied. The millions of returning veterans sponsored by the federal G.I. Bill compounded the situation but they too had difficulty attending the nation's colleges. Waiting lists were long due to the unavailability of space. Shortages affected every level of education. There was an immediate need for more teachers, and obviously, for more schools. The returning veterans were eager to make-up for the years spent at war, not only lost time, but more significantly, lost skills. Training was necessary for re-entry into a changed workplace. Year-round classes, evening school, and specialized programs were in serious demand. These conditions prompted Winship to meet with other area superintendents to discuss a potential solution.

In 1955, Winship called for a meeting of area superintendents in an ambitious attempt to consolidate the independent school districts of Cypress-Fairbanks, Klein, Tomball, Spring, Humble, Aldine, and Northeast Houston, in order to create a community college to serve the needs of area students. Winship recognized from a pragmatic standpoint that the establishment of a local college would not only provide the surrounding school districts with the opportunities of higher education, but also a much needed facility for vocational-technical training. A community college would provide affordable education in a variety of programs within the commuting distance of area residents. Through education and specific training, the opportunities for advancement and better jobs would increase. Winship believed that the programs offered by community colleges "are geared particularly to the needs of the community, and that's where... junior colleges have strength. It will be for this community and it will offer courses in job training for the people of the community.... The challenge of our junior colleges is to meet the needs of our new and complex society where more technicians are required, and that's really the whole reason to offer classes in a great variety of subjects and a great variety of time."[1] Although the 1955 meeting did not result in a formidable plan for the establishment of a college, it did reveal the interest of area superintendents in serving the educational needs of their communities beyond the high school level.

John A. Winship was born in Abilene, Texas on July 4, 1911, and moved to Houston at an early age. He graduated from Reagan High School and continued his education at the University of Houston, receiving a baccalaureate and master's degree. In 1939, Winship became superintendent of the Spring schools. At the time, Spring was recovering from the effects of the Great Depression, the most serious of which was the relocation of the town's lifeblood, the railroad industry, to downtown Houston. Spring remained a small rural community consisting of the vast lands of produce (truck) and dairy farmers. An early progressive civic association, the Houston North Association, described the locale in the following way, "The two best revenue producing industries in the area were tomatoes and turkeys... (it) was primarily an agricultural area."[2] However, the area began to rapidly change after World War II, as the economy recovered and veterans returned home. Beginning in the 1950s, suburbs began to appear in every direction outside the urban center of Houston, encroaching far into the northern communities. The Houston metropolis was rapidly changing, and in sprawling fashion. In a report prepared by Rayford Kay, Harris County Agricultural Extension Agent, it was noted that in 1960, seventy-one percent of Harris County was agricultural land. By 1974, that percentage had fallen to forty-four percent and continued to decline. Kay said that "the sounds of the country, tractors grinding in the fields, cattle lowing as they head for the barn, have been drowned out by the roar of bulldozers clearing away acres of trees (pasture and farmland) for shopping centers...."[3] F.M. 1960 was a new road in the 1950s, though its name continues to reflect its agricultural "farm-to-market" nature. W.W. Thorne remembers F.M.1960 as a "two-lane blacktop road that ran from Humble to Waller."[4] And according to E. M. Wells, former Spring ISD board member, "I always told everybody that when I moved out there I could look up and down Jackrabbit Road and every fifteen minutes I might see a car... now I pull up to 1960 and look both ways and maybe can get on it in fifteen minutes."[5]

E.M. Wells became chairman of the college's preparatory Steering Committee, and the first president of the North Harris College Board of Trustees. Recalling the many years that he worked with Spring ISD superintendent John Winship, Wells said, "He was a real fine superintendent. When Spring was in its infancy, he would coach, he would teach, he would do everything that needed to be done out there... for he was dedicated to the school system."[6]

Winship served as superintendent of Spring schools for thirty-four years, from 1939 until his death in 1973. He witnessed the transition of the Spring school district from "a rural community district with one school building housing all grades (with 11 teachers) to a suburban school district made up of one high school, two intermediate schools, and four elementary schools… with enrollment standing at 4700 students."[7] Winship also witnessed the desegregation of public schools, and specifically assisted in the integration of Spring schools. The oldest school serving black students in the Spring area was the Southwell School, operating from approximately 1910 until integration in 1966. B.F. Clark, the last principal of the Southwell School, credits John Winship for providing employment for all of the displaced faculty members from the Southwell School when it closed.[8]

Throughout the 1950s, Winship continued to express interest in the establishment of a community college for the area. However, the financial support necessary to maintain an institution of higher education was lacking. Spring was a residential/rural community with little commercial base. In comparison, the largest school district in the area, Aldine ISD, became financially bankrupt in 1958, and Aldine schools were closed for a brief period of time as Aldine ISD was unable to pay teacher salaries. Thus, during the 1950s, the timing was not quite right to pursue the establishment of a junior college in the area. But the movement itself never died. As the area and the economy continued to change, John Winship kept bringing the topic up for discussion at meetings with the other superintendents, and board members. Community leaders would raise the matter at area business and civic meetings. Residents would periodically ask "when are we going to get a junior college?"[9] According to the minutes of the Houston North Association, the discussions on the need for a college in the area resulted in the formation of an education committee to study the proposal, a committee on which W.W. Thorne served.

W.W. Thorne, area civic leader and former superintendent of Aldine schools, is regarded as the key founder of North Harris College. A native Houstonian, Thorne was to experience two major historical events that affected the United States in the twentieth century- the Great Depression and World War II. During the depression years, Thorne's family had temporar-

ily worked as sharecroppers in the fields of East Texas. A drought however, had ruined the chance for even meager earnings, forcing the family to return to the Houston area. Thorne graduated from Jeff Davis High School, but any further educational plans were interrupted when the United States became embroiled in World War II. At the conclusion of the war, and upon discharge from the U.S. Navy, Thorne eventually received both his baccalaureate and master's degree from the University of Houston. Thorne became known in the area as a longtime leader in the field of education, heading the Aldine Independent School District for over twenty years.

The experiences of World War II profoundly affected Thorne's future in education. During the war, Thorne served three years in the U.S. Navy as a radar operator aboard the U.S.S. New Orleans, a highly decorated vessel in the Pacific fleet.[10] As a returning naval veteran, Thorne experienced firsthand the effects of postwar federal legislation, particularly through the passage of the G.I. Bill. The G.I. Bill provided veterans with the benefit of higher education, and consequently, caused an educational boom throughout the nation. Thorne credits the G.I. Bill for providing him with the opportunity to complete his education. He recalls, "it was probably the greatest program that the Government ever came up with. I would have not been able to go to college had it not been for the G.I. Bill. The G.I. Bill for a married veteran paid for tuition and the books."[11] At the time, the University of Houston was still a privately supported institution, charging high tuition rates that few could afford. The G.I. Bill provided many veterans like Thorne with the benefit of receiving a college education.

In the postwar period, Houston as a community experienced population growth while still rebounding from war-induced rationing and shortages. Shortages existed of every kind, from food and clothing to housing. Returning veterans crowded the nation's cities and school facilities trying to catch up on the years spent at war. Lack of housing at the University of Houston resulted in many G.I. veterans with families living "in trailers and shacks near the campus" as they completed their degrees.[12] The University had no dormitories at the time. M.M. "Rusty"

Morris, a returning U.S. Army Air Corps veteran and one of the original members of the Board of Trustees of North Harris College, recalls that the University of Houston resembled an "old fashioned mobile home park… In one part of the village were single people and the other part married… You had a waiting list of people to get in there."[13] The postwar problems experienced by the nation's institutions of higher education directly contributed to the growth of community colleges.

President Harry S. Truman had a profound interest in the nation's higher education due to several factors, including personal experience. Truman himself had been denied the opportunity to attend college and complete his education because of the lack of funds. Raised on a farm in Missouri, Truman's small town upbringing was a direct contrast to the Ivy League presidency of Franklin D. Roosevelt. Denied an education beyond high school, Truman was particularly disturbed by the exclusiveness of the nation's many universities and the lack of availability of higher education to the citizens of small towns. Personal experience notwithstanding, the actual catalyst for educational reform was the war itself.

The lingering effects of World War II and the fight against the anti-democratic forces of Nazism and then communism, resulted in the intensification of democracy at home. The postwar world was a time of serious reflection. The changes in foreign policy, the threat of the Soviet Union, the fear ushered in by the atomic age, had redefined the way Americans looked at themselves and the world. Both foreign and domestic policies were directed against the spread of communism. Cold War ideology translated into strengthening our democracy at home, including several important federal initiatives towards educational reform. The postwar emphasis was particularly geared toward the fields of science and technology. As a consequence, higher education was pressed with new responsibilities but lacked the necessary resources.

At the conclusion of the war, Truman attempted to remedy these problems by launching a thorough investigation of higher education. A Presidential Commission on Higher Education, also known as the Truman Commission, was formed to study the problem

and provide some solution. The President's Commission prepared a voluminous study of higher education in the United States. The resulting "Report on Higher Education," published in 1947, revealed that "American colleges and universities face the need both for improving the performance of their traditional tasks and for assuming new tasks created for them by the new internal conditions and external relations under which the American people are striving to live and to grow as free people."[14] The Commission also sought to restructure the nation's higher education system by providing equal opportunity to all citizens. Most significantly, the report revealed an overwhelming support for the nation's fledgling community colleges. Serving all citizens, the community college would provide accessible and affordable education, in contrast to the exclusiveness of the ivory towers. This heightened democratic philosophy, combined with the effects of the G.I. Bill, spurred a national movement in educational reform.

The postwar period of the 1950s affected all Americans as it was a time of unparalleled economic growth and prosperity. Houston and the outlying areas were part of this national trend. The growth of the suburbs and the baby boom all contributed to a new affluence that erased the era of the depression. In education, however, an immediate shortage of both teachers and schools confronted citizens. Local school districts felt the greatest brunt, as student populations continued to increase while resources seriously lagged behind.

Upon graduation from the University of Houston, W.W. Thorne began teaching in the Aldine schools. He became superintendent of Aldine ISD in 1958 when the Aldine school system faced literal bankruptcy. Thorne recalls that although the drive for a community college in northern Harris County began at this time, the problems of the postwar period in education did not yet warrant the development of a community college. According to Thorne, "Aldine had a scholastic population of about 10,000 students. We were growing by about ten percent a year. There was not a bank, not a chamber of commerce, not a city club, not a newspaper. The only commercial establishments in the district included gas stations and grocery stores. We had some produce farmers, we had some dairy farmers, and we had open land. Lots of kids, and very little taxes. And the community, financially, could not afford to support a junior college. It had difficulty supporting the public schools. In fact, a taxpayer's association gained control of the school board and literally shut the schools down. It ran out of money and the schools were closed for it."[15]

Thorne was studying school law at the University of Houston at this time, a class which would provide the solution to Aldine's financial problems. Despite a professor's initial skepticism, Thorne revised an old time warrant bill to fit the needs of the Aldine school district, and presented it to representatives at the State Capitol in Austin. The bill was simultaneously presented to the Texas State House of Representatives and the Senate; and signed by Governor Price Daniel the same day.[16] The passage of the time warrant bill allowed Aldine schools to stay open, as it would be used primarily to pay teacher salaries. $200,00 worth of time warrants were sold door-to-door to members of the local community in denominations as little as $100.[17] The drive and determination to save the Aldine schools had important consequences. Thorne remained superintendent of the Aldine schools for the next twenty years, before assuming the presidency of North Harris College in 1973.

By the 1960s, the northern area had undergone dramatic change from a remote rural setting to a suburban one. The land boom that occurred in the late 1960s was a result of several factors. The construction of an intercontinental airport in northern Harris County and plans for a new mall at Greenspoint attracted land speculators and businesses to the area. The heavily timbered northern area was also attractive to corporate families who relocated from out of state. The proximity to downtown Houston was less than twenty miles, conducive to the establishment of new communities for commuters. Vast tracts of undeveloped land were relatively inexpensive to obtain, and highly coveted along the interstate freeway and Farm-to-Market 1960. The population of northwestern Harris County began to rapidly grow as the building boom transformed the rural landscape.

At the state level, the regulated development of community colleges in Texas occurred during the 1960s, coinciding with the state's population increase, and the motivation of the governor. Under the advisement of Governor John Connally, a formal study was conducted on "Education beyond High School" examining higher education in Texas. The study resulted in the creation of the Coordinating Board of Higher Education in 1965, with a mandate to "provide leadership and coordination for the Texas higher education system, and institutions and governing boards, to the end that the state of Texas may achieve excellence for college education for its youth."[18] The Coordinating Board, consisting of eighteen appointed members, became responsible for a master plan regulating college programs and development in the state of Texas.

Prior to the establishment of the Coordinating Board, community colleges in Texas fell under the jurisdiction of the Texas Education Agency, which regulated secondary school education. This important transfer to supervision by the Coordinating Board officially severed the connection of community colleges from high schools. The transfer to the collegiate level also allowed for an increase in state funding, as the state particularly encouraged the development of specialized technical and vocational programs, areas which senior institutions generally did not offer. Community colleges therefore, assumed a unique purpose which differed from the traditional junior college role. Junior colleges were two-year colleges that specifically provided academic programs to prepare students for transfer to the senior institutions. Community colleges, in contrast, were more comprehensive in scope and diverse in the programs offered. Traditional academic classes were held, plus offerings in technical/vocational training, and continuing education. The variety of programs were particularly geared to the interests and needs of the community, and made community colleges a popular choice for many area students. Though community colleges had been in existence since the turn of the century, their popularity as an institution of higher education was a modern phenomena.

In 1966, encouraged by state reform and local interest, John Winship once again promoted the idea of a community college to area school superintendents and board members, this time requesting that a detailed study be prepared at the University of Houston. Winship approached a graduate education class at the university to prepare a feasibility study on the establishment of a college in northern Harris County as a class project.[19] Population figures were drawn up and overall evaluations conducted to determine if the local community could support a college. The studies were favorable.

Community support for the establishment of a new college had long been gained from several area business groups. Civic associations, such as the Houston North Association and the Tomball Good Roads Committee, had actively promoted the commercial development of northern Harris County. Minutes from the Houston North Association contained several references to studies on the creation of a local college. John Winship's feasibility study was presented to the board of this association, including "the steps that may be taken in order to have a junior college built in the district."[20]

W.W. Thorne's interest in the project was such that the group appointed him chairman of the Education Research Committee. In 1966, the Houston North Association prepared an official resolution in support of a local college stating that "We propose that this association officially go on record favoring the eventual establishment of a Junior College to serve the north Harris County area."[21] Both W.W. Thorne of Aldine and Roy Hohl of Tomball served on the Board of Directors of the Houston North Association. The Tomball Good Roads Committee meeting in 1958, which Roy Hohl headed, had earlier discussed the creation of a junior college for the area. Hohl would become a member of North Harris College's Board of Trustees.

In 1968, a major proposal appeared from downtown Houston for the establishment of a Greater Houston Community Junior College, an extensive countywide community college system patterned after one established in Dallas. This system would include the entire Greater Houston area, consisting of thirteen school districts and extending far into northern Harris County. The earlier push for an independent college to the city's north was temporarily shelved, as northern Harris County rallied behind the new and larger effort. Support for a county-wide system was present in the suburban school districts of northern Harris County which stood to gain a college cam-

pus, but the election miserably failed in the city of Houston.[22] Only twelve percent of the eligible voters turned out to vote. The defeat of the county-wide proposal prompted the northern Harris County school superintendents to act on their own. The drive for an independent community college in northern Harris County, which had started off and on for the past several years, had now gained a new momentum. According to W.W. Thorne, "In 1969 or 70, John Winship and I and some schools from Humble had met and began to say now maybe it's time we started talking about a junior college. Maybe we really could do it now..."[23] The conditions were ideal.

Community interest had been generated by the publicity of the countywide proposal, and frustrated by its subsequent defeat. Northern voters in the school districts of Aldine, Spring and Klein had rallied behind the countywide effort. The failure of the election in Houston only heightened the desire to establish a college of their own to serve northern Harris County needs. A rapid population increase in the suburbs added fervor to the drive.

After several attempts to start a junior college in the area, particularly the failed effort in 1968 to establish a Greater Houston Community College, an executive meeting of representatives from the local school districts was scheduled for October 26, 1971. W.W. Thorne invited the superintendents and district officials of Spring, Humble and Klein ISD to meet at Aldine High School to "discuss the desirability of beginning a study looking toward the possibility of the formation of a union junior college district comprised of the four school districts."[24] The meeting was well attended. Nine school district officials were in attendance from Spring ISD, eight from Klein, eight from Aldine, and three from Humble.[25] It was the unanimous decision of those present to pursue the study looking toward the establishment of a junior college district. This executive meeting resulted in the creation of a Steering Committee consisting of one representative from each of the separate school boards of trustees, two lay citizens, and the superintendent of each district. It was also at this meeting that John Winship recommended that W.W. Thorne act as temporary chairman of the Junior College Study Committee until the Steering Committee could elect permanent officers.[26]

*Roy Hohl, Tomball business and civic leader, accompanied by Jack Frey (right), pushed for legislative reform to allow the inclusion of Tomball into the North Harris County Junior College District.*

The Steering Committee was instrumental in providing the leadership and organization necessary to establish a community college in northern Harris County. Data needed to be collected and reports drawn to present to the State Coordinating Board. Spring ISD board member, E.M. Wells was elected chairman of the Steering Committee, nominated by Spring superintendent, John Winship. Mrs. Louise Panzarella, who proudly recalls serving as the "first woman board member of Humble ISD," served as secretary.[27] The four superintendents of Aldine, Spring, Humble and Klein served as ex-officio members of the Steering Committee. Members representing Aldine on the committee were: Superintendent W.W. Thorne, Floyd Hoffman,

Mrs. Nancy Reeder and Rev. Jack Armstrong. Representing Humble were: Superintendent George Turner; Mrs. Louise Panzarella, Charles Philipp, and Quinn McWhirter. For Klein ISD were: Superintendent Donald Collins, Don Edwards, Freeman Marburger, and Roy Partin. And from Spring ISD were: Superintendent John Winship, E.M. Wells, B.R. Haught, and H.J. Doering.

The group established a Survey Committee, chaired by Floyd Hoffman of Aldine, to study projected enrollment figures, as well as the tax and financing structure of the proposed district.[28] To provide some idea of the size of these school districts in 1969-70, excerpts from the Tax Research Association reveal that at the time Aldine served 19,234 students in average daily attendance; Spring — 1,583; Humble — 2,202; Klein — 2,025; and Tomball — 1,266.[29] Further studies indicated that more than half of the area's high school graduates, "in some instances as many as 60%, stop[ped] their education at the end of high school."[30] This latter disturbing statistic revealed the need, and therefore the intensive drive launched by area superintendents and school board members to establish a college in the area, bringing upper level education courses within the reach of everyone.

In June 1972, Thorne brought the case before members of the State Coordinating Board and the local community. At a Public Hearing on the proposed North Harris County Junior College District, Thorne said, "It bothers me tremendously that about sixty percent of our young people terminate their education at high school. The cost of education is a major factor in this situation. I'm convinced that if we have a community college close at hand, more youngsters can stay at home and be at the entrance to the college in fifteen minutes. To create that, a college can be located that is close to our needs... I'm convinced that if this program is approved by our application for a community college, we'll see that the voters approve it.... It will be the biggest step forward in the education of boys and girls for North Harris County in my lifetime."[31]

The Steering Committee spent one full year compiling data in compliance with the requirements set by the Texas Education Agency and the Coordinating Board of Higher Education. These requirements included appointing a survey committee to prepare an extensive study and feasibility report, launching a petition drive in the contiguous school districts, gaining approval from the TEA, the county, and the state, to hold an election, and lastly, conducting the determinate election itself which would poll the local citizenry. The Chairman of the Steering Committee, E.M. Wells of Spring, recalled the success of the petition campaign, stating that "the first thing we had to do was get ten percent of the voters to sign and we ended up with twenty percent of the voters signing the petition to create a junior college… (it was) then we petitioned the TEA."[32] The petitions revealed the popularity of the idea of a local community college in northern Harris County, particularly in the larger area of Aldine. The superintendents, such as Thorne, had worked closely with the local Parent Teacher Association (PTA) to generate support for the establishment of a college. PTA members of the Aldine school district were reported to have carried the petitions door to door. In the end, the total number of petition signatures acquired was double the mandatory number needed to hold an election. The first hurdle of the process had been taken. With the election scheduled for the fall, a telephone bank was created and campaign brochures entitled "Our Next Big Step" were printed, courtesy of Aldine ISD. Just before the scheduled election date, the Klein school district abruptly withdrew, leaving Aldine, Spring and Humble ISD to continue the drive on their own.

The withdrawal of Klein catapulted Tomball ISD out of the proposed college district picture, at least temporarily. Tomball supporters had been part of the discussions for the college from the onset, as evidenced by the Tomball Good Roads Committee and the work of Roy Hohl. However, Tomball's participation in the establishment of a new junior college district with Spring, Aldine, and Humble ISD, could only be attained if the adjoining school district, Klein, joined. Due to legislative restrictions from the Texas Education Agency, only contiguous school districts could join to form a new college district. The boundary lines of Klein ISD separated Tomball from Spring. At the time, Klein could not become part of the college district, eliminating Tomball from the original group. Klein ISD, though actively involved in the college's Steering

Committee process, withdrew at the final hour due to an unfavorable "straw vote" poll. This action forced Tomball, one of the earliest supporters for the formation of the college, to be excluded from the founding ISD members. Tomball's exclusion from the new college district meant that the community would not be allowed to join until either Klein ISD reconsidered, or state legislation was reformed. Area leaders, particularly Roy Hohl of Tomball, assumed the task of legislative reform. Hohl and others, including Aldine's W.W. Thorne, eventually succeeded in pushing for the elimination of the restrictive passages of legislation calling for contiguous alliance as they applied to Tomball. Fondly referred to as the "Tomball Bill," Tomball joined the North Harris College district in 1982. The Tomball Bill made Tomball the only independent school district in Texas to become a non-contiguous member of a junior college. According to Roy Hohl, that fact is "extremely significant to the Tomball community."[33]

The establishment of North Harris County Junior College occurred through the successful election held October 7, 1972 that revealed the overwhelming approval of the local citizenry of the Aldine, Spring, and Humble school districts. North Harris County Junior College became the first institution of higher education in northern Harris County. It was applauded and promoted as the "biggest bargain in education today."[34] Congratulatory letters were received from members of the State Coordinating Board in Austin, as well as from area community college presidents. With the successful election, a new college district was formed in northern Harris County, a tax rate was authorized, $6.5 million in bonds were secured, which allowed for the immediate construction of a college campus, and the first seven-member North Harris College Board of Trustees were elected by area voters.

The first Board members of the new college district were representatives of the area school boards and the community at large. Several were veterans of World War II. Two had served as officers on the college's executive Steering Committee. E.M. Wells of Spring ISD was elected the first president of North Harris County College's Board of Trustees. Wells had served as chairman of the college's Steering Committee and previously as president of the Spring ISD

*Charter members of the North Harris County Junior College Board of Trustees. Front row, left to right: W.E. Crozier, Assistant Secretary; E.M. Wells, President; Lawrence Adams, Secretary; Charles W. Philipp, Vice President. Second row, left to right: M.M. Morris, Hugh E. Dugan, H.J. Doering.*

school board, serving in close association with superintendent John Winship. Charles Philipp of Humble, served as co-chairman of the Steering Committee. Philipp was a former member of the Harris County Board of Education, and president of the Humble Chamber of Commerce. M.M. "Rusty" Morris was former president of the Aldine ISD School Board, and a U.S. Army Air Corps veteran. Hugh E. Dugan served as a board member of Humble ISD. Henry J. Doering worked for the U.S. Postal Service in Spring. W.E. Crozier was the Vice President of Liberty Savings Association, and a resident of Aldine. Crozier had served during World War II as a cryptographer for Supreme Headquarters of the Allied Expeditionary Force (SHAEF).[35] Lawrence Adams was the Vice President of Peden Industries and also a resident of Aldine.[36]

With the election of these seven men, the first trustees for North Harris College, the momentum immediately began to get things moving underway and quickly. With the college

district established in the fall of 1972, classes were expected to begin in 1973. That left only a few months time to hire administrators and faculty needed to start a college from the ground up. The leadership and dedication of the founding Board ensured that the new college would meet the needs of the surrounding community. Immediate tasks included the formation of committees to select a college president, and a site for the construction of a permanent new campus. The enthusiasm of the first college Board president E.M. Wells and the original Board of Trustees can only be paralleled with that of the first group of administrators, faculty, and staff.

In December 1972, the Board selected W.W. Thorne, as the first president of North Harris College from an applicant pool of approximately twenty candidates. Thorne allowed the college Board of Trustees to continue meeting at Aldine High School until another facility could be found. Aldine High School also housed the first college classes, to be held each day after hours until a permanent campus was built. Aldine H.S. served as the temporary home of North Harris College until the new campus opened in 1976. Temporary facilities were also provided by the area high schools of Spring and Humble, as well as the base in Aldine. This allowed college classes to be held almost immediately, serving area residents beginning in June of 1973. John Winship, the longtime superintendent of Spring ISD, died in April, having witnessed the successful election and the birth of his enduring vision, the establishment of a community college to serve local students and residents north of Buffalo Bayou. In memory of John Winship's role in the founding of the college, one of the first buildings to be erected at the permanent campus site, bore the Winship name. The Winship Building became the center of Science and Technology.

The founding of a "people's college" north of downtown Houston occurred through the determination and drive of many individuals. The community's interests and needs, as reflected by the area school superintendents such as Winship and Thorne, were served well through the establishment of the first college in the area. The popularity of northern Harris County in the 1970s resulted in rapid population growth, and the expansion of commerce and industry. Throughout its existence, the district has been continually challenged with meeting the needs of a growing community. In twenty-five years, the community college district has dramatically changed from one original campus serving the communities of Aldine, Spring, and Humble, into a multi-campus system serving a variety of outlying communities and extending throughout northern Harris County and into Montgomery County. Kingwood College in the east, Tomball in the west, and Montgomery in the north, all have permanent new campuses of their own, as well as outreach satellite centers. The student population has significantly grown from the initial 613 students in 1973. As the district commemorates its twenty-fifth anniversary, statistics reveal the enrollment of approximately 30,000 total credit and non-credit students in the fall semester of 1997. The vision of the original founders, and the continuance of the original mission to serve the needs of the community, resulted in the successful creation of an extensive and comprehensive college system, serving residents throughout the northern Houston area.

## NOTES

[1] John Winship, "Public Hearing on the Proposed North Harris County Junior College District," June 20, 1972. This meeting was attended by members of the Texas State Coordinating Board of Higher Education, the North Harris County College Steering Committee, and members of the community.

[2] Houston North Association, "History of Houston North," *Minutes of Meeting*, November 19, 1971. NHC archives. Mr. Ben Goolsby, member of the Houston North Association Board of Directors, made this presentation.

[3] *Houston Chronicle*, September 13, 1979. As cited in Marilyn D. Rhinehart, "Country to City: North Harris County College and the Changing Scene in Gulf Coast Texas," *The Houston Review*, Winter 1982.

[4] W.W. Thorne, interview with author, Houston, 1996.

[5] E.M. Wells, interview with author, Houston, 1996.

[6] Ibid.

[7] *North Harris County News*, "Thousands Mourn Passing of Superintendent John Allen Winship," May 2, 1973. Courtesy of Joan Link.

[8] Principal B.F. Clark, "The History of Southwell, The Spring School For Black Students," unpublished report, Spring ISD archives. B.F. Clark, interview with author, 1997.

[9] W.W. Thorne, interview with author, 1996. E.M. Wells, interview with author, 1996.

[10] The U.S.S. New Orleans attained 17 battle stars during World War II.

[11] Thorne, interview with author, 1996.

[12] Marguerite Johnston, *Houston, The Unknown City, 1836-1946* (Texas A & M Press, 1991), p.392.

[13] M.M. "Rusty" Morris, interview with author, Houston, 1996.

[14] President's Commission on Higher Education, *For American Democracy, A Report of the President's Commission on Higher Education* (New York: Harper & Brothers, 1947), Volume One, pp.2-3.

[15] Thorne, interview with author, 1996.

[16] Ina Bott, "Thorne, Aldine Citizens Helped Bring School District Back From Bankruptcy," *North Freeway Leader*, May 7, 1977.

[17] Ibid.

[18] Dale F. Campbell, "Texas," as found in Ben Fountain and Terrence A. Tollefson, ed., *Community Colleges in the United States: Forty-Nine State Systems* (American Association of Community and Junior Colleges, Washington, D.C., 1989), p. 218.

[19] Elemer Bertelsen, "Dream of Junior College For Northside Coming True," *Houston Chronicle*, June 17, 1973.

[20] Houston North Association, Director's Meeting, *Minutes*, October 29, 1965. The Education Committee for the establishment of a junior college district was created at this meeting. Each of the four local school districts was represented.

[21] Houston North Association, *Minutes*, January 28, 1966.

[22] Thorne, interview with author, 1996; Greater Houston Community Junior College Commission, Local Survey Report, 1968. NHC archives.

[23] W.W. Thorne, interview with author, 1996.

[24] Junior College Study Committee, *Minutes*, October 26, 1971.

[25] Due to a conflict in schedule, the superintendent and several board members from Humble ISD could not attend the first meeting.

[26] Junior College Study Committee, October 26, 1971.

[27] Louise Panzarella, interview with author, 1996.

[28] Junior College Steering Committee, *Minutes of Meeting*, December 9, 1971. *Houston Post*, "Report on New College Ready," December 30, 1971.

[29] Figures are drawn from a July 1971 report by the Tax Research Association on public schools in Harris County, as cited in *Houston Post*, "At Schools, Money Talks," December 25, 1971.

[30] Junior College Steering Committee, "Junior College Fact Sheet," 1971. Courtesy of E.M. Wells. Refer also to Truman Commission Report.

[31] W.W. Thorne, "Public Hearing on Proposed North Harris County Junior College District," held at Aldine ISD Administration, June 20, 1972. NHC archives.

[32] E.M. Wells, interview with author, 1996.

[33] *The News*, January 13, 1982.

[34] Junior College Steering Committee, campaign brochure, "Our Next Big Step," 1971. NHC archives.

[35] W. E. Crozier, interview with author, 1996.

[36] Junior College Steering Committee, "Our Next Big Step," 1971.

[37] Junior College Study Committee (Executive), *Minutes*, October 26, 1971. NHC archives.

[38] North Harris County Junior College Committee, Steering Committee, Local Survey Report, July 21, 1972.

# THE HISTORY
# OF NORTH HARRIS COLLEGE

*The Land, The People, The College*

by Theresa Kurk McGinley

*"Be the good Lord willing, if our luck holds and the creek don't rise,*
*we will have a junior college in North Harris County this fall."*[1]
-W.W. Thorne,1972

races of the dense loblolly pine forest that once dominated northern Harris County still exist on the campus of North Harris College. The campus land, bound on the east by Turkey Creek, totaled at purchase 185 acres. It was considered then a remote wooded site located twenty miles north of downtown Houston. The land was purchased in 1973 from a group of investors collectively known as the Turkey Creek Ranch Company. The site was chosen due its geographic location as the approximate center between the three school districts responsible for its creation: Aldine, Spring, and Humble ISDs. At the time of purchase, the heavily wooded tract had no access road other than rural Aldine-Westfield. Nearby Farm-to-Market (F.M.)1960 was also a two-lane road, referred to by locals as Jackrabbit Road. The closest subdivision was Memorial Hills, and the closest shopping area was Northline Mall. The Greenspoint area was not developed until the mid-

*North Harris College, the first and largest campus of NHMCCD, opened its permanent new facility off Aldine-Westfield in 1976.*

*Dr. McGinley is professor of history at North Harris College, and serves as the Project Director and Editor of the NHMCCD Commemorative History.*

*Northern Harris County was a rural area of dairy and truck farms.*
COURTESY: ELMER BECKENDORF

1970s land boom, prior to which the land was predominantly in use as pasture. The history of North Harris College begins with a history of the surrounding communities, as one is rooted in the other.

Northern Harris County has been described as the wilderness, full of timber, prairie, agriculture, rural farms or pastureland far removed from the sprawling downtown core of the city of Houston. At one time, the creeks near the piney woods held an abundance of game and wildlife-including wild turkey and white-tailed deer. Bald eagles were seen in the winter months as they annually migrated from the north, following other wintering birds, and feeding from the many local tributaries including Turkey, Spring, and Cypress Creeks.[2] Area farming families recall Aldine-Westfield as a shell road connecting several agricultural communities. The major crossroads was Bammel Road, serving as the east-west thoroughfare until replaced by Farm-to-Market 1960. The local area abounded in farms of all types, particularly family truck farms and dairies. On and near college grounds extending from the Aldine area, Westfield, and into Spring, were generations of German farmers and dairymen living off the land. The history of the surrounding areas is rich in culture and lore, rapidly changing and often overlooked as time and progress erase the original landscape.

Historically, the Houston area and northern Harris County were originally part of Stephen F. Austin's colonization attempts of Texas, begin-

ning with the legendary Old Three Hundred families that settled in the 1820s. With permission gained from the Mexican government, Texas land was parceled into large tracts consisting of one league (4,428 acres) set aside for cattle ranching, and one labor of land (177 acres) set aside for farming. Most of the early settlers sought land parcels along the creekbeds, and early colonization maps show the largest parcels being alongside the area's rivers, creeks, and bayous. Austin's colonization efforts in northern Harris County are revealed in the familiar names of Frederick Rankin, and David Harris (brother to John Harris for whom the county is named), members of the Old Three Hundred families to settle in Texas.[3] The Kuykendahl brothers also received land grants to the area during this early period. One of the largest land grants, five leagues of land, was awarded to a former Mexican official, Victor Blanco in 1831. This large parcel of land extended from the present-day George Bush Intercontinental Airport east through Highway 59 in Humble. During the Texas Revolution of 1836, the pivotal Battle of San Jacinto occurred just south of Houston. It was here that Texas commander, General Sam Houston defeated the Mexican Army under General Antonio Lopez de Santa Anna, and secured the independence of Texas. In preparation for this final battle of the revolution, General Houston marched his troops from New Kentucky near Tomball, crossing Spring Creek in his descent toward San Jacinto.[4] The city of Houston was then founded by two New York brothers, John and Augustus Allen, who shrewdly named their new town after the hero of the Battle of San Jacinto. Houston became one of the first capitals of the Lone Star Republic, a promising commercial center situated on the meandering banks of Buffalo Bayou. As an independent republic, Texas offered substantial grants of land as rewards to veteran soldiers of the Revolution, as well as incentives to new immigrants. The opening of a Land Office in Galveston/Houston, further encouraged settlement of the abundant public land surrounding the new urban center.

The Republic's constitution entitled settlers to "first-class" headright certificates similar to Austin's—one league and one labor of land for the head of a family (approximately 4,600 acres), and a third of one league for a single person. In northern Harris County, the lands along Spring, Cypress, and Willow Creeks were disbursed as headright grants offered by the Republic of Texas. Individuals such as Ambrose Mays received a league size first-class headright located along Aldine-Westfield closest to college grounds. This survey extends north beyond Cypress Creek into the areas of Timberlane subdivision. Lexington Woods is located on the former Howard Decrow survey, another first-class headright grant. The land surveys date from 1838 to 1842, when the Land Office first opened. Calvin Richey, whose father Hiram escorted the Austin colonists from Louisiana, settled and farmed a large tract of land near present-day Richey Road and Interstate 45. Another large land grant, on Willow Creek between Tomball and Spring, was awarded to Elizabeth Smith, a widow of a Texas Revolution veteran. John Frederick Schlobohm, a German immigrant and a war veteran, was one of the earliest known settlers to homestead in the Aldine area near Green's Bayou. Settlement increased when Texas was formally admitted into the United States in 1845. The population of the new state

was officially tabulated by the U.S. Census taken five years later, revealing the names and occupations of the area's early settlers.[5]

After attaining statehood, public lands in eastern Texas were further distributed to encourage internal improvements such as through the construction of railroad lines. Railroad companies received generous land grants for every mile of track laid.[6] The development of the railroad directly affected several northern Harris County communities. Although the first railroad charter in Texas was issued in 1836, plans for railroad construction were frequently interrupted due to internal disputes and lack of financing. The first railroad line, extending from Harrisburg and Galveston to the Brazos River, (today's Union Pacific) was completed just prior to the Civil War. Other railroad companies, such as the Houston Tap & Brazoria Railroad, owned extensive portions of Texas land for development, including the area where North Harris College now stands.[7] The Houston Tap & Brazoria Railroad was chartered in 1856. After the Civil War, the railroad became the property of Jay Gould's International and Great Northern Railroad (I. &

*Area dairy farming.*
COURTESY: LESSIE UPCHURCH

*The Carl Theiss Homestead,
built in 1929. Located on North
Harris College grounds,
the homestead is representative
of the many family truck farms that
existed in northern Harris County.*

COURTESY: MARILYN THEISS KRON

G.N.) which constructed railroad lines extending north from Houston. The industrialization of the South, via the construction of extensive transportation lines linking the markets of the North and South with the West, occurred during the Reconstruction period. The resulting "railroad boom" in Texas lasted over a decade until 1882. Aldine, Westfield, and Spring, all became railroad towns along the I. & G.N. encouraging further settlement and trade.[8] At the turn of the century, railroad roundhouses, cattle pens, saloons, general stores, opera houses, hotels and depots were to be found around these area stops. Records reveal that there had been sawmills harvesting the abundant timber, gristmills, blacksmith shops, as well as churches and schools, located around these northern farming communities.

Although considered a wilderness by many Houstonians, northern Harris County was settled by enterprising farmers, both truck and dairy. Truck farmers grew a variety of produce for market. The farms of northern Harris County would not produce the quantity of cotton of the Brazos area, but they would yield award-winning vegetable and fruit produce needed by the city of Houston and other areas.[9] Many local products were shipped by rail outside the state to markets in St. Louis, Chicago, and New York. Corn, sweet and Irish potatoes, tomatoes, and cabbage, to name a few staples were important area crops. John M. Robinson, of the founding family of Old Town Spring, recalls that his father had shipped the first boxcar of Irish potatoes to northern markets in 1899. In 1932, that number increased to twenty-six boxcars of produce.[10]

After World War II, area truck farmers suffered due to increased competition from the Rio Grande Valley. Unable to get local vegetable crops to market first, many became dairy farmers. According to Elmer Beckendorf, a dairyman and descendant of an early pioneering German family to the area, "there were about 500 dairies operating in Harris County in 1955."[11] Many of these were located in northern Harris County. The dairies, five located within the immediate vicinity of the college, supplied Houston with milk and milk products.[12] The closest was the Essman Dairy which consisted of property that extended from old Bammel Road to North Harris College grounds, through what is now the Wood Creek subdivision. Operating in the 1920s, the Essman dairy had at one time 580 head of cows on approximately 660 acres of land, a little over a section.[13] The Essman Dairy reached the westernmost portion of North Harris College land. Grazing cows and open pastureland were once found where today's athletic fields are located. Further west, rice fields were located along Hardy Street and the railroad, from Aldine into Spring, as well as on either side of Interstate 45 near Richey Road. On Hardy going north, cotton was grown in the fields between Westfield and Spring. Additionally, remnants of pecan orchards can be seen throughout the area, particularly off Aldine-Westfield and along Bammel Road. The old pecan groves are visible reminders of the area's agricultural past. At one time, the pecan groves on Bammel were interplanted with tropical Satsuma oranges. Prior to the invention of the car, area farmers traveled by mule-drawn wagons for a two-day drive to Houston to market their goods. Traces of the farming community still exist in the northwest area, though they are rapidly disappearing in the changing suburban landscape. In many instances, the old farms and groves are being bought out and replaced by new subdivisions or commercial interests, permanently eradicating the vestiges of the area's rural history.

On North Harris College grounds is the Carl Theiss homestead which can be viewed from Aldine-Westfield Road near Turkey Creek. The Theiss family is one of the oldest German families to settle in northern Harris County, and a large number of descendants still reside in the

*Top, right: Descendants of early German settlers to northern Harris County. Family members, Frederick Wilhelm Bode and Louise Strack Bode. Theiss Homestead, North Harris College grounds.*
COURTESY: MARILYN THEISS KRON

areas of Spring and Klein. Carl Theiss was a descendant of Johann Theiss, who emigrated to the United States in the first wave of German immigration to Texas in the mid-1800s. The homestead of Carl's father, Martin Theiss, son of Johann, is located nearby off Theiss Road. The farmhouse located on college grounds, flanked by large pecan and oak trees, was built by three family members, Carl Theiss, his brother, and future brother-in-law, in preparation for Carl's marriage to Meta Bode.[14]

The Theiss homestead was one of several German family truck farms that dotted the northern prairie in the 1920s. Aside from raising cattle and hogs, the primary interest and livelihood was agricultural produce. The Theiss farm yielded turnips, cabbage, potatoes, and squash among other vegetable goods. Marilyn Theiss Kron, born in the homestead, recalls that "during the spring and fall you could smell the fresh plowed fields ready for planting. Blackberries grew in abundance along the road, and on our way home from school we would pick berries in our lunch buckets. At the same time you would have to watch for our Uncle Otto Theiss' cattle herd he would drive from Theiss Road past our house to a pasture he owned on the corner of Aldine Westfield and Farrell Road."[15]

Directly across from the Theiss homestead, and sharing a well, was a one room rural schoolhouse known as the Hartwell School. Prior to the establishment of independent school districts, northern Harris County had rural common schools. The Hartwell School was located in rural school district No. 29, Aldine. Four schools, indicating a large rural district area, were listed in county school records in 1910. These schools were Aldine, Higgs, Westfield,

*Top, left: Truck farm staple—a giant turnip held by Marvin Theiss, 1946. Theiss Homestead, North Harris College grounds.*
COURTESY: MARILYN THEISS KRON

*Below: A "Mule Slide" transports baskets to the field for harvest. Howard and Marvin Theiss ride to the fields. North Harris College grounds.*
COURTESY: MARILYN THEISS KRON

and Hartwell.[16] The Hartwell School was relocated during the depression years to Bammel Road on the extensive Herman Kies property. The school no longer exists.

The farms nearest the Theiss homestead were the Kies Farm located to the north (where apartments now stand), and the Baumgartner Farm which was located across Aldine-Westfield, bound by Turkey Creek. The latter farmhouse "sat back from the road with a long lane leading to it. There were woods on the left of it and fields on the right."[17] Arlene Schultz, who spent much time there as a child, recalls the farm well. Her grandfather, Willie Baumgartner, had truck farmed the sixty acres of land "using a team of mules and a wagon, although he had a tractor."[18] A neighbor and kin to the Theiss family, Arlene states that her grandparents "lived on a working farm, one that remained working until Grandpa's death in 1967. I was the oldest grandchild…. I used to help harvest tomatoes in the summer months, and also drove the tractor through the fields."[19] The Baumgartner farm produced cabbage for fresh sauerkraut, cucumbers and dill for pickles, potatoes, and other standard truck farm crops including fruit such as peaches and melons. The next farms were the Schindewolf farm and Saathoff (Koinm) dairy, located in a row further down Aldine-Westfield Road on the other side of F.M. 1960. Only the farmhouse and a few outbuildings of the Saathoff dairy still stand, the grounds appropri-

ately in use today as pasture by Spring ISD's Future Farmers of America.

The early permanent settlers of northern Harris County, particularly in the areas of Spring, Westfield and Klein, were predominantly German farmers who emigrated to the United States in two waves beginning in the 1840s. Escaping the hardships of Europe, the Germans immigrated as entire family units searching for economic opportunity and political freedom. Landing in Galveston and purchasing acreage sight unseen from railroad or land agents, they traveled to northern Harris County where the heavily timbered land, deemed unsuitable by most immigrants, was offered for quick sale between 10 and 25 cents an acre. One early settler wrote this account to his family in Germany describing the forests of Texas in present-day Spring.

"Texas is an excellent country where the people can live well… here in general each man has his own forest and that is not difficult because the forest and land is not as expensive as in Germany…. The forests do not have any owners, only the United States of America."[20]

Historically, the earliest German immigrants settled in Rosehill near Tomball. From Tomball, the German families migrated further east into the Spring area as the population increased, along with the corresponding need for more farmland. Family names such as Theiss, Beckendorf, Wunsche, Mittelstaedt, Kaiser,

Kleb, Klein, and Hildebrandt… distinctly reveal the German settlement in northern Harris County. The northern farming communities were tight-knit, with settlers establishing churches and schools nearby, in an attempt to preserve their German heritage. For many farmers, life off the farm centered around the church. Social activities as well as education often occurred on church grounds. Serving the early German families of the area were Trinity Lutheran Church (1874) in Klein, followed by St. Matthew's (1886) located off of Hardy Street in Westfield. Both were originally wooden structures with prominent bell towers. The oldest church to serve the Westfield area is the Church of Christ, founded in 1873, and located along the railroad tracks. The nearby Mueschke community cemetery contains the prominent old families of West, Boettcher, and others who once settled in Westfield. Family-run sawmills and gristmills supplied the local community with lumber, and meal. Food supplies, such as meat, were often shared amongst several farming families. Traditions such as hog-killing time meant that families would withstand the winter months through the distribution of meat, and the production of smoked sausages.[21]

The German farmers remained virtually undisturbed until the Civil War interrupted their relatively pastoral existence. Mustering companies for the Confederacy were formed on the banks of Cypress Creek. One post, Camp Cypress, was the principal mustering station

*Above: The Klein community. Kleb House. German settlements existed throughout northern Harris county from Spring to Tomball. Descendants of several pioneer families still reside in the area.*

COURTESY: KLEIN, TEXAS HISTORICAL FOUNDATION

"for recruits from outlying farm communities north of Houston."[22] Though many German settlers opposed secession and the south's "peculiar institution" of slavery, it is known that Friedrich August Wunsche, grandson of one of the original settlers of Spring, joined the military ranks of the Confederacy. Other settlers contributed to the war effort in a variety of ways, such as through the blacksmith work of forging "spurs and bridles for the southern army."[23] An important contribution of the area was the establishment of a gunpowder mill that existed on Spring Creek in Tomball. It served the Confederacy until 1863, when an explosion took the lives of several prominent area sons.

In 1871, during the postwar Reconstruction period, the International and Great Northern Railroad installed a major railroad switch from Houston through Spring. The influence of the railroad on the northern communities was enormous, as towns were born where depots stood. The towns of Spring, Westfield, named after early settler Gate F. West, and Aldine, earlier known as Prairie Switch, were officially established alongside the railroad lines. The urban center of Houston was drawn closer, and increased a reciprocal trade of goods and supplies.

Other industries also developed in these northern regions as a result of railroad transportation opportunities. Bammel and Westfield would become future oil boom towns, initially considered as extensions of the Humble oil fields.[24] Due to the shipping of goods provided by the railroad, the area's timber industry experienced tremendous growth at this time, changing from community sawmills to larger corporate-run industries. Water drawn from Spring Creek at the Spring depot supplied steam locomotives on their way to and from downtown Houston. Several major lumber mills existed in the woodlands nearby, all located near railroad connections.[25]

Lumber production was the earliest major industry of northern Harris County. Thick forests of hardwoods and pine extended into this area of eastern Texas, creating a lucrative timber supply. The timber was used extensively in the early formative years for railroad construction. Towns to support the industry quickly appeared. A large company town of 450 workers, for example, existed in nearby Montgomery County for the Grogan-Cochran

Lumber Company.[26] Sawmills were found at close distance to each other in intensive market competition. A number of farming families had originally established their own local sawmills out of necessity. With the appearance of large lumber companies in the area however, many residents sought additional incomes by working in company lumberyards. In nearby Spring, located along the railroad tracks, the Bayer Lumber Company operated an Excelsior Mill in 1927, and then a sawmill, harvesting the pines and hardwoods so prevalent in the area. The Boettcher Sawmill operated closest to the present site of the college, and a "dinky track" was reported to have transversed college grounds near the Theiss homestead transporting timber from the woods to the mill.[27] The Boettcher Sawmill was located on Hardy directly across

*Above: The town of Spring.*
COURTESY: JOHN M. ROBINSON

*Below: The Spring Train Depot.*
*The railroad industry was responsible for the formation of several local towns—such as Spring, Westfield, and Aldine.*
COURTESY: JOHN M. ROBINSON

*Above: Westfield commerce. Tautenhahn & Son, General Store. This store existed on the corner of Bammel and Hardy Street. It was one of several businesses that fronted the railroad tracks.*

COURTESY: REBECCA TAUTENHAHN STRACK STONE

*Below: Westfield, Texas. Mueschke House on Humble-Westfield Road. Local railroad workers, and oilmen from the Humble fields, "roomed" at this home.*

COURTESY: REBECCA TAUTENHAHN STRACK STONE

from the present-day Westfield-by-the-railroad. Today, only a railroad spur remains. The Tautenhahn Sawmill once operated in the woods on the western side of the tracks. Earlier mills include the Bender Sawmill of a large estate near Humble, operating in the woods on Bender Lake.[28] Nearby Bordersville housed the workers of Edgar Border's sawmill.

The extensive railroad connections, so vital to these mills, transported the harvested lumber to markets worldwide. At the turn of the century, the railroad further expanded and the Fort Worth Texas and Brazos Valley Line intersected with the I. & G.N. railroad line. Spring became a major switchyard with fourteen tracks. A large roundhouse, no longer in existence, once rested on the intersecting tracks.[29] The result was a boom town of approximately 2,000 people, containing railroad workers as well as the local farmers and sawmill workers.[30] As an indication of its rapid growth in the railroad era, Spring had three local schools serving the growing community in 1912. One school was built on Hardy Street Road, and another was located off Aldine-Westfield. For transportation, two members of the Wunsche family reportedly "built the first school bus from a used Model B Ford Truck."[31]

Like Spring, Westfield was a farming community that changed with the advent of the railroad and the discovery of oil. At the turn of the century, Westfield was referred to as the West Oil Field, housing oil workers from the Humble wells. Due to the railroad and timber industries, Westfield, as did most of the other railroad stops, bustled with commercial activity. "By the 1890s it had cotton gins, sawmills, gristmills, and railroad tonnage that rivaled Spring's. Cotton, lumber, cattle and hides were loaded onto freight cars from Westfield's mammoth warehouses and cattle pens...."[32] Cattle were watered at these area stops, as well as inspected.

According to Rebecca Tautenhahn Strack Stone, descendant of Westfield's prominent Tautenhahn family, "area families, such as the Mueschke's, rented rooms to railroad employees and others. Double-door farmhouses often contained one room set aside exclusively for "roomers."[33] A county deed shows the original railroad plan for the town of Westfield. The town would consist of two large blocks, with a Morris Street located in between. Soon afterward, the construction of family homes occurred along the railroad tracks not far from the Westfield train depot. Local families recall the plantation-style, two-story Tautenhahn home located on the corner of Hardy and Bammel Roads. Surrounded by lush exotic foliage, the Tautenhahn home also sported a family of peacocks. A large Osage orange tree marks the corner where the house once stood.

Today, the Hardy Toll Road towers over the former backyard. The home has been relocated

to another location and is still in the possession of the Tautenhahn family. A two-story brick General Store, a sawmill, and large parcels of land on either side of the tracks were also owned by the Tautenhahns of Westfield. Other prominent two-story homes included the Boettcher house, and the Louisiana style Mueschke home on Humble-Westfield. Neither the businesses nor these particular homes exist today, although the library has named its local branch in honor of Baldwin Boettcher. Two of Westfield's smaller Tautenhahn houses were relocated and are currently in use in Old Town Spring.

The town of Westfield was officially established in 1870, coinciding with the opening of a post office. The Boettcher Sawmill and family home existed across the railroad tracks from the Tautenhahns. A row of warehouses and a commissary partially blocked the sawmill on this eastern side.[34] Westfield's wooden train depot, feed store, one-room post office, two-story brick buildings, have vanished from the area. Only

the pecan orchards continue to dot Bammel Road all the way to the modern Interstate 45. Prior to the existence of F.M. 1960, Bammel Road was the way to cross the two-lane freeway at this northern junction. At the time, Interstate 45 was called Highway 75. A stop sign, then a traffic light, marked this formally peaceful and ground-level crossroads.[35]

Located further to the south and closest to the city of Houston is the Aldine community, originally settled in the 1830s along Green's Bayou. The area's early settlers were also predominantly farmers with expansive fields of assorted vegetable produce. At the turn of the century, this rural community was advertised nationwide by land developers in Houston. To attract settlers, Aldine was promoted as a garden paradise with a climate similar to Florida. The area attracted enterprising farmers who grew crops that were somewhat different from the norm. Fig and orange groves were found in the Aldine community between traditional truck and dairy farms.

*Tautenhahn Sawmill.*
*Westfield community.*

One promotional billboard of 1909 read: "Aldine—11 miles to the city, Good Roads, Makes Famous Skinless Fig Preservatives, Fig Orchards, Garden Lands, Orange Groves, Small Farms, Large Quick Sure Crops."[36] The soil was promoted as fertile and suitable for speculative investment. Though annual freezing temperatures eradicated the orange grove ventures, magnolia figs thrived. A large fig cannery, touted as the "oldest and largest fig preserving plant in Texas and America" was the J.C. Carpenter Fig Company.[37] The cannery existed in Aldine until the 1920s when the Great Depression caused several area industries to collapse. Located near the railroad, figs were transported to Houston and out of state markets by rail. For many years, the fig orchards and cannery provided employment to area residents.

Oil proved to be the largest and most productive industry of northern Harris County, affecting the areas of Humble, Westfield, Bammel, and Tomball. The discovery of "black gold" in Humble at the turn of the century, the oil deposits found in Westfield and the Bammel area, and the strikes in Tomball which occurred later during the Great Depression, all transformed the relatively small rural communities into industrial bases. As the nation switched from coal to petroleum, the rich oil fields of Texas became its major supplier. These oil pro-

*Right: Aldine, 1912. Corn and other crops grown in Aldine and Spring supplied downtown Houston and elsewhere with vegetable produce. Schleuter collection.*

COURTESY: HOUSTON METROPOLITAN RESEARCH CENTER, HOUSTON PUBLIC LIBRARY.

*Below: Cabbage fields in Aldine. Schleuter collection.*

COURTESY: HOUSTON METROPOLITAN RESEARCH CENTER, HOUSTON PUBLIC LIBRARY.

ducing regions, located north of Houston, ushered rapid modernity to the farming communities. The construction of the transcontinental Houston Natural Gas pipelines, and the massive underground storage tank facility in Bammel off of Kuykendahl Road, provided significant employment in the area. The abundance of oil and natural gas found in the clay earth of northern Harris County contributed to make Houston an international city, as investors worldwide sought to purchase area land and gain on mineral rights. Then the Great Depression came, creating a temporary setback.

During the depression years of the 1930s, Houston's northern farming communities were able to survive as they always had, off the produce of the land. Though times were hard for many local families, the farmers themselves rarely suffered from hunger. Beef clubs, in which area farmers rotated the cuts of beef so that each family would receive a different cut, ensured that local families had fresh meat every week. It was area industry, particularly that associated with the railroad, that was most affected by economic change. The railroad towns which housed railroad and lumber work-

*Above: Aldine, Texas. The J.C. Carpenter Fig Cannery. The cannery was located near the railroad and operated until the Great Depression. Schleuter collection.*

COURTESY: HOUSTON METROPOLITAN RESEARCH CENTER, HOUSTON PUBLIC LIBRARY.

*Below: The Aldine community. Aldine farms and "garden lands" were promoted for development by E.C. Robertson in 1909. The area was known for its fig orchards and "famous skinless fig preserves."*

COURTESY: ELIZABETH BATTLE, ALDINE INDEPENDENT SCHOOL DISTRICT

*Aldine School District #29, 1913.*

COURTESY: ELIZABETH BATTLE, ALDINE
INDEPENDENT SCHOOL DISTRICT.

ers did not fare well. The local economy collapsed when the railroad relocated its services to downtown Houston. The major roundhouse in Spring shut down, hotels and businesses closed, and the result was a virtual ghost town. Changes incurred at the federal level, regulating the minimum wage, also affected the area's largest employers. Local businesses and industries, such as lumberyards, could no longer compete since they could not afford to pay workers the required minimum wage. The resulting loss of jobs meant a serious decline in population and funds, as many moved to the urban centers in desperate search of employment. Hobos temporarily moved in, riding the trains in the hope of finding odd jobs for food from the many local family farms.[38] Other problems followed.

The serious decline in community population and funding were issues that dramatically affected the local rural schools. The threat of school closure was omnipresent. The northern communities, such as Spring, remained small after the railroad's relocation, reverting back to the simpler times of a rural farming community. Crime did not escape the area, nor strict adherence to prohibition. A local depression-era legend exists of the renowned outlaw team of Bonnie and Clyde in what is called today, Old Town Spring. During the Great Depression, Bonnie Parker and Clyde Barrow were purportedly to have held up the Spring State Bank, making off in a Model A with $7500, a large sum of money for the time.[39] According to Arthur Bayer, of the Bayer Sawmill in Spring, Bonnie and Clyde "had parked at Spring Creek and got stuck...."[40] John M. Robinson added that "Clarence Booker, the driver of a Wunsche wrecker, pulled them out of the sand and was tipped $5.00" for his services, a significant sum for the 1930s.[41] Booker had personally described the incident to Robinson.

By the Second World War, northern Harris County was still regarded as located a world away from downtown Houston. The impact of the war and particularly the postwar decade of the 1950s, brought about profound and permanent changes to the northern rural landscape. The wartime need for natural gas resulted in the formation of several large oil corporations and the construction of an eastern gas pipeline. The Tennessee Gas Transmission Company, known later as Tenneco, was formed in 1944. Tenneco operated a "1265 mile pipeline to West Virginia. By 1957, (Tenneco), the first transcontinental company to tap the Gulf Coast fields, possessed 9811 miles of lines."[42] The construction of the transcontinental pipeline provided vast opportunities for employment during the war years.

World War II impacted the nation as a whole by reversing the tide of the Great Depression. The lean years of the depression were finally over, and returning veterans eagerly sought new opportunities offered in federal programs of education and housing.

Consumerism was on the rise, and suburbs of G.I. and tract houses were found throughout the area, extending at a rapid pace into the outlying regions of northern Houston.

One of the key pieces of federal legislation passed after the war was the G.I. Bill, which provided returning veterans with the opportunity to complete their interrupted education. The G.I. Bill directly affected the growth of the nation's educational facilities, particularly in the area of higher education. At the federal level, President Harry Truman authorized a special commission to comprehensively study higher education, analyzing the existing structure, identifying its problems, and providing a workable solution. The result was a voluminous report calling for sweeping changes. The study disturbingly revealed that many high school students did not have the means or the opportunity to continue their education. Universities were located too far away, and were too expensive for average families. As a result, the many opportunities awarded to those who graduated with college degrees were denied the nation's students who could not continue their schooling due to lack of funding or accessibility.

In Truman's Commission Report, a heightened democratic philosophy fostered by the war emerged on the domestic level. Involvement in the Second World War against the forces of fascism, the ensuing Cold War and the struggle against the Soviet Union, caused serious reflection upon ourselves as a democratic society. The result was the development of several major policies, including one on the protection of human rights. The concern with human rights after the war, and the spirit of egalitarianism, helped alter traditional views of women and minorities. This heightened democratic philosophy particularly affected the course of higher education. Although community colleges had been in existence before, the sense of urgency to make higher education available to all peoples, as expressed in the postwar Truman report, permanently transformed the role of community colleges in the United States. The community college movement was formally launched. As found in the president's report, the word "com-

*Humble Oil Well.*
NORTH HARRIS COLLEGE FILES.

*Humble Oil Fields, Humble, Texas.*
*Schleuter collection.*

munity" was to be highlighted in the label "community colleges," accentuating the belief that in a democratic society, education should be made available to all citizens "regardless of race, faith, sex, occupation, or economic status." The report stated that:

"By allowing the opportunity for higher education to depend so largely on the individual's economic status, we are not only denying to millions of young people the chance in life to which they are entitled; we are also depriving the Nation of a vast amount of potential leadership and potential social competence which it sorely needs."[43]

Throughout postwar America, students were returning to school in greater numbers than ever before. College attendance was particularly affected, due in large part to the returning veterans. Statistics from the Truman Report reveal the dramatic increase in college enrollment that took place.

"In 1900 fewer than 250,000 students, only 4 percent of the population 18 through 21 years of age, were enrolled in institutions of higher education. By 1940 the enrollment had risen to 1,500,000 students, equal to a little less than 16 percent of the 18-21 year olds. In 1947, enrollments jumped to the theretofore unprecedented peak of 2,354,000 although approximately

1,000,000 of the students were veterans, older than the usual college age because World War II had deferred their education. The situation in the fall of 1947 gives every indication that the school year 1948 will witness even larger enrollments."[44]

A myriad of problems immediately surfaced with the implementation of the G.I. Bill. There were not enough teachers, classrooms, or schools to accommodate the returning veterans. The postwar baby boom would only further intensify the problems already facing existing educational facilities.

By the 1960s, Houston like other large urban centers, responded to this education crisis with the establishment of several new schools and institutions in the area. In Aldine, the student population dramatically doubled from 10,771 students in 1961 to 20,307 only seven years later.[45] The need for a community college in the area appeared soon afterward, as the establishment of community colleges south of Buffalo Bayou followed the national trend. San Jacinto College was established in 1960, and Lee College, though established in 1934, began to offer technical-vocational education in 1963.[46] The federal emphasis on education as a democratic right fostered the creation of other local institutions of higher education. The community college, unlike the university, came to be regarded as the people's college, pragmatic in purpose, and distinctively a grass roots institution.

The first meetings calling for the establishment of a community college in northern Harris County began in the postwar period of the latter 1950s. The northern communities, although experiencing some change, remained relatively small. The town of Spring, which was home to John Winship, one of the earliest promoters of a community college in the north, boasted a population of 500 in 1950, but would witness tremendous growth in the next two decades.[47]

North Harris College was the result of the overall federal and state changes in education that occurred due to the impact of the Second World War. The generation that was largely responsible for the creation of the institution had experienced the war years and their postwar impact. W.W. Thorne, the key founder of the college, and many of the original Board members, were World War II veterans directly affected by both the benefits and initial problems that resulted from the G.I. Bill. The area's school superintendents, particularly Winship and Thorne, were daily exposed to the limitations in their own school districts, the constant need of funding, and overall most sensitive to the needs and future of their own high school graduates. The drive for accessible and affordable education came from the very individuals who had experienced the many changes brought about in the postwar era, and persistently worked toward a solution.

As urban Houston experienced rapid growth in both population and industry, the northern fringe was likewise changing. The land along both sides of Jackrabbit Road, today's F.M. 1960, was being developed. The vegetable farms and cattle ranches were making way to new commercial enterprises. A large parcel of rural land on F.M. 1960 was purchased and developed by two pro-golfers creating one of the first major commercial and recreational ventures in northern Harris County.[48] This area became known as Champions, home of a golf course and an exclusive development. At the time, many locals thought the idea of a golf course being built in a rural area was foolhardy. "They are going to lose their shirts. People out there wear overalls and ride horses, they don't play golf."[49] Champions Golf Course however, opening in 1958, attract-

ed relocating corporate families and businesses to settle in the secluded northern sector. The area's farms were rapidly being purchased and replaced by other large subdivisions and businesses. The attractiveness of the area was found in its "country-like" setting, and distance from downtown Houston. Ten years after the opening of Champions Golf Course, the Goodyear Blimp "America" established a large base headquarters off of I-45 in Spring, "becoming the single biggest industrial taxpayer in the Spring Independent School District."[50] No longer in operation today, the distinctive Blimp flying overhead was the area's favorite attraction for over twenty years.

Houston's northern farmlands, forests, and prairie, were rapidly being bought out by businesses and developers all along the major freeways. By the 1960s, plans had been made to create three man-made lakes within the vicinity of Houston, Lake Houston in the east, and Lakes Livingston and Conroe to the north. Lake Conroe, a San Jacinto River Authority project in conjunction with the city of Houston, began in 1960 as a water supply reservoir for Houston. The project was completed in 1973. At that time, "21,000 surface acres of land were inundated with water... it was all timber and pastureland."[51] An old railroad tram that had once transversed the land taking hardwood to a local sawmill, found a new home beneath the waters of Lake Conroe. The creation of lakes attracted developers and businesses, as well as provided area residents with recreational water activities from fishing to sailing.

The greatest amount of population growth experienced by northern Harris County would occur in one decade's time, from the latter part of the 1960s through the 1970s. This was the result of several factors. In 1969, an international airport was built in northern Harris County, originally named Jetero (Jet Era) Airport. Today, George Bush Intercontinental Airport is the home of a major air carrier, Continental Airlines, and provides transportation services worldwide. Construction of a new modern airport dramatically affected the surrounding community through increased land and industrial development. Investors bought large tracts of land within close proximity of the airport. A new premiere shopping mall, to be located off of Interstate 45, was advertised as the largest shopping center in the southwestern United States. Greenspoint Mall was to encompass a total of 140 acres. At the time, the closest mall for area residents was Northline Mall located closer to Houston. Greenspoint Mall, in planning stages in 1974, was completed in 1976.

Other improvements included flood control. The relocation, straightening and/or cementing of local bayous and creeks, was a temporary attempt to contain the annual flooding of the banks. At the time, the channeling improved the quality of the land enough for quick sale. The land and building rush that occurred throughout northern Harris County in the 1970s was the result of the availability of inexpensive and wooded land, the proximity of the new airport, road improvements (including an outer loop Beltway), plans for the largest mall in the south (Greenspoint), local flood control, and distance from the city. Corporate relocations of businesses to the northern sector, followed national urban patterns where corporations preferred to locate in more attractive and exclusive outerbelts. Businessmen found the northern setting attractive and safe for the well-being of their families. Most of the subdivisions of the area can be dated back to the 1970s, causing an abrupt change in the landscape from rural to modern suburban.

Despite the growth of area businesses, as far as higher education was concerned, the northern sector was still regarded as too far away, and too remote from the city of Houston. Downtown Houston understandably received top priority, although most institutions of higher learning including several community colleges, were already located there and further south of Buffalo Bayou. It was the impetus of northern Harris County educators, civic leaders, and concerned citizens in the area's local communities that pushed for the establishment of a college to serve the northern sector.

John A. Winship, superintendent of Spring Independent School District, was responsible for promoting initial interest for the creation of a community college in northern Harris County. Winship foresaw the change of the northern communities from rural to commuter districts. At the time, Spring was a small community with little commercial base. There was no separate high school, and all classes from kindergarten to high school were held in one building. As the area began to change and the population increased, Winship promoted the need for a college through meetings with the superintendents and board members from the surrounding school districts of Aldine, Tomball, and Humble. Winship recognized that his graduating students had too far to travel for the benefits of higher education. Likewise, he believed, technological programs should be offered nearby to provide greater opportunities and result in higher paying jobs. Winship particularly emphasized that the citizens of the area "were paying state taxes that helped support junior colleges in other sections of the state... they deserved one of their own."[52] In 1966, Winship approached a graduate education class at the University of Houston to develop a feasibility study for the establishment of a college in the area. The findings of this study provided the necessary information to present to local business leaders and local school boards, allowing for future planning. Winship's study was also presented to the Houston North Association, a civic organization of which Roy Hohl of Tomball, and W.W. Thorne of Aldine were active leaders. But a series of drawbacks occurred in the initial college drive.

In 1968, a serious attempt was made in downtown Houston to create a Greater Houston, 13-district, countywide community college system patterned after one established in Dallas. Serving on the Steering Committee of this early proposal were three northern Harris County school superintendents: John Winship of Spring ISD; W.W. Thorne of Aldine ISD; and George Turner of Humble ISD. Roy Hohl of Tomball, serving as president of Houston North Association, was also a member of this committee. Although the countywide proposal failed in Houston, the northern response to the community college movement was a positive one. In the initial petition drive, the citizens in the largest area school district of Aldine, collected 4,810 signatures of a required 1,096.[53] The voters in the northern communities had overwhelmingly approved the establishment of an institute of higher education for the area in the county-wide election. Although the proposal failed to pass in Houston, the 1968 election served to strengthen the determination of the northern communities to establish a junior college district of their own.[54]

W.W. Thorne, superintendent of Aldine Independent School District, was the builder of Winship's vision to establish a community college to serve local students. Thorne had served as superintendent of the Aldine schools since 1958, assuming the superintendent's position when Aldine schools were closed and the Aldine school district was virtually bankrupt. Through tenacious drive, Thorne turned the school district around, and into one of the most progressive in the state. To solve the bankruptcy problem, Thorne approached the Texas state legislature with innovative ideas on funding. Time warrants were issued to community residents who Thorne credits with literally saving the Aldine schools.[55] Of Thorne's many accomplishments as Aldine's superintendent, it is reported that an average of one new school building was constructed per year, meaning that over sixty percent of all Aldine schools were built during Thorne's administration.[56] Along with his dedication to education, Thorne served as a leader of the Houston North Association. Involved in many civic issues, Thorne became the most active crusader in leading and organizing the effort to establish a community college in northern Harris County. Aldine High School became the base headquarters for meetings with local superintendents and area residents, and organization of the legal data needed to create such an entity.

The process to establish a community college in the state of Texas is squarely based on statute. Through important revision of state legislation via the Acts of 1969, community colleges were placed under the supervision of the newly established Coordinating Board of the Texas College and University System (1965). This centralized system enabled community colleges to develop according to a master plan, regulating course offerings, as well as increasing state aid. Prior to this time, community colleges were governed by the Texas Education Agency, supervisor of public schools.

The establishment of the Coordinating Board had an important effect on the development of community colleges in Texas. Community colleges were no longer regarded as extensions of

high school, but as distinctive upper level facilities offering a variety of programs to serve student needs. The responsibilities of the Coordinating Board range from the evaluation of programs, to regulation in the establishment of new community college districts.

During the 1960s, Texas experienced rapid population growth with the population doubling in the ten year period 1965-1975. New college campuses were needed to provide widespread access to higher education for the growing numbers of high school graduates.[57] According to a master plan prepared in 1969 by the Texas Coordinating Board entitled "Challenge for Education," junior colleges would be located "within easy distance of all Texans who could logically benefit from attending."[58] The State Coordinating Board was responsible for authorizing an election to establish a junior college district after determining that certain conditions had been met, and that it was both feasible and desirable to establish the proposed new district. If the Coordinating Board authorized the election, a majority of the electors in the proposed district voting in the election, would determine the question of creation of the junior college district, the election of the original trustees, and the questions of issuing bonds and levying taxes.[59]

Because of the rapid population growth in northern Harris County, the voters in three school districts- Aldine, Spring, and Humble, led by their superintendents and board members, petitioned for the establishment of a community college in their area. The drive began in earnest in 1971 with the establishment of an Executive Steering Committee. Members on the committee were selected from the three local school districts. Each of the district's Board of Trustees had one member; two lay citizens from each of the three districts; and the three school district superintendents who served as ex-officio members of the committee.

Tomball Independent School District sought inclusion into the district in 1972, although support for a community college could be found earlier in the initial talks of the late 1950s. Members of the Tomball Good Roads Committee such as Roy Hohl, were most supportive of these early discussions on a community college. But Tomball's inclusion in the new college district could only be attained if the adjoining Klein ISD became part of the district. Due to the limitations of the law at the time, with a policy that forbade non-contiguous districts from joining, Tomball ISD, was not allowed to become part of the proposed new school district at its formation. The administration of Klein ISD was initially in favor of inclusion in the new college district. In fact, the school superintendent of Klein, as well as several KISD board members, had served on the college's Steering Committee. However, Klein withdrew support for the college in April 1972, just six months prior to the election, after an unfavorable straw vote poll. Officially, Klein indicated that "…our action in withdrawing at this time is a decision based on what we feel is best for the Klein school district, considering all of the many factors of increasing student enrollment, rising taxes, the lack of an adequate industrial and commercial tax base…."[60] At the time, Klein was experiencing rapid population growth and concern over their own schools prevented their full commitment to the college team. The withdrawal of Klein ISD only temporarily eliminated Tomball from entrance into the college district. W.W. Thorne from Aldine, Roy Hohl from Tomball, and key state and local representatives would eventually be able to eliminate the non-contiguous restriction of state legislation through the passage of what is fondly referred to as the "Tomball Bill." Tomball would enter the college district in 1982, and a new campus, Tomball College, would open four years later in 1986.

With the Steering Committee formed in 1971, the leadership of the college drive was in place. The administrators of Aldine and Spring ISDs were most responsible for the organization and direction of the drive. The largest area district, Aldine ISD, served as base headquarters. Meetings with the area superintendents and board members were held, studies prepared, and literature produced advertising both the benefits and need for a local college district. E.M. Wells, representing Spring ISD, served as the chairman of the Steering Committee, with John Winship, superintendent of Spring ISD, serving as ex-officio member. The groundwork of feasibility studies and survey reports had to be done according to the guidelines prepared by

the Texas State Coordinating Board. The support of the community was evident from the onset. Petitions were carried "door to door," circulated within the Aldine community via the tireless work of individual PTA members and others, beginning in April 1972. The signatures collected on the petitions were well in excess of what was needed to call for an election. For example, Aldine ISD required 4,500 signatures, and received 6,000 showing tremendous community support.[61] Other community colleges located in the southern Houston area offered support and advice toward accomplishing the final goal. Lee College's president, Raymond Cleveland, wrote "…This letter is just to let you know that all of us at Lee College are pulling for you as you map your strategy for election day…. We believe in the Community College and are willing to work for it…. Best of luck."[62] The petitions and local survey report were subsequently presented to the Coordinating Board of the Texas College and University system for approval to hold an election. By June of 1972, the Harris County Commissioner's Court was asked to call an election for the creation of a new junior college district in northern Harris County. The election would determine whether the citizens of the outlying communities were in support of such an entity.

The election, held October 7, 1972, overwhelmingly approved the creation of North Harris County College. The election set a tax rate, approved a bond issue, and elected the first seven members of the Board of Trustees. A college had been born due to the grass roots efforts of the community and the keen leadership provided by both the superintendents and board members of the local school districts.

North Harris County College District, created by the citizens in 1972, embraced all the territory contained in the Aldine, Spring, and Humble school districts. An area that consisted of approximately 256 square miles in northern Harris County, with an estimated population of 160,000 people.[63] With the establishment of a new college district, the election also provided for immediate leadership through the selection of seven men to serve as the original Board of Trustees. These members were: E.M. Wells from Spring, Charles W. Philipp from Humble, M.M. Morris from Aldine, Hugh E. Dugan from

Humble, Henry J. Doering from Spring, W.E. Crozier from Aldine, and Lawrence Adams from Aldine. Several former board members and officers of the founding ISDs, Spring, Aldine and Humble, were represented on the first college Board of Trustees.[64] Three of the board members: E.M. Wells, Charles W. Philipp, and Henry Doering served on the college's Steering Committee, with E.M. Wells serving as its president. Wells would become the first president of the North Harris College Board of Trustees.

With the passage of the college election in October, the time for celebration was short-lived. In less than one year's time, a college was to be up and running. The workload for the first board was overwhelming but exciting. Wells recalled the enormity of starting a college, and one of the first obligations, "now we were sitting there with seven trustees and no college, no chancellor... and the TEA asks me for a proposed budget for the next biannual!"[65] Other pressing tasks included the simultaneous search for a college president and a campus site, committee work that would begin immediately.

The first Board of Trustees meeting was held October 12th in the Board Room of Aldine High School, at the extended invitation of W. W. Thorne. Subsequent board meetings continued to be held at Aldine H.S., until a permanent location for the new college could be found. At the first meeting of the board, it was recommended by president, E. M. Wells, that the oath of office be administered to the new Board of Trustees by Aldine superintendent W.W. Thorne. The original North Harris College board members represented the community at large, some were business leaders, one a postman, but the majority had served as officers or president of the local school boards. The immediate responsibilities of the first Board of Trustees were the selection of a president, and a site for the new college. Separate committees were formed to handle those tasks. W.E. Crozier headed the site selection committee; and Hugh Dugan chaired the presidential search committee. From a pool of approximately twenty candidates for the office of president, on November 30, 1972, the board extended the offer of presidency to W.W. Thorne.

Thorne became the first president of North Harris College at the following board meeting held December 14, 1972, after giving an unex-

pected notice of resignation to the school board at Aldine ISD. Thorne had served as superintendent of the Aldine schools for over fifteen years. News of Thorne's resignation reportedly "came as a shock to (Aldine) board members, some of whom have served with him for ten to twelve years. They regretfully accepted the resignation...."[66] Marion Donaldson, Thorne's longtime secretary at Aldine ISD, accompanied Thorne to his new position, serving as first executive secretary to the first college president.

Being involved in the birth of a college

*North Harris College founder and first president, W.W. Thorne.*

required hitting the ground running. Aside from paperwork and bond sales, a staff had to be assembled and instructional programs developed from the onset. A central office for the new college was established off I-45 in the International Plaza building, at the time, "the tallest building out there."[67] According to Dr. Bob Williams, "on a clear day, downtown Houston was visible from the Plaza building."[68] Greenspoint Mall and the surrounding business complexes had not yet been developed on the open pastureland. Karen Kincheloe remembers that charter faculty fondly referred to International Plaza as the "white house."[69] This building, which no longer exists, housed the administrative offices for the college. North Harris charter member Dr. Joe McMillian, stated that he was interviewed at the "white house" when "at the time, it was Dr. Airola, Mr. Thorne, and Lester Burks, and their secretaries. These were the (first) six employees."[70]

By the end of December 1972, with the college district in existence for two months, the architectural firm of Koetter, Thorpe and Cowell (KTC) had been selected to assist the college board in site selection and building design of a permanent college campus.[71] Until that time, Aldine High School would serve after hours, beginning at four o'clock each day, as North Harris College. Dr. Roy Lazenby, one of the charter administrators, noted that his office was located "in a little elementary school, Carroll Inez Elementary, just south of Aldine High School, where (we) had leased some classrooms at the back of the school. Two classrooms. One side would be for admissions, registrar, and my office; the other classroom would be for faculty. That became our home for three years from 1973 through 1976.... We were there, had offices there all day long, and then moved our offices at four o'clock in the afternoon to Aldine High School, room

504, and had offices there until ten o'clock, four nights a week, (for) we had four classes a night, four nights a week."[72]

The founding administrators included W. W. Thorne, President of North Harris County College; Dr. Joe Airola, Dean of Instruction; Lester Burks, Dean of Vocational-Technical Education. Richard Curd served as Business Manager; Dr. Roy Lazenby, Director of Student Personnel Services; Dr. Larry Phillips, Financial

Aid Counselor; Susan Pearson, Counselor; and Anne Trammell, Head Librarian. The first Division heads were: Dr. Joe McMillian, Chairman of the Division of Mathematics, Science and Physical Education; Mr. Victor Watson, Chairman of the Communication and Arts Division; and Dr. Nellie Carr Thorogood, Chairman of the Division of Business and Technology. Jack L. Foreman was hired as the Director of Continuing Education. Charter full-time faculty members included: Audra Brewster, Cosmetology; Charles Chance, Instructor of English; John C. Eudy, Instructor of History; Dr. Mari Jon Filla, Instructor in Business Education; Karen Kincheloe, Instructor of English and part-time Public Relations director; and Brian Wilson, Instructor in Business Education and Mid-Management. Support staff included: Marion Donaldson, Secretary to the President; Edwina Clement, Secretary to the Dean of Instruction; Lela Meader, Secretary to the Registrar; Charlene Johnson, Business Office; and Hazel Woods, Accountant.

The first students to attend North Harris College were registered for non-credit continuing education classes that began in June of 1973.

Initially, North Harris College assumed responsibility for the Adult Education program offered at Aldine High School upon retirement of the program director, Mr. Chandler. These first continuing education classes were held in the evenings at Aldine High School. Many of the first students were enrolled in subjects such as bookkeeping and shorthand.[73] They were typically non-traditional college students, usually older, determined, having full-time jobs and families to support, and hence, more serious about their study. W.W. Thorne recalls, "We didn't have any kids right out of high school. All the students were working adults that were going to school at night. One of the most amazing things to me was when I was at the University of Houston, if that professor was five minutes late getting to class that was an excuse for us to go.... At Aldine High School, if that professor was five minutes late, I had a group of students down in my office wanting to know where that professor was.... That was a refreshing difference and it makes a difference in the way you do things...."[74]

One class had been held earlier in March at the request of the Humble Chamber of Commerce. The Chamber requested that North

Harris College develop a Defensive Driver Training Program, to be established "as soon as possible."[75] The first class of the junior college had been in fact held at Humble High School on April 10, 1973 six months after the college had formed. Twelve students had enrolled in Defensive Driving.[76]

In the fall of 1973, the first comprehensive programs for both academic credit and continuing education non-credit courses were offered at North Harris College. These classes were to be held in the evening at several area sites, including the high schools of Aldine, Spring and Humble. The first college registration was held in the Aldine High School cafeteria, amidst warnings that there was a hurricane or tropical depression in the Gulf of Mexico. Dr. Roy Lazenby recalls that it "seemed like every registration we had in the first two or three years, at least for the Fall semester anyway, there was always a hurricane or a depression in the Gulf.... I think that's where we got our nickname, the Hurricanes."[77] Despite the bad weather, registration numbers were promising, 239 students enrolled in non-credit classes alone.

The first North Harris College catalog was printed in 1973, listing the programs of instruction, and a description of college courses offered at several temporary locations. President, W.W. Thorne welcomed the first students with the following Foreword:

> *Welcome to North Harris County College! As a member of the first student body of this institution, you are joining with the faculty and staff in a pioneering effort to develop an outstanding college to serve the needs of the citizens of this area. You will be helping to set the pattern for the hundreds of thousands of students who will follow you in the years to come....[78]*

North Harris College received Correspondent Status with the Southern Association of Colleges and Schools, the first step of the accreditation process. This meant that academic credits earned at North Harris would be fully transferable to other colleges and universities within the state. Programs were designed to meet the requirements of the State Coordinating Board. The total headcount in both credit and non-credit courses for the first fall semester of North Harris County College was over 600 students, a figure that exceeded all expectations, particularly in view of the limitations imposed by the offering of night classes and the interim use of local public school facilities to hold classes.

Aldine High School was being renovated at the same time that North Harris College began operations. A new school library was projected to open in the fall of 1973. North Harris College was able to secure one room adjacent to the Aldine H.S. library for the start of its own library collection.[79] The college's Board of Trustees authorized $50,000 for the purchase of an opening day collection for the college, a collection that consisted of nearly 4,500 books.[80] The first college logo was also being developed at this time by Floyd Hoffman, a member of the college's founding Steering Committee, and a commercial artist. Hoffman donated his talent and service to the college district.[81] The first North Harris College logo was a bold letter N with an arrow pointing north and upwards.

Plans for the construction of a permanent college campus were underway since the founding of the college in October of 1972. The selection of an architectural firm occurred by December of that same year to assist in site location. The committee work and land reports secured by the NHCC Board of Trustees and president W.W. Thorne, allowed for the purchase of a wooded 185 acre tract off of Aldine-Westfield Road, located northwest of the Intercontinental Airport. The land was primarily selected due to its central proximity between the local school districts of Aldine, Spring and Humble. The architectural firm of KTC was responsible for the evaluation of several sites, taking into account such aspects as student accessibility, population distribution, traffic, the environment, and size. With the college's service area encompassing 254 square miles, the geographic center was considered to be an ideal location. Five sites were evaluated based on the

*The original North Harris College logo was designed by board member, Floyd Hoffman.*

above criteria. Of the five, one site of 125 acres was offered to the new college at no cost.[82]

One month prior to the election forming North Harris County College, Friendswood Development Co. and the King Ranch approached the Steering Committee with a generous donation of land. Located northeast of Humble in the master planned community of Kingwood, "a 175-acre site has been reserved for an education complex... 125 acres of land (is) available to proposed North Harris County Junior College...."[83] In 1972, the site was considered by the architectural firm as too remote for the construction of the new college.[84] The Board of Trustees, meeting in closed session, decided to purchase a site that was more conveniently located. Referred to as "Site 2," consisting of 186 acres in Aldine ISD, this location received the highest ratings from the architectural firm, particularly in view of accessibility. This parcel of land was located west of Aldine-Westfield Road and just south of a "proposed major thoroughfare" known as F.M. 1960.[85] The proposed deepening of Turkey Creek would provide site drainage, and the only noted drawback would be noise control due to the site's proximity to the Intercontinental Airport. Based on the architect's report and recommendation, the 186 acre parcel of land was purchased in

May of 1973 from a group of twelve investors known collectively as the Turkey Creek Ranch Company. This extensive land holding "in the middle of nowhere" contained a combination of loblolly pine forest in the northeastern half, prairie and swamp land toward the west. Although the low lying areas had to be filled prior to construction, the pine forest was from the beginning to be protected as much as possible during the construction phases. Most area builders at the time found it much easier to eradicate the trees, rather than to build around them. The wooded campus setting that is so distinctive of North Harris College was the result of careful planning and concern for preservation.

Projections for the opening of the permanent campus of North Harris College were for the fall semester of 1975. At that time, both day and evening classes would be made available to all students. President Thorne publicly reassured citizens in the fall of 1974 that "although with the opening of the college buildings, morning and afternoon classes will be held, there will be a high percentage of evening classes to accommodate working students."[86] North Harris continued to offer evening classes at off-campus locations to accommodate the area's working students, a precedent that would continue twenty five years later.

With the architectural firm in place in December of 1972, and the site selected and purchased in May of 1973, architectural plans for the new college were then drawn. The blueprints called for a two-story structure of modern design that would be built in several phases. Bids for the construction of Phase One were collected from several area building firms. Fleetwood Construction Company of Houston was awarded the campus building contract in January of 1974. The contract stipulated completion dates, as well as an addendum listing conditions for the site clearing. Phase One of the college was to be completed by August 15, 1975, with the builder given 540 days to complete the project upon notice to proceed.

Phase One of North Harris College specified the construction of four buildings: Academic, which included Admissions as well as a Learning Resource Center; Science and Technology; Vocational-Technical; Mechanical; and Central Receiving. Of the four, the first building to be erected was the one-story Vocational-Technical building to allow for technical programs to be offered such as welding, auto mechanics, and air-conditioning. In the fall of 1973, the Board of Trustees had decided prior to actual construction, that the Science and Technology building would be named the John A. Winship Science and Technology Building in honor of the Spring superintendent who envisioned the establishment of a community college in northern Harris County. Winship passed away after a lengthy illness in April of 1973. Six months prior to his death, Winship was able to see his vision become a reality, with the successful election ensuring the creation of the North Harris College district that included Spring ISD. At this time, the Board also agreed that the library of North Harris College, would be named the Marion H. Donaldson Memorial Library, in honor of W.W. Thorne's longtime and dedicated secretary.[87]

Environmental concerns were clearly addressed both in the planning and building stages of the college following Environmental Protection Agency guidelines. An addendum to the builders contract ensured the protection of the area's many trees. All existing trees indicated to remain were to be protected via the installation of temporary barricades, and any trees damaged during the construction of the college were to be repaired or replaced under architectural guidelines.[88] The parking areas "will be interspersed with green landscaped sections to break the severity of the asphalt surface, as well as to create a cooling naturalistic effort and to blend with the rest of the wooded 185 acre site."[89] The architectural firm KTC, recommended the natural tones of the exterior light brown brick in order

to blend into the surrounding wooded landscape. Airline noise control was also an important consideration in the planning stages of the buildings. Thorne described the structural thickness of the walls and roof of the new buildings, "the four and one-half inch concrete roof and the exterior walls, having an air cavity between the brick and masonry block, which was then covered by two thicknesses of sheetrock, will serve to keep out the noise."[90] Likewise, windows were kept to a minimum in order to contain the noise level as well as to conserve energy. The classrooms would have "one wall of vivid color to accent the others in off-white, and one would also contain a permanent mounted screen to use with audio-visual equipment. Several types of materials were blended. The vinyl covered walls, light brick, terrazzo floors were coordinated to accent the harmony of the various textures."[91] The one accent wall of vivid color, caused some friendly debate amongst board members, several of whom were Texas A & M alumni. The several accent paint selections did not include the Texas A & M color of maroon. As a practical joke, Thorne had one room in the new college painted completely in maroon, the storage closet located near the President's office.

Construction of a paved access road off of Aldine-Westfield (today's W.W. Thorne Drive) was of first concern, and work began immedi-

ately after purchase in 1973. The roadwork, including the construction of a bridge over Turkey Creek, allowed for preparation of the building site, clearing and leveling, proper drainage, as well as providing water and sewer supply. Several delays occurred during the construction phases due to bad weather. As construction of the new facility proceeded, college classes continued to be held at area schools.

The first commencement of North Harris College students occurred on May 9, 1975 with

*Above: Academic Building.*

*Below: Courtyard Amphitheater.*

*An aerial view of North Harris College. The location in a pine forest prompted founder, W.W. Thorne to call North Harris "the little college in the woods."*

*Opposite: Founding President W.W. Thorne presents Marion Wilson, the first student to graduate from North Harris College, with an Associate of Science degree, May 9, 1975. The First Commencement Ceremony was held at Aldine High School.*

COURTESY: W.E. CROZIER

the ceremony held at Aldine High School. The first graduating class consisted of a total of sixty-four students. The commencement address was given by the Honorable Mark W. White, Jr., at the time, Secretary of State for Texas. The first student to cross the stage and graduate from North Harris College, received an Associate of Science degree. The A.S. degree was conferred to one student, Marion May Wilson, who went on to graduate from Rice University with a degree in science. Fourteen students received the Associate of Arts degree. Six received an Associate of General Studies. The majority of the first class of North Harris College graduates received Certificates of Competency. These certificates were awarded to forty-three students enrolled in the programs of Cosmetology and Institutional Food Service. Joyce Brown and Joyce McQueen were among the recipients of the first North Harris certificates. Joyce Brown recalls that, "after the ceremony, the Aldine ISD food service had refreshments for us. They made petit fours and on top was a tiny rolled up diploma tied with black ribbon, inside was Class of 1975. I kept that diploma for many years."[92] Joyce McQueen reflected on the college's accessibility and location, stating that "when North Harris College offered its classes at Aldine H.S.... I was elated. I was working on a

certificate in Institutional Food Service at San Jacinto College. Since I live in Aldine, that was a long drive for me."[93]

Vocational nursing was one of the early popular programs offered at North Harris College, coinciding with the establishment of a new area hospital. The first capping ceremony for Vocational Nursing students occurred in January 1975, when twenty-five students, "the first nursing class" completed their pre-clinical work and were awarded with nurse's caps. Marie Bayard, coordinator of nursing education, Lester Burks, Dean of Technical-Vocational, and Carol Bary, nursing instructor, presented the students with their caps.[94] This was a well publicized event as students entered the health profession. Students in training worked at Houston Northwest, Parkview Hospital, and other area locations.

Houston Northwest Medical Center opened in 1973, the same year that North Harris College began offering classes. Similar to the description of college property, the land purchase for this hospital site occurred in 1971 when founder, Dr. Edward Roberson, and a group of other doctors, "purchased 60 acres off a two lane farm-to-market road called Jackrabbit Road. Back then, the site was nothing more than a cow pasture in a remote area of Greater

**The First Graduating Class of North Harris College**

MAY 9, 1975
*Commencement Address by the Honorable Mark W. White, Jr., Secretary of State for Texas*

**ASSOCIATE OF SCIENCE**
Marion May Wilson*

**ASSOCIATE OF ARTS**
Frances Derring Anderson
Marilyn Ann Barnes
Ronald Eugene Brannon
Fay Sylvia Buenger
Beverly A. Chapman*
Estaban Galvan
Pamela Denise Gilmer
Althea Lynn King
Elizabeth E. Kuhn
Martha C. Michels
Brenda Sue Salyers
Michael Allen Shomaker*
Warner L. Williams

**ASSOCIATE OF GENERAL STUDIES**
Roy Blasingim
Sidney Michael Cates
Delwin W. Davis
Rudi Nan Lee
Jo Anne Metcalf*
Katherine Ann Nelius

*Member of Phi Theta Kappa Honor Society

**CERTIFICATE OF COMPETENCY**

**COSMETOLOGY**
Theresa Lynn Atkinson
Jessie Jeanette Briscoe
Janis Lane Bryan
Charlotte A. Burk
Dora Estell Cuellar
Henry A. Dean
Ernest Lloyd Diggs
Maurice Delores Ellis
Rena M. Flores
Penny Fuller
Teresa Gonzales
Janis Darlene Goynes
Diana Lynne Haude
Barbara J. Headrick
Alice L. Humphries
Janice Thomasena Jager
Nilda Norma Leza
Sunny G. Morgan
Alfred Grant Pebworth
Cindy Mills Pierce
Joyce Marie Qualls
Barbara Ann Sheffield
Jo Ann Tindol
Debra Lynn Wright

**INSTITUTIONAL FOOD SERVICE**
Mayola Nolin Brewer
Joyce Brown
Betty Crawford
L.E. Franklin
Shirley Harrington
Lue Hicks
Dorothy Johnson
Joyce McQueen
Rose Norman
Evelyn Pearson
Mary Raley
Sydney Bessent Redding
Anna Stafford
Cleo Thomas
Irene Vaughn
Ella Walker
Annie M. Williams
Frances Worn

Houston… there were no other medical facilities nearby. The people who lived in the area had no place to go when they needed medical attention."[95] Louise Panzarella of Humble, who served on North Harris College's founding Steering Committee, concurs, recalling that her husband, an M.D., traveled "all the way from Humble" to deliver babies in Spring. Panzarella said that before the hospital was built, the "need for doctors was so bad… that he was overwhelmed with patients. It was a grave situation, because there was no one here."[96] The establishment of an area hospital and the subsequent need for nurses meant that college classes for

*Above: First North Harris College Vocational Nursing Graduates, 1975. Marie Bayard (right) congratulates honor students, Tempie Neal of Aldine (center), and Jo Benson of Spring.*

*Below: The Hurricanes Basketball Team. Back row, left to right: Basketball Coach, Rich Almstedt, Lee Hightower, Ben Mosley, Cornell Harrison, Ray Matlock, Charles Taylor, Jerry Dobbs. Middle row: Barry Ross, Michael Witchet, Frank Skero, Michael Joseph, Danea Wilkerson. Front row: Michael Walter, Billy Hampton, Dwight Thomas, and team supporter, Rusty Hawkins of Humble.*

these early programs were generally full. According to Lester Burks, "Marie Bayard… and her instructors always had good success with their students passing state boards… that was a measurement of how well the program was going."[97] The next step, and the much anticipated North Harris Associate Degree Nursing Program, began in 1978. Carol Singer served as program director, and was joined shortly afterward by Marianne Malague and Dr. Nockie Zizelmann. It is fondly reminisced that "the first

class of 36 nursing students were chosen by lottery. Names were placed in gelatin capsules drawn by community representatives."[98] The Associate Degree Nursing Program continues to be a highly respected program for students seeking a career in the medical field.

Intramural and intercollegiate sports started in the fall of 1975. Until the construction of a permanent gymnasium on campus, the Bender Gym in downtown Humble was leased by the college for use by the NHC physical education department. The North Harris "Hurricanes," clad in silver and black uniforms, were the college's first and only intercollegiate basketball team. The Hurricane name was derived from the first registration of North Harris College students, held during a tropical depression. Coaching the popular Hurricanes was Rich Almstedt. Almstedt recalls, "We were on a pretty tight schedule as our players had to practice at Bender in Humble and then drive to evening classes over at Aldine High School. Our first team was made up of players from Forestbrook, Smiley, Sam Houston, Aldine, Aldine Carver, Klein and Humble…. It was really quite exciting playing in Humble because we drew good crowds from the local community."[99] The Hurricanes were supported on the sidelines by a squad of North Harris cheerleaders, sporting bobby socks, sad-

dleshoes and black and white uniforms that displayed a megaphone containing the letters of NHCC. The cheerleaders were selected by a committee of faculty and staff. Lynn James, a graduate of Klein High School served as the first captain of the cheerleading squad.[100]

Dr. Bob Williams, served as North Harris' first athletic director, and was responsible for recruiting several local area athletes. North Harris' first basketball team included former captains from area varsity teams, such as Aldine's Frank Skero and Klein's most valuable player, Michael Witchet.[101] The Hurricanes competed with other junior college teams around the Houston area. A track and field team, coached by Dr. Bob Williams, began competing in early 1977. At that time, a competitive golf and tennis team were also in the planning stages.[102] The intercollegiate sports program, popular at its inception, was eventually unable to compete with the scholarships and benefits

provided by other area community colleges. Although intercollegiate sports at North Harris were short-lived, the physical education department continues to offer a variety of programs pertaining to health and fitness. The development of a one mile jogging trail that loops around the forest patches off of W.W. Thorne Blvd. attracts students, faculty, administrators, and area residents.

In 1980, the much anticipated cultural Fine Arts Center opened at North Harris College. This occurred at a time when most senior level universities were cutting back funding on programs in the arts. The Fine Arts Center was heralded by president Thorne as "the only structure of its kind between Buffalo Bayou and Dallas."[103] The Fine Arts Center, a $2 million dollar project, included a 350-seat Performing Arts Theater complete with orchestra pit. The center houses rehearsal halls, music practice rooms, art studios and an impressive art gallery designed

*North Harris College, the first campus of the college district, opened its new facility in 1976.*

*Above: NHCC Cheerleaders, in school colors of black and white, supported the Hurricanes basketball team, 1977. Lynn James, captain (center front). From left to right: Valerie Shannon, Jan Dean, Gloria Young, Vicki Keilman, Paddy Woods.*

*Right: Dr. Bob Williams was North Harris College's first athletic director, 1974.*

for artists and students to exhibit their work. Dr. Joe Kaough has served as the longtime director of the theater, offering productions from Neil Simon comedies to dramatic classics. "The first production at the college featured a guest appearance by the Academy award winning actress, Mercedes McCambridge. The production was *Look Homeward Angel*," Kaough recalled.[104] The college offered productions in the Performing Arts Theater as well as a more intimate setting in a smaller theater in the round, called the Arena Theater. The Arena Theater initially began as a dinner theater that board members, faculty, and area residents found particularly attractive. Here students were able to experience the artistic difficulty of performing to a circular audience.

New Caney and Tomball ISDs became part of the college district in 1981 and 1982. Statistics for 1982 show that the student population at North Harris College swelled to "more than

8,000 taking credit classes and 8,500 taking non-credit classes," a significant increase from the 640 students who first registered in 1973.[105] With the expansion of the college district to include five member ISDs, North Harris College had nearly doubled its geographic size in the first ten years of its existence. Land purchase and final plans were approved by the board for the construction of a second campus in Kingwood, and plans were already underway to build a third campus in the near future, in Tomball. North Harris College was on its way to becoming a multi-campus system.

In August 1982, W.W. Thorne chose to retire after serving the local community for a total of thirty-six years in the field of education. As first president of North Harris College, Thorne had seen the birth of the college and the dramatic change from serving 640 students to over 16,000 in the college's first ten years. The college had grown to serve other areas, from northern Harris County and extending into southern Montgomery County. North Harris College, the original campus established to serve residents north of Aldine and into Spring, had outgrown

its facility by 1981. Rather than enlarge the main campus, plans for the construction of a smaller east campus near Humble were made under Thorne's direction. At the same time, hope existed that a west campus in Tomball would also become a reality. A college system of multiple campuses would ensure accessible education to all students, reduce commuting time, provide small student-teacher ratios, and prevent overcrowding of existing facilities. The "Tomball Bill," promoted by Tomball's Roy Hohl, Jack Frey, as well as W.W. Thorne and others, passed the state legislature in 1981, allowing Tomball ISD to finally enter the college district family via election in 1982.[106] Securing Tomball's inclusion, it was that same year that Thorne chose to retire.

Founder and first president W.W. Thorne was succeeded by vice president and former Dean of Instruction, Dr. Joe Airola. It is Airola who is recognized as the first Chancellor of the North Harris County College District. NHCCD officially became a multi-campus district in the fall of 1984, with the opening of a second campus in southeastern Montgomery County. Initially

*The Fine Arts Center houses a professional Art Gallery and Performing Arts Theater, North Harris College.*

called the East Campus of North Harris County College District, today the campus is known as Kingwood College. The groundbreaking ceremony for the construction of a new second campus occurred in the spring of 1983. Brad York, president of the NHCC Board of Trustees at the time, remarked that with the establishment of a multi-campus district, "North Harris County College has reached a new benchmark in its ten year history."[107]

The decision to create a multi-campus system rather than enlarging the capacity at North Harris College was a philosophical one. According to Dr. Airola, "the deciding factor had to do with the fact that we wanted to be close to the community, if you're too big you tend to forget that."[108] In keeping with the mission of North Harris College, the institution was founded on the principle of serving the community. The rapid growth of the northern sector war-

ranted the establishment of a multi-campus system. Airola served as president of North Harris College for two years before his appointment as Chancellor in January 1984. At that time, Dr. Larry Phillips, formerly Dean of Instruction, assumed the presidency of the South Campus. Recognizing the continued growth pattern of the college district, Phillips remarked that "the challenge is to keep up with the area's growth with new facilities, new campuses. I feel the plans we have made will cope with the need for post-secondary education here."[109] The third campus, Tomball College, located on the western edge of the district on Highway 249, opened in 1988. Tomball College serves the residents of Tomball, as well as the outlying communities of

Decker Prairie, Magnolia, Klein and Cy-Fair.

As Chancellor, Dr. Airola managed to bring about an important partnership at the North Harris College campus. Our Lady of the Lake University in San Antonio had expressed interest in opening a Houston branch at North Harris College, to provide area students with alternative ways to complete their four year degrees.[110] At the time, there were no bachelor degree programs available in northern Harris County. Sister Elizabeth Anne Sueltenfuss, president of Our Lady of the Lake University, and Dr. Antonio Rigual, vice president of Institutional Advancement, came up with the idea of a joint public/private educational program.[111] In an agreement with North Harris College in 1986, Our Lady of the Lake University would use the campus facilities on Saturdays. This university extension at North Harris College allowed many area students to continue their education at both the senior and graduate levels. In 1991, OLLU's Houston Weekend Programs held at the college, offered graduate degree programs such as the M.B.A., and in 1996, the M.A. in

Human Sciences and the M.S. in Psychology. Several students received institutional sponsorship from NHC/OLLU for the completion of their degrees.[112]

In 1987 under Airola's direction, the NHC Board of Trustees shrewdly purchased an entire office building located in a prime commercial area off of Beltway 8 near Greenspoint Mall. At that time, many of Houston's office buildings were left vacant and bankrupt due to the harsh conditions imposed by a poor economy. Houston's major oil and gas companies abruptly downsized, forcing many individuals to lose both their jobs and homes. Bank foreclosures occurred in commercial and residential housing, and many office buildings stood empty throughout the greater Houston area. The building in which the District Office is located became available as the result of a bankruptcy situation.[113] The District Office building serves as the administrative center of the expanding college district, housing the Chancellor's office as well as the Trustees Boardroom. Continuing education and other classes, including the establish-

*Above: First Chancellor, Dr. Joe Airola and NHCC Board of Trustees President, Brad York (left) view the site of the proposed East Campus, 1983. The second campus of the college district, the East Campus (today's Kingwood College) established NHCC as a multi-campus district.*

*Above: North Harris College in the winter.*

COURTESY: DREW HAZZLERIGG

ment of a northern branch of the University of Houston, were eventually held at this location.

In 1991, Dr. John E. Pickelman became Chancellor of the North Harris Community College District upon the retirement of Joe Airola. Dr. Pickelman served as president of Galveston College since 1983, and in several administrative capacities at the Dallas County Community College District. As Chancellor of NHMCCD, Pickelman is responsible for implementing even further expansion of the district in geographic size, decentralizing the college district with emphasis on individual campus communities, as well as internal modernization through the establishment of a technological infrastructure connecting all college campuses and district.

The emphasis on decentralized operations was a distinct change from former administra-tions. Pickelman believed that as the service area of the district continued to grow, individual college campuses needed to "work separately for local effectiveness" and be sensitive to the needs of the particular communities that they served.[114] The initiatives under Pickelman's leadership include the establishment of Montgomery College in The Woodlands, the Carver Center in the Acres Homes area, and the development of The University Center.

The University Center, located in The Woodlands, is considered to be a premiere facility in the state of Texas. Six senior universities have formed an important partnership with the North Harris Montgomery Community College District, providing area students with the opportunity and incentive to complete their baccalaureate as well as master's degrees. According to Dr. Pickelman, "For more than 20 years, north

Houston community leaders have looked forward to building an upper-level university in the area. The University Center will be a technologically advanced facility, and its scope will extend to the six university campuses and our four community colleges through interactive means...."[115]

Change reached every level. The original campus, North Harris College, received a new college president and the first selected from outside the original system. Dr. Sanford C. Shugart, a native of North Carolina, replaced Dr. Larry Phillips, and immediately began the implementation of plans for the improvement of the original campus. Shugart is responsible for the college's outreach initiative which includes the establishment of two off-campus satellite centers designed to further serve the Aldine community. Regular campus bus transportation was also introduced via Metro service. A strategic master plan, which includes expansion and renovation of the North Harris College campus, provides a clear vision for the college future. Based on architectural drawings, the proposed expansion of North Harris College includes a new and separate three-story Library, an advanced Technology Center, a Child Development Lab School, extensive restructuring of the existing campus facility adding classrooms and science labs, as well as increased and covered parking areas. More than 200,000 square feet of new buildings will be added to the existing 468,000

square foot NHC campus, which is already one of the largest two-year campuses to serve the Houston area.[116]

In May of 1991, an election held in Conroe ISD resulted in the addition of a new school district to the North Harris College system. The college district was expanding further into bordering Montgomery County following population growth. To reflect its expanded geographic service area, the college district name officially changed. The new name, North Harris Montgomery Community College District, reflects a multi-campus system that serves an area of approximately 1,000 square miles, and over a million residents. In 1996, two additional school districts, Willis and Splendora, voted to join the college family.

As these changes occurred, the official logo of North Harris College also became outdated and was modernized to reflect the decentralization of the multi-campus system. From the bold letter N pointing upwards, a new artistically lined star on different colored squares coincides with each individual campus. North Harris College is represented by the color red; Kingwood- green; Tomball- maroon; and Montgomery- blue. In the reorganization process, each college campus was to retain its own identity rather serve under the umbrella of the North Harris College name. North Harris College, the original and largest of the campuses, had been referred to as the South Campus of the North Harris County College District. The directional names were replaced by community ones during Airola's term of office. Tomball College was the exception, as it was the only campus of the district located adjacent to a

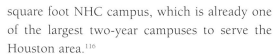

*Top: Dr. John E. Pickelman, Chancellor of NHMCCD.*

*Bottom: The District's new logo.*

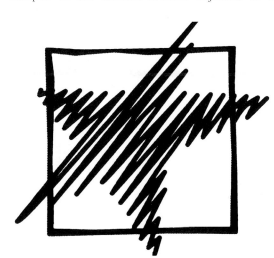

opened in the summer of 1995 with a dedication speech delivered by the Governor of the State of Texas, George W. Bush.

The innovative University Center located near Montgomery College officially opened in January 1998, providing state-of-the-art and one-step learning. Baccalaureate and advanced degree programs from several senior universities, including Texas A&M, the University of Houston, and Sam Houston State, will be offered in conjunction with the community college. Area students will not need to commute at long distance or at great expense to complete their degrees. The groundbreaking for The University Center occurred in the spring of 1996. Heralded as "the first in the state of Texas," The University Center has established a bridge between the modern community college and senior universities.[117]

From the start of North Harris College in 1972, the district has grown to include four permanent college campuses, The University Center, as well as several satellite outreach centers providing academic, vocational, and continuing education to area residents. The original

town. During Pickelman's administration, a new fourth campus opened called Montgomery College serving students in southern Montgomery County. Montgomery College, located in the master-planned community of The Woodlands,

founders of North Harris College, who had boldly envisioned bringing higher education to the local community, never anticipated the tremendous geographic or physical growth that the college district has made. In the words of founder, W.W. Thorne, "I don't know of anything that I would have done that I enjoyed more, or that I'm more proud of, than association with this school. They told me, some of my colleagues who were junior college presidents here, that when we were trying to get this one (started), they said it will be bigger than you can imagine. You're just not thinking big enough.

Well, I kind of took that with a grain of salt. But I don't think anybody in their wildest imagination conceived of what would happen to this institution. It has been more than most anybody thought...."[118] Twenty-five years, a quarter of a century of service to the community, is only yesterday in the lifetime of an institution. What is important to measure is how many lives were changed as a result of the educational experience. The number of students who have passed through the community college doors is immeasurable. The college experience remains one of enrichment, and is profoundly rewarding.

# NOTES

[1] W.W. Thorne, Superintendent of Aldine Independent School District. Letter addressed to Members of the Steering Committee, School Board Members, Proposed Junior College Board Members, July 25, 1972. North Harris College, LRC Archives.

[2] Gary Clark, naturalist and descendant of Lemm family, interview with author, 1996.

[3] The Old Three Hundred colonists were predominantly Southerners. Frederick Rankin was from Kentucky; but David Harris was born in New York. The three Kuykendahl brothers, Abner, Joseph, and Robert, were also from Kentucky.

[4] At New Kentucky, a historic settlement near Tomball, General Houston was informed of Mexican Army movement. New Kentucky was settled around 1826 by pioneer Abram Roberts.

[5] The U.S. Census of 1850 identifies the following early settlers as being from Germany: Strack, Thaisz/Theiss, Meyer, and Wincher/Wunsche. From Louisiana were the Ritchie/Richey family, and the Sellers. The majority were listed as farmers.

[6] Initially eight sections of land were granted for every mile of track laid, this number doubled prior to the Civil War.

[7] Harris County, County Clerk's Office, Archives. Deed from Houston Tap & Brazoria Railroad Company, 1862 to Darius Gregg survey. Trace of North Harris County College Deed conducted 1996.

[8] This railroad line is the oldest of the Missouri Pacific system (today's Union Pacific) found in Texas.

[9] In 1995, Harris County ranked tenth in a listing of the top ten rice-producing counties in the state of Texas. Wharton and Colorado counties ranked first and second, with Brazoria fifth. Agricultural Report, *Houston Chronicle*, 1996.

[10] John M. Robinson, descendant of Spring family which started the Robinson Addition, now Old Town Spring. Interview with author, 1996.

[11] Elmer Beckendorf, interview with author, 1997. Mr. Beckendorf has served on the NHMCCD Board of Trustees since 1985, and is a descendant of August Beckendorff, who emigrated from Germany and settled northern Harris county in the mid-1800's. Mr. Beckendorf's grandfather established a dairy in 1907.

[12] The Essman Dairy was located off Humble-Westfield Road; Saathoff Dairy on Aldine-Westfield and Treaschwig; Greggson Dairy on Hardy near Westfield; Spears Dairy, which bottled its own milk; and Davis Dairy on Hardy. Interviews with Marilyn Theiss Kron, Arlene Schultz, Marvin Theiss, and Rebecca Tautenhahn Strack Stone, 1996.

[13] James King, current owner of subdivided Essman property, in interview with author, 1996.

[14] Marilyn Theiss Kron, daughter of Carl and Meta Theiss, interview with author, 1996.

[15] Ibid.

[16] L.L. Pugh, County School Superintendent, "Report of Harris County Schools For Year Ending August 31, 1910," page 101. Courtesy of Rebecca Tautenhahn Strack Stone.

[17] Kron, interview with author, 1996. Willie Baumgartner was her uncle.

[18] Arlene Schultz, interview with author, 1996.

[19] Ibid. The Schultz family is kin to many of the major German family groups (Theiss, Baumgartner, Hildebrandt, Beckendorf) who settled northern Harris County.

[20] Peter Wunderlich, *Letters*, May 6, 1853 and April 13, 1857. As cited in Diana Severance, "Klein, Texas" (Klein Historical Foundation, 1994), pp.48-50.

[21] Sausage making was "an art brought from Europe by the immigrants and virtually unknown to the southern Anglo-Americans," according to Terry Jordan, *German Seed in Texas Soil* (University of Texas Press, 1966), p. 153.

[22] *Texana*, Vol. 8, p.353; as cited in Bill Winsor, *Texas in the Confederacy* (Hillsboro, Texas, 1978), p.15.

[23] German settler, Herman Strack of the Klein area. As cited in Diana Severance, "Klein, Texas" (Klein Historical Foundation, 1994), p. 4.

[24] The Bammel farm community extended from the dirt road, Kuykendahl and today's F.M. 1960, to Cypress Creek. Bammel Road was the major thoroughfare prior to the construction of F.M. 1960. It connected Bammel with Westfield and Humble. "Oil bearing sands" were discovered in 1938.

[25] 1889 first Lumber Mill in area; Bayer's Lumber Mill 1927; Bender's Sawmill; Klein Sawmill; Boettcher Sawmill, majority located in Spring-Westfield area where East Texas Big Thicket timberline extends furthest south.

[26] Research information from Texas Forestry Museum, Lufkin, Texas. Statistics reveal that in 1928 this one Company Town of the large Grogan-Cochran Lumber Company, located near Magnolia, had 450 employees; 175 in 1934; and 400 in 1940.

[27] A "dinky track" was a small railroad track used to haul logs from the woods to the sawmill. Interview with Marvin Theiss, 1996.

[28] Arthur Bayer, interview with author, Spring, 1996. See also Gladys Hildebrandt Tullos, "A German Family Contributes to the Development of Spring. My Family Heritage," no date, p.3. Spring ISD archives.

[29] North Harris County Branch of the American Association of University Women, *The Heritage of Northern Harris County* (1977), Spring, p.84. Also, John M. Robinson, interview with author, 1996.

[30] Charlene Ragsdale, ed., *Spring: Lofts and Lore*, compiled by the American Cultures Class, Spring High School South, 1977-1978 (Houston, Texas, 1978), p.9. Spring ISD archives.

[31] Spring ISD, "Spring: An Area of Growth and Change," p.7.

[32] *The Heritage of North Harris County*, (1977), Westfield, p.79.

[33] Rebecca Tautenhahn Strack Stone, interview with author, 1996.

[34] Ibid., 1996.

[35] Arlene Schultz, interview with author, August 1996.

[36] E.C. Robertson, "Aldine in Midwinter, As Portrayed by Kodak," (February 1909), photograph. Courtesy of Elizabeth Battle, Aldine ISD archives.

[37] E.C. Robertson, "All Doubts Dispelled by the Doubters Themselves," 1909, promotional pamphlet. Courtesy of Aldine ISD. The Aldine preserved figs were also reported to have won the "highest prize at the St. Louis World's Fair."

[38] The problem of hobos riding the trains resulted in a railroad detective stationed in Spring. From interview with John M. Robinson, 1996.

[39] The robbery occurred May 1932 at the Spring State Bank, $7500 was stolen from the vault. "Bonnie and Clyde Hit Spring Bank," *The Lion*, Spring High School, April 18, 1973.

[40] Arthur Bayer, interview with author, 1996.

[41] John M. Robinson, interview with author, 1996.

[42] David McComb, *Houston: A History* (University of Texas Press, 1969, 1981), p. 129.

[43] *For American Democracy, A Report of the President's Commission on Higher Education* (also called the Truman Commission), 1948, Volume I, p.29.

[44] Ibid., Volume I, p.25.

[45] Aldine ISD Election Pamphlet, "Aldine, A Future with a Plan"(1973), refer to graph on student enrollment. Election would provide for the construction of several new schools, including "4 elementary schools, 2 middle schools…" and improvements on existing others.

[46] Donald Whisenhunt, *The Encyclopedia of Texas Colleges and Universities, An Historical Profile* (Austin, Texas: Eakin Press, 1986).

[47] Margaret Smith,"Significant Dates in the Development of the Spring Community," The Spring Historical Museum, 1996.

[48] Jimmy Demaret and Jackie Burke were responsible for Champions Golf Course, 1958.

[49] W.W. Thorne, interview with author, February 2, 1996.

[50] Houston North Association, "North Houston's Urban Pioneers: The Houston North Association 1962-1984." Pamphlet, LRC Archives, North Harris College.

[51] H.E. Barrett, interview with author, San Jacinto River Authority, Conroe, Texas, March 21, 1996.

[52] *Houston Chronicle*, June 17, 1973. "Dream of Junior College for Northside Coming True."

[53] Klein 212 (of required 141); Spring 250 (of required 140); Tomball 301 (of required 156). "Report of Petition Signature Tabulation, 13 districts." Greater Houston Community Junior College Commission, The Local Steering Committee, *Local Survey Report*, Submitted to Coordinating Board, July 15, 1968.

[54] *The North Freeway Leader*, October 5, 1972. "Voters to Decide on Four Propositions at Polls."

[55] W.W. Thorne, interview with author, 1996.

[56] *The Houston Post*, August 2, 1972. "Local Educator College President."

[57] Dale F. Campbell, Asst. Commissioner Texas Higher Education Coordinating Board, "Texas," as found in Ben E. Fountain and Terrence A. Tollefson, *Community Colleges in the United States: Forty-Nine State Systems* (American Association of Community and Junior Colleges, Washington D.C., 1989), p.221.

[58] Kathleen Bland Smith, "Crossroads in Texas" as found in Roger Yarrington, ed., *Junior Colleges: 50 States/50 Years* (American Association of Community and Junior Colleges, Washington D.C., 1969), p. 147.

[59] Campbell, p. 222-223.

[60] April 11, 1972 Letter from Edwin Theiss, President, Board of Trustees, Klein ISD to E.M. Wells, Citizen's Committee, Union Junior College. LRC Archives- North Harris College.

[61] *The North Freeway Leader*, June 15, 1972. "Junior College Proposal To Go Before State Board."

[62] Letter from Raymond Cleveland, President, Lee College to E.M. Wells, Chairman of North Harris County College Steering Committee, July 21, 1972. Courtesy of E.M. Wells.

[63] Letter from W.W. Thorne to Mayor of Houston, Louie Welch. March 1, 1973. NHC-LRC Archives.

[64] E.M. Wells served as president of the Board of Spring ISD; M.M. Morris served as president of the Board of Aldine ISD; and Hugh Dugan served as secretary of the Board of Humble ISD. In addition, Charles Philipp served five years on the Harris County Board of Education. From "Our Next Big Step," campaign literature promoting the establishment of North Harris County Junior College, 1972; NHM-CCD archives.

[65] E.M. Wells, interview with author, Houston, Texas,

[66] *North Harris County News*, "Thorne Leaves Aldine Post For Junior College Presidency," December 13, 1972. See also *Houston Chronicle*, "Aldine School Chief Quits to Head College," December 13, 1972.

[67] Lester Burks, interview with author, Houston, Texas, March 1996.

[68] Bob Williams, interview with author, April 1996.

[69] Karen Kincheloe, interview with author, February 1996.

[70] Joe McMillian, interview with author, 1996.

[71] Koetter, Tharp & Cowell. Letter to Mr. E.M. Wells, president of the Board of Trustees, North Harris County College, December 18, 1972.

[72] Roy Lazenby, interview with author, April 1996.

[73] North Harris County Junior College, Board of Trustees, *Minutes*, February 8, 1973, p. 3.

[74] W.W. Thorne, interview with author, February 1996.

[75] North Harris County Junior College, Board of Trustees, *Minutes*, March 8, 1973.

[76] Ibid., April 12, 1973.

[77] Roy Lazenby, interview with author, 1996.

[78] *North Harris County College Bulletin*, 1973-1974, Foreword, p. 6.

[79] North Harris County Junior College, Board of Trustees, *Minutes*, October 11, 1973, p. 3.

[80] *Houston Post*, "Library to be Shared by Aldine High School," August 2, 1973.

[81] Michael Green, Associate Vice-Chancellor/Research and Planning, correspondence with author, 1996. Floyd Hoffman became an early member of the North Harris College Board of Trustees.

[82] *Houston Post*, "JC Trustees Vote To Buy Land, Turn Down Donation," February 9, 1973.

[83] Jack Byrd, Manager, Friendswood Development Co. and the King Ranch, Inc., Letter to Mr. R. McWhirter, North Harris County Junior College Steering Committee, September 8, 1972. NHMCCD Archives.

[84] Koetter, Tharp & Cowell, Architects and Planners. *Report: Site Evaluation for North Harris County Junior College*, 1972.

[85] Ibid, Evaluation of Site 2.

[86] *The News*, December 4, 1974. "NHCC Construction Showing Progress."

[87] North Harris County Junior College, Board of Trustees, *Minutes*, November 8, 1973, p.2.

[88] American Institute of Architects, General Conditions of the Contract for Construction, Standard Form of Agreement Between Owner and Contractor, January 11, 1974. Building Contract, North Harris County Junior College and Fleetwood Construction Company, "Site Clearing, 1.03 Protection." NHMCCD District Archives.

[89] *The Northeast Sentinel*, November 11, 1975. "NHCC Campus Nears Finish."

[90] Ibid., W.W. Thorne remark.

[91] *The News*, "New College Campus To be Ready for Occupancy in June." November 12, 1975. W.W. Thorne remark.

[92] Joyce Brown, correspondence with author, January 1997.

[93] Joyce McQueen, correspondence with author, April 1997.

[94] *The News*, "Capping Ceremony Held For NHC College's First Vocational Nursing Grads," January 22, 1975.

[95] Dr. Edward Roberson, as cited in Houston Northwest Medical Center's "Twenty Years in Pursuit of Medical Excellence," 1993. Courtesy of Houston Northwest Medical Center.

[96] Louise Panzarella, interview with author, 1996.

[97] Lester Burks, first Dean of Vocational-Technical Programs, interview with author, 1996.

[98] Peggy Aalund compiled this information from a nursing reunion held in the summer of 1996. Submitted by Joy Tichenor to author.

[99] Rich Almstedt, correspondence to author, 1996.

[100] *The Humble News-Messenger*, "New Cheerleaders", February 2, 1977.

[101] *The North Freeway Leader*, "NHCC Organizes First Basketball Team," October 9, 1975.

[102] Ibid., "Sports Program… Expanded," January 27, 1977.

[103] *Houston Post*, "Up in North Harris County, the Arts Never Had It So Good," December 1, 1980.

[104] Joseph Kaough, interview with author, North Harris College, April 1, 1996.

[105] *Houston Post*, "President of NHCC Retiring, But Plans to Keep Options Open." April 18, 1982.

[106] House Bill #389 (The Tomball Bill), was introduced by Representative Don Henderson in the House, and Senator Walter Mengden in the Senate. The Tomball Bill revoked the existing law on contiguous school districts. *The News*, January 13, 1982.

[107] *News-Messenger*, April 28, 1983.

[108] Dr. Joe Airola, interview with author, Houston, February 1996.

[109] Dr. Larry Phillips, NHCC Office of Public Information, January 30, 1984. NHC archives.

[110] Airola, interview with author, 1996.

[111] Geraldine Gallagher, North Harris College, *Houston Chronicle*, April 9, 1997. Theresa McGinley, interview with Dr. Adrian Shapiro, Assistant Academic Dean, Our Lady of the Lake University—Houston Weekend Programs, 1997.

[112] Dr. Adrian Shapiro, interview with author, 1997.

[113] Airola, interview, 1996. The land alone has doubled in value since purchase.

[114] John E. Pickelman, North Harris Montgomery Community College District, *Vision Statement*, 1996.

[115] John E. Pickelman, North Harris Montgomery Community College District, "Message from the Chancellor," *Maxim*, Vol.4, No.3, 1996.

[116] "North Harris College Expansion in Works," *1960 Sun*, August 27, 1997.

[117] Pickelman, *Maxim*, 1996.

[118] W.W. Thorne, Interview with author, 1996.

# KINGWOOD COLLEGE

### The College in the Woods

by Link Hullar and Dean Wolfe

*"Beginning in the fall of 1984, the College district will have two campuses to serve its students. The original campus is the South Campus and the new campus at 20000 Kingwood Drive is the East Campus. Classes will be offered on the new campus for the first time during fall registration. Specific classes to be offered will be listed in the printed fall schedule."*[1]
—BULLETIN 1984-1985, North Harris County College District

While the above announcement was certainly not the first the people of our college district had heard regarding the new East campus, it was the first mention of the future Kingwood College in the college's official annual *Bulletin*. Construction was underway at the selected site at the extreme west end of Kingwood Drive, administrators were on board, and the process of selecting faculty and staff had begun. The fall semester of 1984 marked the expansion of the North Harris County College District along with the beginnings of a new "multi-campus" approach to serving the people of our communities in Harris and Montgomery Counties.

*Link Hullar and Dean Wolfe are professors of history at Kingwood College.*

The site selected for construction of the new East campus was suited for the rapidly developing area of east Harris and south Montgomery counties. Conveniently located just north of the San Jacinto River to the west of U.S. 59, the college site was designed to attract students from Humble, Kingwood, New Caney, Porter, Splendora, and other communities along the U.S. 59 corridor. With the cooperation of the Friendswood Development Company, which had already begun an aggressive building program in the planned community of Kingwood, north of Humble, in 1971, the college became situated among the tall pines of this rural, east Texas location.

One Kingwood resident, Bob Colt, moved into his home off Sorters Road in 1980. Mr. Colt recalls that "Sorters was a disaster; filled with potholes. They resurfaced it about 1983." He remembers that "it was all woods...pines, oaks, magnolias, but mostly pines. There was also a lot of brush and vines." The woods along Sorters Road held abundant wildlife. Mr. Colt has seen many animals such as muskrat, beaver, fox, alligators, bobcats, wild hogs, and numerous deer. "There was a family of beaver in the low marshy area just across the road from the college up until just this past year, and I still see deer from time to time," he commented. As many area residents are aware, "the river is filled with fish. I've caught bass, carp, perch, and cat fish in the San Jacinto."[2]

In addition to describing the wildlife and woods where the college campus is now located, Mr. Colt added that there are stories of Spanish gold lost in the general area around Kingwood College. "There's supposed to have been a Spanish expedition through here that was attacked by local Indians. They dumped gold and cannon in a lake in this area, but no one has ever found it." However, he quickly pointed out that "around 1900, a wood cutter found a gold bell that dates from around that time period." In the old days, barges used to transport goods on the San Jacinto River, and Mr. Colt recovered a two hundred pound anchor along the banks of the river near his home. In closing, this Kingwood resident reminded me that the "livable forest" is still filled with snakes, "copperheads, ground rattlers, coral snakes, and all sorts."[3] Indeed, the area surrounding Kingwood College is a beautiful region inhabited by a variety of wild life and covered in trees and plants. A second glance at the region, however, reveals a heritage that is just as colorful as the east Texas landscape.

Over a century before the establishment of Kingwood College, or nearby Humble for that matter, East Texas developed through a kind of "colonial experience" that lasted from the 1830s to about 1876. The economy was an extractive one based on farming, slavery, cotton, timber, or whatever wealth could be produced from the land. In 1824, the Mexican government issued a land grant to Davis Harris "for one league of land" in what would become northeast Harris County.[4] Farming and ranching were essential to the Humble area. Nineteenth century "husbandry" wasn't very scientific either. In those days, cattle and "pineywoods rooters" (hogs) all grazed in large common herds. Although pioneering cattlemen exhibited an entrepreneurial spirit, they were not opposed to sharing their grazing lands, corrals, and the work of roundups, brandings, and marketing chores, too.[5]

Describing the lives of the Humble area pioneers is far easier than finding the elusive "why" they pioneered this East Texas frontier. In 1828, according to one account of early Humble, friends of pioneer Joe Dunham advised him to move to the area from Liberty for "safety reasons." Rumor had it that the "Mexican Army under the command of General Santa Anna would be passing through the area." Knowing the dangers and disruptions of an invasion army, Dunham took the path of least resistance, and made life *here* rather than *there* in Liberty.[6]

About sixty years later, another founding father, J.H. Slaughter, camped on the banks of the San Jacinto River after a laborious day of rafting logs. While building his fire, "he noticed bubbles seeping from the bank." Slaughter then spent the rest of his life trying to strike it rich in the oil and gas business.[7] Moreover, one imagines that "other reasons" had a gravity-like pull on the pioneers who came and stayed in the Humble area. People had a tendency to grow and fit those spaces and times they called life.

Mrs. Rose Hamlin is a wonderful example of a rich talent who grew into an opportunity. She opened the first Humble one room school in 1887 "with about a dozen pupils." Once the community had fifty residents, she made herself teacher and principal for her twelve students. In the Humble school, as with most of East Texas, the school year

lasted about four months. The Humble one room school's first graduating class was composed of three graduates, two were twins named Edith and Ethel.[8] Even in these early days of public education there were concerns about the social adjustments of the children. One student named N.E. "Bob" Smith had other ideas. He earned the distinction of being Humble's first drop-out. Taking matters into his own hands, he moved to Houston and earned his own diploma called millionaire.[9]

Other early families in the Humble area included the Morgans, Jones, Sabens, and Garners.[10] But the single most important pioneer was the "vagabond fisherman" P.S. Pleasant Humble and his wife Jane. As with many who migrated here in the early 1830s any opportunity was a good opportunity. And like many of the East Texas founding fathers, Humble wore many hats and could be called many things—both good and bad. For Humble, time and destiny intersected on the San Jacinto river. So important is the man that years later when the founders of an oil company looked for a name that symbolized their vision, Pleasant Humble stood head and shoulders above the rest. One of the greatest statements made about Humble reads "Humble, Texas isn't named after Humble Oil and Refining Company, it's the other way around."[11]

Humble worked as a homesteader and farmer but is best remembered as a gifted and enterprising entrepreneur. He immediately realized that residents would have to cross the San Jacinto river, so he opened a ferry boat. By doing so, he and others took the first steps in promoting this vital lifeline to the Houston economy. But Humble's entrepreneurial spirit didn't stop at ferrying and farming. In 1886, when Tom F. Shelton's dream of a post office was endangered by his untimely death, Pleasant Humble "stepped up to the plate" so to speak, and created his own post office that linked his community to the outside world.[12]

Humble must have been a popular founding father. After all, he had been entrusted with a paper lifeline that expressed the communities collective hopes, dreams, loves, and losses. The new postmaster operated out of his own home, "later moved to an abandoned box car, and then to the Bender Commissary." One eyewitness revealed the simplicity of life in Humble's new "Post Office." In reality it consisted of two boxes labeled INCOMING and OUTGOING and "each person examined the incoming basket in search of his own mail." Later, Humble served as lawyer and Justice-of-the-Peace. By 1905, "Uncle Plez"

*Town founder, Pleasant Humble, and others on Main Street. Humble, Texas.*
COURTESY: THE HUMBLE MUSEUM.

*The train depot in Humble, Texas.*
COURTESY: THE HUMBLE MUSEUM.

as his friends called him, met a series of misfortunes that included the death of his beloved wife Jane and son. In 1907, failing eyesight caused his move to his brother's residence in Silsbee, Texas, where he died in 1912, at the age of 77.[13]

Humble's life is important to this informal history of the area, because he bridged the colonial and transitional eras. Equally at home in each epoch, he helped unleash the vital forces that would define the Humble community and simultaneously gave its history a legacy we are honored to call our own.

1877 is an important year for Humble and East Texas for a number of important reasons. On the national level, the ordeal of the postwar Reconstruction period ended. In this larger perspective, the nation could heal, grow and unite around the dynamic power of industrialization. For East Texans, the 1870s unleashed a barrage of economic forces. Lasting until the 1930s, the era would dramatically impact the daily lives of Humblites by applying, as one historian notes, "the range of modern technology to the bulk of its resources."[14]

In other words, the Humble community smoked, chugged, and gushed to glory. Humble's transitional economy took off with timber and seized her glory with "black gold." Before the oil boom, Humble and East Texas had long leaf pine, hardwoods, and narrow gauged railroads that connected its economy with Houston and other markets. For Humble and her timber economy, the Houston East and West Texas Narrow Gauge Railroad (HE & WT) acted with a springboard effect, propelling the local economy toward a "jump off" to prosperity. From the vantage point of this history, the early development of Humble is indeed exciting, but we must not forget the dangers of this narrow gauge railroad from heat, smoke, and burning embers caused many to informally rename the HE & WT, "HELL EITHER WAY."[15]

Railroads meant general progress that contributed to the Humble boom. Bridges and trestles were built. The most famous area bridge had to forge the San Jacinto crossing. The bridge was made by the Cincinnati Bridge Co. and shipped here at the cost of $7000. Upon viewing the progress, one Humble resident was moved to say the bridge made for an "impressive sight."[16]

By 1880, the railroad connected Livingston with Moscow, and then Nacogdoches in 1883. Despite obvious inconveniences, railroads brought adventure, sightseeing, and leisure from the world of work. In 1878, for example, one could steam to San Jacinto Springs for a roundtrip fare of 50 cents for adults and 25 cents for children. At the destination, one traveler remembered fishing, swimming, boating, and a St. Louis band to serenade its patron each afternoon and evening. To preserve the dignity of the male and female spheres, one participant remembered that "no drinking of spirits was allowed."[17]

The railroads and the timber industry fed off each other, pushing the economy into higher gear. By 1894, the railroad had been transformed through adoption of a standard gauge track. Communication with the "outside world" increased while the quality of life, in what would become the "Livable Forest," gave its citizens a growing sense of pride. One Humble resident observed that within the short distance between Humble and New Caney, "five sawmills were there, operating along the right-of-way with a combined capacity of 100,000 feet of lumber per day."[18] The sawmill communities were so large that they operated their own schools, commissaries, and churches. The last of the local sawmills was operated by Ed Borders from which the Bordersville community still exists. The mill formally closed in 1949.[19]

Without a doubt, the oil boom produced the most significant and colorful chapter of the Humble area. The discovery of natural gas in the Humble Oil field in the 1890s, and its first well in 1902 put the name of this east Texas town on everyone's lips. Humble's spirits and hopes for riches reached frenzied proportions with its first gusher in 1905. In June of that year "production had soared to 2,800.000 barrels" and the town claimed a population of 15,000 residents.[20] This first boom couldn't last, but fortunately, a second one in 1914, and yet another in 1929 created a level of wealth and opportunities that are legendary to the "oil patch." It truly was a great run for oil men such as Barrett, Staitti, Granberry, and Higgins.[21]

After 1900, one area of Humble called Moonshine Hill gained the reputation as "one of the toughest towns in the state." A virtual tent city, it could boast over 40 saloons and a marshall by the name of Danger. Oil derricks were everywhere. In fact, parts of Humble were under pools of oil. Sometimes, wells came in at a rate of "one each day" according to Humble docent, Mary Lawson. One anonymous source remembers that one could cross the street climbing "derrick to derrick without touching the ground."[22]

Sometimes more than oil gushed from the earth. To the chagrin of Nick Lambrecht who

*Humble Oil Well.*

drilled a well near the "corner of FM Road 1960 and North Houston avenue," fate aimed at his pocketbook and hit the bathtub. This new hot water strike gave Humble its first bath, and for just 25 cents, "wildcatters" could get a bath with all the appropriate amenities. Today the water still flows as do the great memories of Humble's oil boom.[23]

But the legacy of the oil boom is more than a *Houston Chronicle* headline that reads, the "Story of Humble is Saga of Oil Rigs, Pool and Multimillionaires."[24] In a larger perspective, the boom years represent just one of many great chapters in the east Texas "Book of Life." And just as important as the oil barrels filled, lumber cut, cattle grazed, and milk gallons produced, new philanthropic traditions secured opportunities for education, medicine, charity, and government. If Humble, according to one source, had the reputation as a "Millionaire Maker," those same oil dollars produced a stone and mortar legacy in Houston and Humble that include the Niels Esperson building, Hermann Hospital, Herman Park, West Building, and the San Jacinto Hotel.[25]

The history of the North Harris Montgomery Community College District has been document-

*Promotion of Town Lots, 1886.*
*Humble, Texas.*

COURTESY: THE HUMBLE MUSEUM.

ed elsewhere in this volume. Our focus in these pages is the development of the East Campus, now known as Kingwood College. Dr. Joe Airola was chancellor of the college district when the East Campus opened its doors to the public in 1984. Dr. Airola recalls that our college district leadership made the decision early to be responsive to the needs of the communities in our service area. He attributes the concept of an East Campus to W.W. Thorne and the Board of Trustees. "They had a vision," observed Dr. Airola, "and the idea evolved from there." The vision was carried forward under the capable leadership and direction of Dr. Airola, who took charge of making the dream a reality.[26]

The college was designed to fit comfortably among the trees and brush of the beautiful countryside. With construction underway, an administrative team was selected to supervise the new college. Lester Burks, charter member of North Harris College as former Dean of Vocational/Technical Education, was selected as the college's first President. Dr. Nellie Carr Thorogood, also a charter member of North Harris, became the first Dean of Instruction. "Lester and Nellie were a good team," observed Dr. Airola.[27] These sentiments were repeated by virtually every person interviewed in researching this chapter. President Burks is consistently viewed as the man "in charge;" he is remembered as pleasant, kind, and likable, but also as a strong

leader who was thorough, knew what was happening around the college, and attended the multitude of details involved in daily operations. Dean Thorogood, who became Kingwood's second President, is warmly remembered as a visionary. Dr. Scott Nelson, Professor of Government, described Dr. Thorogood as "exciting" while Patsy Talbert, Division Assistant for Liberal Arts, called her "fun."[28] Dr. Joan Samuelson, Professor of English, described Nellie Thorogood, as "warm, brilliant, and visible."[29] Dr. Rose Austin, Dean of Educational Resources, added that "Nellie always thinks outside the box."[30] The respect and affection for these early college leaders is evident in the manner they are so warmly and fondly remembered. Furthermore, the results of their efforts in this college community are obvious as the standards of academic and instructional excellence established so early in this institution's history.

When the college began classes in August of 1984, construction of the buildings was not yet completed. Dr. Airola was determined to begin classes on schedule in spite of building delays so while the basics were in place there were many remaining details to be finished during the first weeks of classes. "The construction people thought we were bluffing," Dr. Airola stated with a good-natured smile, "but we moved in and began classes. They had to work around us."[31] In fact, Dr. Thorogood distributed plastic "hard-hats" for the faculty and staff to wear as a symbol of the on-going building that continued into the early weeks of classes.[32] Steve Davis, Associate Dean for Liberal Arts, recalls "I had to briefly stop class one day to ask some workers if they could delay a noisy project taking place near my classroom."[33] Elizabeth Lunden, Director of the Learning Resources Center, commented that the LRC was not completed so that the college opened with few resources available to faculty and students.[34] A final anecdote from this hectic period comes from the Interim Vice President for Instruction, Katherine Persson, who remembers that her class was temporarily disrupted one morning while workers installed a chalkboard in her classroom. "I had to help them hold the board in place," Ms. Persson smiles while relating to the incident, "the men were too short to hang the board in the proper position on the wall."[35] These hectic days of construction, registration, and first classes were underway, but the challenge of building a community college had only just begun.

"I taught a U.S. History class at 7:30 on the Monday morning that classes began," Steve Davis observed. "I remember being very conscious that I was part of something, that I had been present at the beginning."[36] Something had certainly begun in this community. "There was so much to do and so few of us to do it," summarized Professor Samuelson.[37] The new college was much smaller than the more established South Campus, but had many of the same responsibilities such as committee assignments, registration, office duties, and other similar administrative, instructional, and clerical functions. With a much smaller number of instructors, administrators, and staff people on board, many people engaged in a wide variety of jobs and roles at the new East Campus. Professor Scott Nelson, for example, served as the first Faculty Senate President, the first sponsor for Phi Theta Kappa, taught a full load of Government classes, and served on a variety of committees.[38] Joan Samuelson observed "We did whatever needed to be done. I even brought a vacuum from home one day," she went on to add, "and we all were happy."[39]

Dr. Nellie Thorogood commented on the atmosphere of the new college. "There was a trust factor here," she said, "we were all in this together. We were having a good time and it showed."[40] Lee Topham, Professor of Mathematics, remarked upon the "can do" attitude of the new college. As an example of this positive approach, Professor Topham related the decision to move away from the "main frame" approach to computer education and to embrace personal computers in our college classrooms. "This was a radical departure from the traditional approach in 1984," Dr. Topham reminds us, "everything was main frame then."[41] This college's ability to envision the future and move toward that vision has been a

*Groundbreaking ceremony, 1983. From left to right: Dr. Joe Airola, NHCC president and first Chancellor is accompanied by NHCC Board members: Roy Hohl, Secretary; Lou Shirley, Assistant Secretary; charter members W.E. Crozier and Charles Philipp; and David Robinson.*

hallmark of its success. This "vision" combined with that "can do" attitude have created a reputation for excellence that permeates the community served by Kingwood College.

In addition to the college's fine facilities, the rural location has always been an important element in the Kingwood's "charm" and attraction. In the early years of the East Campus this rural atmosphere was often enhanced by "visitors" from across the San Jacinto River. When the water level of the river became low, cattle grazing on the other side would cross the river and wander on to the college campus. Dr. Thorogood was working late in her office one evening when she received a frantic call from the library. She arrived on the scene to find a cow with her nose pressed against the glass of the LRC building seemingly interested in "people watching." On several occasions, our police officers had to assist in driving cattle from the commons area and the large student parking lot across Sorters Road from the main campus. These evening "cattle drives" were only one of our connections with the rural communities surrounding Kingwood College.[42]

Lester Burks, who served as the first college president from 1984 to 1987, was then followed by Nellie Carr Thorogood from 1987 to 1991. Dr. Thorogood had been one of the college's founding administrators as the first Dean of Instruction. Much of the college's creative energy and innovative approach had derived from the early leadership of the dynamic Nellie

*Donning hard-hats, Dr. Joe Airola, Chancellor, and Dr. Nellie Thorogood, welcome students to the East Campus. Dr. Thorogood became the second president of Kingwood College.*

Thorogood. Dr. Thorogood was responsible for the decision to "integrate" faculty into the academic community across disciplines. The traditional organization for colleges called for faculty to be divided into groups along academic subjects and disciplines with a sharp division between vocational/technical areas and academics. Dr. Thorogood chose to abandon tradition in organizing faculty in office areas that were multi-disciplinary and cut across academic as well as vocational/technical lines. This approach brought about a unified faculty with a strong understanding of the total mission of this institution.[43] As a college president, Nellie Thorogood would carry on with this type of forward thinking, unconventional approach to the challenges of the college and community.

As president, Dr. Thorogood was everywhere. You might find her in the cafeteria, walking the grounds, visiting with support staff, or as all the "veterans" remember, in a meeting.[44] Regular and lengthy meetings were an important part of this president's college community. Not only was everyone kept informed and up-to-date on everything happening at the college, but Dr. Thorogood promoted an "open, free exchange" of ideas and opinions on all important subjects that impacted the institution. From "brain-storming" new concepts to working out the details of programs and policies, Dr. Thorogood sought maximum involvement from all concerned.[45] "It was my goal to build an instructional team," Dr. Thorogood observed. From all accounts, she was extremely successful in accomplishing this goal. All of those "on board" during these years in Kingwood's development, relate stories of this "team" spirit.[46] Joseph Minton, Professor of English, said "Nellie was a joy" and Joan Samuelson summed up this president's tenure by saying "we were never bored, Nellie was always exciting. She was a fine president."[47]

While the administration provided leadership, it was the faculty that brought to Kingwood College a strong identity focused upon instructional excellence. One faculty member relates, "It was clear to me in the interview process that teaching excellence was the norm; it was an expectation of anyone who came to teach at the East Campus."[48] Professor Lee Topham commented that the founding faculty was "as good as I've ever seen," and those sentiments have been repeated by all those interviewed for this project.[49] This tradition of quality instruction has carried forwarded throughout changes in administration. Throughout the years, Kingwood faculty has evidenced strong academic credentials as well as scholarly research and an active role in professional organizations. However, the primary focus of Kingwood College as a teaching and learning institution has never been neglected. "My first semester at the college Joan Samuelson and Joseph Minton approached me one day in the commons area," an early faculty member reports. "They simply wanted to tell me they heard good things about me from students. Both of these colleagues were a strong, positive, encouraging force for teaching excellence."[50] The faculty at Kingwood College has increased in numbers and diversity, but that standard of excellence established by those founding "teachers" and scholars has not been altered by that growth. As much as any other feature, this is what makes Kingwood a unique and distinctive institution.

In 1991 Steve Head became the third president of Kingwood College. Dr. Head had joined the college district in 1984 as the Director of Financial Aid at the South Campus. He was very active in the early formation of the new East Campus and assisted with the development of the college's student services and financial aid offices. After serving as the Dean of Student Services at North Harris College, Dr. Head came to Kingwood as president in the summer of 1991 under the new chancellor, Dr. John Pickelman.[51] A new era of innovative leadership was about to begin for the college in the woods.

Early on in his administration, Dr. Head became aware of Kingwood's "low profile" in our service area. Some of the region's residents called the college "the best kept secret in Kingwood." He began to make plans to make Kingwood College an important part of people's lives throughout the communities of Atascocita, Humble, Kingwood, Splendora, New Caney, and the 59 corridor. Among Dr. Head's first priorities was the consistent use of news releases to keep the people of our neighborhoods informed regarding events at the college. Regular features and calendars in the community newspapers put upcoming events in the hands of area residents and also reported activities by way of follow-up on "who, what, when and where" at Kingwood

*Dr. Steve Head, the third president of Kingwood College.*

College. People not only came to discover the "secret" but they began to recognize that exciting things were constantly taking place at their community college.[52]

In addition to making people aware of what was already happening at the college, Dr. Head concentrated his efforts on integrating the institution into the community while developing working relationships with groups and individuals throughout our service area. Under his leadership, Kingwood College has become a community center for the fine arts, particularly the dramatic arts, and a wide variety of businesses and organizations. Dr. Head has been actively involved in community projects and became Chairman of the Board for the Humble Area Chamber of Commerce in 1996.[53]

Not only did Kingwood College take an active part in the region under the new administration, but the institution also moved into a fully-functioning, independent role within the North Harris Montgomery Community College District. Founded as the "East Campus" with origins at the South Campus, Kingwood had often been in the position of a "branch campus" within the district. However, with the opening of Tomball College, the plans for the new Montgomery College , the arrival of Dr. Pickelman and Steve Head upon the district scene, the "East Campus" identity was forever in the past. Dr. Head aggressively pursued and accomplished a separate identity for Kingwood College complete with a full-service approach to the entire spectrum of college life.

## KINGWOOD COLLEGE FOUNDING FACULTY & STAFF

**Lester Burks**
Founding President

**Rose Austin**

**Mary Beleele**

**Steve Davis**

**Nora Diaz**

**Carol Goldsby**

**Shirley Grant**

**Jean Hayden**

**Reba Kochersperger**

**Bill Leach**

**Elizabeth Lunden**

**Ann McCormick**

**Greg Mitchell**

**Scott Nelson**

**Katherine Persson**

**Joan Samuelson**

**Patsy Talbert**

**Lee Topham**

**Sherry Young**

From admissions to graduation, all aspects of the college experience became available under the supervision of Steve Head. The "East Campus" had truly become Kingwood College.[54]

One of the founding faculty members at Kingwood College is Dr. Rose Austin, now Dean of Educational Resources. Over the years, Dr. Austin has served the college district in a variety of teaching and administrative roles, but her leadership at Kingwood College remains a constant source of satisfaction. Dr. Austin commented recently upon a change in how our community views Kingwood College. "At first," she observed, "the community college was viewed as a second choice, but now we are often seen as the college of choice. We have so much to offer." Dean Austin was quick to point out Kingwood's quality instructors, small class size, and low costs, but went on to add "we are expanding our horizons to include a traditional college cultural environment as well as quality learning experiences. We have a full-range of activities related to the arts, music, plays, and exhibits not to mention a growing number of active student organizations such as Phi Theta Kappa and our Student Government Association. In fact, Fran Manwarring of our PTK Chapter was elected the International President of PTK for the year 1996-1997." In addition to Kingwood College's quality instructional and campus programs, Dr. Austin pointed to the expansion of opportunities for people throughout the communities served by the college. "Through distance learning, community partnerships, and outreach locations such as the Humble Center at Deerbrook Mall we are providing more ways for more people to learn than ever before." Indeed, with programs such as dual credit agreements involving high schools, weekend college schedules, and night high school, the college continues to grow in numbers as well as to diversify the student population. "We have many nontraditional students here," Dr. Austin observed, "and we are able to provide quality instruction through both the traditional classroom experience as well as a wide variety of flexible methods including television, independent study, and the internet."[55] From approximately one thousand students in 1984 when the college held the first registration for classes at the new campus, Kingwood College has grown to accommodate well over three thousand students by 1996; this is really only a portion of what this college has come to mean in the surrounding communities.

Penny Westerfeld, Dean of Community Education, points out that more than three thousand additional students take advantage of Community Education classes through Kingwood College each year. In our technology areas, both credit and non-credit hardware, is "state-of-the-art" according to Westerfeld. "We have a college-wide commitment to the finest technology in our facilities. Our local business community can depend upon us to provide quality training for present and future employees." Through Community Education classes the college is able to offer "short-term professional training and retraining to meet the ever changing demands of the work force," the Dean added. In fact, Kingwood College offers unique, technologically advanced programs such as desk top publishing, computer graphic arts, and Novell Networking (one of only two such programs in the state leading to Novell Certification). Small businesses make up such an important part of the surrounding communities that Kingwood College has established the Business and Industry Institute, which operates under the direction of Dean Westerfeld through the Community Education division. "Not only can we train employees on site," the C.E. Dean comments, "but we can create and design training for area employees here on our campus as well. Many area businesses prefer to have their people come here to enjoy the peaceful beauty of our grounds and the fine facilities we can offer." While support for business and industry is a major commitment for the college, another innovation for Community Education is the Summer Youth Program. Each summer over three hundred public school age students come to the Kingwood campus to participate in classes ranging from "Drama Camp" to foreign language instruction to photography and much, much more. "Community Education offers a great many opportunities for every age and type of individual in our service area," concluded Dean Penny Westerfeld.[56] Without a doubt, the quality programs of this division have been a major factor in the expanding role Kingwood College plays throughout the communities that surround the college nestled in the piney woods of east Texas.

The year 1994 was especially important in the

history of Kingwood College as it marked the tenth anniversary of the founding of the college. A celebration was held on September 29, 1994 for all to share the joys of this day and to see just how far the college had come in those ten years. The immaculate buildings and grounds were an outward manifestation of the quality the community had come to expect from Kingwood College. The beautifully landscaped campus provided a glorious setting for the afternoon festivities. Green and white balloons decorated the campus where music and refreshments combined to create an atmosphere of joyful celebration.[57]

While there was a good deal of fun and entertainment for those present, there was also a formal ceremony lead by Dr. Steve Head, college president, and Dr. John Pickelman, the district's chancellor. At this ceremony, the founding faculty and staff were honored as well as the first two college presidents, Lester Burks and Dr. Nellie Carr Thorogood. Dr. Head commented that "it has been a real pleasure working here. Becoming president of this campus has been like getting behind the wheel of a Cadillac." Lester Burks observed that, "Those folks who started this so many years ago would never have

imagined or guessed at the growth that has transpired." Dr. Pickelman added "We are proud of Kingwood College and what it has accomplished…. It is a major jewel in the District's crown." It was left for Dr. Thorogood to sum up the feelings of so many present when she quoted a song from the Grateful Dead. "What a long strange trip it's been," she said, and then went on to add, "Seriously, history will record that Kingwood College is different because the people here have made it different. We are delighted to look to the future."[58]

Sometimes, however, the assessment of a college community must come from sources other than those neatly summed up as programs, state-of-the-art technologies, or degrees conferred. In late 1994, as the college celebrated its tenth anniversary, larger events intervened, and the outcomes of those events temporarily redefined leadership roles, learning relationships, and priorities of this "College in the Woods." Unfortunately, rains and floods devastated the Kingwood area at the same time the college community celebrated the joy of a job well done. Summing up the situation, Dr. Chris Martin, professor of mathematics, remembers going to class

*Kingwood College celebrates its Tenth Anniversary of service to the community in 1994. To the right are Dr. Steve Head, president of Kingwood College and Dr. John E. Pickelman, NHMCCD Chancellor.*

with a great lecture only to find a student body ravaged by one of the worst floods anyone could remember. "Basic human needs really replaced what I wanted to do," he recalled with his usual sunny disposition. "In light of the events of that fall, we had to meet student needs first, even if it meant amending the syllabus,"[59] Martin remembers. Sondra Whitlow, then Dean of Community Education, observed that "water was up to the back door, the parking lot was flooded, and the workers I was so concerned about, were handling all the problems caused by the flood!"[60] Kingwood College Librarian Charles Gillis lost his home, but he could find some peace and companionship when his cats were rescued from the chimney top after three-and-a-half days![61]

Losing a home is bad enough, but Linda King, then a Kingwood College student, would be evacuated not once, but a total of four times![62] Normal institutional routines were disrupted and sometimes stopped. Faculty Senate Officers Rich Almstead and Brian Shmaefsky remembered that security officer J.D. Adams had been flooded in. With no other officers to relieve him, he kept his watch. For over two days, he ate out of the cafeteria snack machines and slept in one of the hospital beds in the Technical Building.[63] Despite these and other disruptions, the good news is that the Kingwood College community found ways to cope and even persevere.

A torrent of water washed out the San Jacinto bridge cutting off Kingwood. Then, to the north, New Caney Creek overflowed its banks slicing vital links to those communities. For a few days, Kingwood found itself literally surrounded and inundated with water. For this college community, many members found that needs and desires that centered around learning were superseded by the most basic needs for food, shelter, and transportation. Suddenly the challenge of educating and administering were considerably imperiled by human needs called hunger, shelter, and even survival.

Much of this college community's response to the "Floods of '94," can be summed up by a rather substantial file folder of documents that illustrate the efforts of the Faculty Senate, Student Services, President Steve Head, Financial Aid Services and Brenda Niekamp who coordinated the relief effort.[64] Moreover, countless individuals gave whatever it took to ease the countless tragedies of our college community. Betty Shafer, Administrative Assistant, related that "Dr. Head was adamant about doing whatever it took" to meet the crisis for members of Kingwood College community.[65]

Examples of generosity abound. Private and institutional donations "provided everything from sheetrock to shampoo," said Niekamp.[66] When one needy family requested a TV, President Steve Head donated his.[67] In another case, when a student relocated to high ground without plumbing, a "Port-a-Potty" made the transition easier."[68] In another case, when a big and tall man needed clothing, arrangements were made with Wal-Mart for his needs. Sometimes, families lost everything, and in those cases, volunteers supplied basic needs that sometimes included Christmas presents, cleaning labor, or even disinfectants. Flood victims remembered that the smallest of needs such as "dry socks and underwear, were in abundant supply," Linda King recalled.[69] Candace Washburn, Kingwood Academic Advisor, did whatever it took as well. Sometimes we even "withdrew" students so that their refunds could purchase food and necessities."[70] In less dire circumstances, according to Sondra Whitlow, schedules were rearranged or classes postponed to fit students' needs.

The floods of '94 affected the Kingwood College community in various ways. Some were merely inconvenienced, others were impacted by fears and disorders that linger today. Yet, it remains clear that without the help of students, faculty, administrators, and other community groups, the flood victims would have been impacted more severely.[72] In fact, the care, and desire, to meet the crisis on all fronts, represented a kind of "validation experience" that may very well have galvanized the community together in ways never imagined. Carolyn Wade, Director of Financial Aid, expressed the Kingwood spirit of giving and sharing when flood victims showed her pictures of their devastated homes. "On one hand we in the office were depressed and devastated," she explained, "but on the other hand, I was deeply satisfied that we could call on the faculty and college resources to meet some big needs I never imagined."[73]

This college community could feel deep satisfaction for its enthusiastic response to the October flood. And if the tragedy occurred almost immediately after the ten year celebration,

it didn't "rain on the parade" either. In fact, the spirited response reaffirmed the commonly held idea that Kingwood College and the surrounding community is "special" for many reasons. But the most important. reason is a bedrock desire to keep that vital "something" alive for those who would choose to live, study, work and prosper in this "College in the Woods."

And finally, this community rebounded strongly to the call of Hollywood and the filming of the Kevin Costner hit movie "Tin Cup." The gymnasium of Kingwood College served as the local recruiting post for movie "extras." Hardly had the flood waters receded when students, staff, professors, could brag about their "casting call" or moment of fame as an extra.

The appearance of the "circus... of eighteen wheelers with catering trucks... and trailers for the stars and crew" did wonders for everyone's spirits.[74] Privately, professors complained that students were cutting class to experience the glitz of Hollywood stars Kevin Costner, Don Johnson, Cheech Martin, or a host of touring PGA professionals. But more than anything else, everyone would agree that while the "Floods of '94" tested our heart and soul, the filming of the "Tin Cup" made us smile again. Laughter really is the best medicine.[75]

The future looks bright for Kingwood College. Enrollments continue to increase in both credit and non-credit classes, while the college ties to surrounding communities grow stronger. President Steve Head observed that "Kingwood College will continue to become more integrated into the community. While our main focus will remain a strong academic transfer program, we will continue to expand our excellent technological base, health careers, contract training with area businesses, and our cultural activities." Under Dr. Head's leadership, Kingwood College will begin a major building program. In 1996, the college district purchased forty additional acres east of the current college campus. Upon this site will be a multi-purpose student center building. This new structure will house student services, a student center, and facilities for use by the growing fine arts programs at Kingwood. Scheduled to open in 1998, this new building is the first of a projected three additional structures planned for Kingwood College; the others include a new classroom building and a new Learning Resources Center.[76] By all standards of measurement, Kingwood College's history is a history of growth, expansion, and improvement. From a rural setting amidst the pine forest of east Texas, a college grew to become a cornerstone of a community.

# NOTES

[1] North Harris County College District, *Bulletin*, 1984 - 1985, p. 13.

[2] Bob Colt, Interview by Link Hullar, 1996.

[3] Colt/Hullar

[4] Humble Museum, "The Humble, Texas Area: A Brief History" (pamphlet). Humble, Texas.

[5] Ibid.

[6] Humble Museum, "Humble, Texas" File.

[7] Ibid.

[8] Ibid.

[9] Humble Museum, "Education" File.

[10] Ibid., "Humble" File.

[11] Ibid.

[12] Ibid.

[13] Ibid.

[14] David G. McComb, *Houston: A History* (Austin: University of Texas Press, 1981), 6-7.

[15] Ibid.

[16] Humble Museum, "Railroad" File.

[17] Ibid.

[18] Ibid.

[19] Susan Thobe, "FM 1960: From Farms to a Very Hot Market," article courtesy of Spring ISD.

[20] Humble Museum, "Humble, Texas Area."

[21] Thobe, "FM 1960."

[22] Ibid.

[23] Ibid.

[24] Humble Museum display.

[25] Humble Museum, "Humble File."

[26] Joe Airola, Interview by Link Hullar, 1996.

[27] Airola/Hullar

[28] Scott Nelson and Patsy Talbert, Interviews by Link Hullar, 1996.

[29] Joan Samuelson, Interview by Link Hullar, 1996.

[30] Rose Austin, Interview by Link Hullar, 1996.

[31] Airola, Hullar

[32] Nelson/Hullar

[33] Steve Davis, Interview by Link Hullar, 1996.

[34] Elizabeth Lunden, Interview by Link Hullar, 1996.

[35] Katherine Perrson, Interview by Link Hullar, 1996.

[36] Davis/Hullar

[37] Samuelson/Hullar

[38] Nelson/Hullar

[39] Samuelson/Hullar

[40] Nellie Carr Thorogood, Interview by Link Hullar, 1996.

[41] Lee Topham, Interview by Link Hullar, 1996.

[42] Thorogood/Hullar

[43] Nelson/Hullar

[44] Lunden/Hullar

[45] Samuelson/Hullar

[46] Thorogood/Hullar

[47] Joseph Minton, Interview by Link Hullar; Samuelson/Hullar.

[48] Link Hullar, personal recollection, 1996.

[49] Topham/Hullar

[50] Hullar, personal recollection

[51] Steve Head, Interview by Link Hullar, 1996.

[52] Head/Hullar

[53] Head/Hullar

[54] Head/Hullar

[55] Austin/Hullar

[56] Penny Westerfeld, Interview by Link Hullar, 1996.

[57] Cynthia Calvert, "Kingwood College Celebrates 10 Years," *Humble Observer*, 5 October 1994, p.1-3.

[58] Calvert, "10 Years."

[59] Chris Martin, Interview by Dean Wolfe, 1996.

[60] Sondra Whitlow, Interview by Dean Wolfe, 1996.

[61] Charles Gillis, Interview by Dean Wolfe, 1994.

[62] Linda King, Interview by Dean Wolfe, 1996.

[63] Brian Shmaefsky, Interview by Dean Wolfe, 1996.

[64] Kingwood College, "Flood File," Kingwood, TX.

[65] Betty Shafer, Interview by Dean Wolfe, 1996.

[66] Brenda Niekamp, Interview by Dean Wolfe, 1996.

[67] Ibid.

[68] Ibid.

[69] King/Wolfe

[70] Candace Washburn, Interview by Dean Wolfe, 1996.

[71] Whitlow/Wolfe

[72] Ibid.3

[73] Carolyn Wade, Interview by Dean Wolfe, 1996.

[74] Diane Blanco, Interview by Dean Wolfe, 1996.

[75] Ibid.

[76] Head/Hullar

# TOMBALL COLLEGE

*Making a Field of Dreams a Reality*

by Rebecca L. Tate and Douglas S. Boyd

In the 1989 movie *Field of Dreams*, the protagonist Ray Kinsella is inspired by a voice that he cannot ignore to pursue a dream that will change many lives. His quest involves turning his simple cornfield into a place where dreams can come true, and in the course of pursuing his dream, he convinces others to make his dream theirs and to make that dream a reality.[1] Like Kinsella, Roy Hohl, lifetime resident of Tomball, was inspired by a dream—the dream of a community college district that would touch many lives by providing desperately needed higher educational opportunities in the Tomball area. Through his leadership, he convinced others of the dream's validity. Wide-spread community enthusiasm then led to Tomball's becoming part of the North Harris County College District in 1982. The fulfillment of that dream of educational opportunities became even more complete when a few years later the district Board of Trustees chose Tomball as the site for the new college that was needed to meet the spurt of growth in the northwest. A beautiful tract of land was chosen, land lush with fields of bluebonnets, dotted with pecan trees, and grazed by an occasional deer. There in those fields of bluebonnets, Tomball College was created, a place where the citizens of the commu-

*Dr. Rebecca Tate and Douglas Boyd are professors of English at Tomball College.*

special rapport and the many partnerships that exist between it and the Tomball area.

Because of the college's strong community connection, the rich history of the Tomball area is worthy of close examination. The original inhabitants of the area were a tribe of Indians, the Orcoquisacs, who had a village on Spring Creek, which forms the college's northern boundary and is the dividing line between Harris and Montgomery counties.[2] The solitude of the Orcoquisacs was interrupted by a visit by the famous explorer La Salle, who had earlier discovered the mouth of the Mississippi River. In 1687, he reportedly crossed Spring Creek, which he called d'Eure River. Sometime later, the Spanish also explored the area, naming the creek "Arroyo de Santa Rosa de Alcázar."[3] One of the earliest settlements on Spring Creek was by Joseph House, who received his survey of land in 1825 from the Mexican government.[4] Also in 1825, Stephen F. Austin led the families of his "second colony," who made their homes east and west of Tomball on leagues of land on either side of Spring Creek, which provided water for sawmills and cattle.[5] These settlers, whose European roots were in England, Scotland, and Ireland, arrived from other southern states. Later immigrants to the Tomball area and other

nity could come to achieve their own personal dreams through education. Because of its connection to the community that dreamed about it and worked ceaselessly for it to become reality, Tomball College finds its unique identity in the

Rolling Prairie, to This--in Five Months--How's That For

Texas, When It Was Only Five Months Old.    In this Picture You can See About Half of the

parts of Texas were from Germany, including the family of a current Board of Trustee member, Elmer Beckendorf.[6]

After its initial settlement, the Tomball area mixed history with legend as it played a small role in the drama of the Texas War for Independence. Legend has it that at a site about eight miles west of Tomball College, the same area near where La Salle crossed Spring Creek, the Texas army stopped on April 16, 1836 to rest while fleeing the troops of Santa Anna.[7] After hearing the reports of Santa Anna's movements from his scout, Deaf Smith, Sam Houston contemplated his choices: "Houston pondered the fork in the road. The road to the left would take them to safety; the road to the right, to Harrisburg, could mean defeat. He shared his momentous decision with no one until he gave the command, 'Columns right!'" As a result of that decision, Santa Anna was later defeated at San Jacinto, helping to open the west to settlement. In fact, the settlement of the Tomball area itself has its roots in the war because the city of Tomball was later founded on land given to William Hurd in return for his "service as a privateer captain during the Texas War for Independence."[8]

Later the Tomball area had an explosive association with another war, the Civil War. In what is now Spring Creek Park, a marker notes the site of a mill that produced gunpowder for Confederate cannons during the war. The mill operated from 1861 until 1863, when it exploded, killing three men from area families: William Bloecher, Adolph Hillegeist, and Peter Wunderlich.[9]

After the Civil War, the industries of cotton and cattle led to a railroad boom that in the early 1900s gave birth to and twice christened the town. Because Tomball is the highest point in Harris County and slopes gradually downhill towards Galveston, a geographic feature that allowed a locomotive to haul more, the Trinity and Brazos Valley Railroad (T & BV Railroad) bought land in the old William Hurd survey and created a freight station in the area; with the railroad came a cotton gin, stock pens, a water station, a roundhouse, storage tracks, a telegraph office, and a depot (which was recently relocated to Burroughs Park).[10] With the railroad workers came hotels, shops, and saloons. But

the bustling area needed a name, so the first townsite company called the town "Peck," in honor of the railroad line's chief civil engineer.[11] The town retained the name less than a year because another townsite company came in and renamed the town. On Dec. 2, 1907, Peck became "Tomball"—after Thomas H. Ball. Once an attorney for the T & BV Railroad, Ball was credited with directing the railroad through the area. Ball was also a three-term mayor of Huntsville, a former Congressman, and "Father of the Port of Houston."[12] Despite the prosperity Ball helped bring to the town and to Houston, Tomball may have derailed his further success. In 1914, Ball ran for governor of Texas on the Prohibitionist ticket, but pictures of the four saloons in Tomball helped his opponent, James E. Ferguson, defeat him.[13]

Later the failure of the T & BV Railroad's business, precipitated by the uncertainties of World War I, caused the railroad boom to bust.[14] However, in 1933, with the discovery of oil, the town's population tripled, and it was at this time that the city incorporated.[15] This boom provided citizens an interesting benefit: one of the oil companies in the area, Humble Oil and Refining Company, agreed to provide free oil and gas to Tomball residents in exchange for drilling rights in the city, prompting *Ripley's Believe It or Not* to highlight Tomball as "the only city in the world with free water and gas and no cemetery."[16] The fringe benefit of free gas continued until only a few years ago when, because of a reduction in the flow of gas, the town had to install gas

*Tomball Train Depot, 1912.*
COURTESY: LESSIE UPCHURCH

meters and begin charging residents. Additionally, an article in the May 1946 issue of *Cornet* magazine dubbed Tomball "Oiltown, U.S.A.," and by the 1950s, oil and gas flowed from over four hundred wells in the Tomball area.[17] In fact, some wells continue to produce today.

Once the town was grounded in a strong economy, community leaders were ready to

*First Oil Strike in Tomball, Texas, 1933.*

make a concerted effort to improve educational opportunities in Tomball. After all, long-time residents Elmer Beckendorf, a member of the community since 1947, and Roy Hohl, a member of the community since his birth in 1921, had been heard to frequently lament the dearth of higher educational opportunities in the Tomball area.[18] As Hohl was fond of noting, "There wasn't anything but a high school north of Buffalo Bayou."[19] Recognized need and earnest wishes turned to feasibility reports in the mid-1960s as Tomball and other communities began to act on a need for higher education. In fact, Hohl, as a resident of Tomball and president of the Houston North Association, took an active role as a member of the Greater Houston Community Junior College Commission that in 1968 created one of these feasibility reports.[20] Thus, it is no surprise that in 1971 when a move was made to turn the dream of a community college district into a reality, Tomball Independent School District (Tomball ISD) sought to join Humble, Spring, Aldine, and Klein ISDs in a bid to form a college district. In spite of wide-spread community enthusiasm, Tomball was eliminated from the district bid with the withdrawal of Klein ISD. Although initially interested, Klein at the time was in a fast-growing mode; property taxes had very little industry base. So in a straw vote, the residents of Klein said no. However, since state law mandated that the ISDs forming a college district must be contiguous and since Klein was the ISD that connected Tomball with the other districts, Tomball was eliminated.[21]

Undaunted by this setback, the Tomball community was still determined to become part of the college district that was formed in Oct. 1972. Finally, the solution was found; thanks to the dedication and insight of Roy Hohl, working in tandem with Don Henderson, state representative for Tomball, and other community leaders such as Diane Holland, Poley Parker, and Hap Harrington, a special bill was introduced and passed in the spring 1981 session.[22] This unique bill, which fit no other district in Texas, would allow the Tomball community to call a special election to become part of the college district. Following the passage of the bill, colloquially known as the "Tomball Bill,"[23] the Board of Tomball ISD passed a resolution expressing its desire to be part of the district. Petitions were then circulated throughout the community. In a very short period of time, the petitions were signed by enthusiastic residents; the issue was brought before the Tomball voters in January 1982; and the proposal passed 338-100, a significant 3 to 1 margin.[24]

Glad to be a part of the district and to have access to quality, affordable education, the people of Tomball were delighted when growth in the northwest corridor indicated the need for a new college. The Tomball Community Advisory Committee, led by Elmer Beckendorf; Dr. Joseph Airola, serving as the first district Chancellor; and the District Board of Trustees, lobbied by its newest member Roy Hohl, all agreed that the new college should be located in Tomball.[25] Accordingly, in 1985 the 143-acre site was purchased for over three million dollars[26] with bond money from a 1981 district referendum. Initially, the board looked at three sites: Telge Road and FM 2920, FM 2978, and Highway 249.[27]

The site at Highway 249 was chosen for several reasons. Located on a major thoroughfare, the site was very visible with easy access.[28] Being adjacent to the city meant cost savings because the city accepted a request from the district to annex the land and provide utilities.[29] Additionally, the site provided room for expansion as well as good drainage into Spring Creek, which marks the northern boundary of the land.[30] In fact, the college's land drains so well—with a drop of approximately seventy-five feet from the highest point on the site to the lowest—that it necessitated the installation of a concrete riprap to break the force of water draining from the property.[31]

A final and very important attraction of the land is its natural, beautiful setting. Although the area was once "open rolling prairie land . . . fringed by beautiful hardwood and pine timber,"[32] by the time the land had been purchased by the college district, the land was long-fallow farm land surrounded by towering pines. This lush setting that the Board of Trustees saw was covered by fields of natural bluebonnets and albino bluebonnets,[33] accented with towering pecan trees (and to this day, every November, Tomball citizens come out to the campus to pick up pecans).[34] In this bucolic setting, deer dashed

from the woods through the bluebonnets and yellow coreopsis. Even after the college was built, employees would often look out their windows in the early morning to see deer darting across campus.[35] Indeed, in the first year of the campus, the employees rescued a fawn on the campus grounds after fire ants had stung it.[36]

Later to enhance the natural beauty of the land, the community and the college planted a number of trees. The first addition was approximately fifty pink crape myrtles lining both sides of the drive near the southeast entrance. Also, the college planted four oak trees near the southwest entrance to honor four people: Dr. Roy Lazenby, founding president of Tomball College; Dr. Joseph Airola, chancellor at the time the college was built; Lela Meader, Dr. Lazenby's longtime secretary who helped found the college; and Troy Carpenter, maintenance employee who served the college in its first several years of operation. In early 1996, Texaco then added to the existing dogwoods by donating fifty saplings, which were planted around the perimeter of the drive.[37]

In addition to being both beautiful and practical, the land acquired for the college has an interesting genealogy of its own. The college's 143-acre site was part of the original Joseph House survey of 1825. In 1840, the land was purchased by Jacob Voebel, who operated a

*Welcome sign displays community support for Tomball College.*

*Right: An early photograph of the Jacob Vobel Home, Tomball College grounds.*

COURTESY: LESSIE UPCHURCH.

*Below: The Jacob Vobel Homestead with Tomball College in the background.*

sawmill, held dances, and sold whiskey. Soon after moving onto the land, Voebel pegged together a two-room home out of cypress wood. This home, though ramshackle, still nestled among the college's pecan trees up until a few months before the new college opened. The largest of the pecan trees, which still stands, probably was planted at the corner of the house by Friedrich Brautigam, who bought the land from one of the Voebels' children in 1892 and owned it until 1917, when Roy Irvine purchased it. Brothers Biaggio and Luke Tinirella owned the site next, and early in 1985 their heirs sold it to the college district.[38] Soon after, on November 19, 1986, the district held its groundbreaking.[39] At that ceremony, the college received a plaque in honor of the Texas sesquicentennial, now displayed at the college's main entrance; its inscription, which reads in part, "The Community and the College / Guardians of the Past / Partners in the Future," gives evidence of the special bond between Tomball College and the community. Later, when workers began to clear the land for construction, the district discovered that the area contained a legacy from the era of Tomball's oil exploration and production: an Exxon pipeline had to be moved from a parking lot.[40] And in the area beneath what is now the commons area, oil well piping had to be cut back to a depth of twenty feet in case the building settled and the pipe did not: for the architects, the mental picture of an oil pipe "sculpture" suddenly sticking up through the floor in the Commons in the indefinite future was not a pretty one.[41]

After the purchase of the land, the architectural firm of McKittrick Richardson Wallace

Architects (now RWS Architects) was chosen to design Tomball College as a campus that reflected the special connection that the new college would have both with the community and with the college district. Indeed, the choice of RWS Architects reflected that desired spirit because not only did the firm design Tomball College, Kingwood College, Montgomery College, and the University Center, but it also has had a long-standing relationship with Tomball ISD, planning the nearby Tomball junior high among other projects.[42] Once chosen, the firm was given the charge by Chancellor Airola to use a "megastructure" design for Tomball College because his philosophy, unlike W. W. Thorne's, who was chancellor when North Harris College was built, focused on a single comprehensive building rather than multiple buildings. As he envisioned the new college, the building in its first phase included not only classrooms, but also labs, some physical education facilities, and a food service area.[43]

Keeping their charge in mind, the design team first considered a "Y" design (which would have been appropriate, considering the questioning nature of education), but ultimately arrived at a "cruciform" shape in which four wings, each wing named for one point of a directional compass, radiate out from a central commons area.[44] By combining the space desig-nated for a dining area, a student lounge, and a registration area, the architects could justify cre-ating a soaring atrium reminiscent of the nave of a cathedral.[45] As a result, this cruciform design uniquely demonstrates the philosophy of the Tomball community in its reverence for educa-tion; at the same time the design reflects the mission of the college employees: the four wings radiate educational opportunities to the four corners of the community, and the Commons which is at the center or heart of the college rep-resents the college's sense of community. Thus, it is no surprise that the Commons has proved popular, both with the community and with stu-dents who enjoy socializing and relaxing there.[46] Notably, even before the college opened for the first full semester, the Tomball Chamber of Commerce held its Business Expo in the Commons. Other community groups have held luncheons, and there have even been two wed-ding receptions.[47]

The unique megastructure design, marked by symmetry, harmony, and attention to detail, has made Tomball College an award-winning build-ing. For example, the college's cruciform shape is repeated in other elements of the building such as the frosted glass of the dance room, the glass inset of the Commons' banister, and the grouping of four windows above the building's main entrances. Employees of the college even

*Tomball College under construction*

refer to the classroom off the second floor of the commons area as the "cathedral room" for its high sloping ceiling. The repeated use of tile at the entrances, the floors and pillars in the Commons, the sign along Highway 249, and the side of the second floor breezeway in the south wing increase the sense of harmony.[48] Another interesting feature of the building is the use of two different colored mortars to add variety to the brickwork. The result of this unity of design and attention to detail was a number of awards including the Merit Award for Architectural Excellence in School Design from the TASB/TASA (Texas Association of School Boards/Texas Association of School Administrators).[49] As an interesting side note, there is a delightful story about how the color was chosen for the rails and banisters in the buildings. According to apocrypha, the administration and the Board of Trustees had chosen the palette of colors—hues of aqua, gray, and mauve—but they could not find the perfect color for the rails. The color was discovered when Chancellor Airola, while on a walk about the grounds with the architects, had an epiphany and turned to one of them and said he wanted the rails to be the color of the sweater the architect was wearing. The architect then took the actual sweater to paint stores all over town until he found a perfect match.[50]

Although the design was perfect for the philosophy of Tomball College, and indeed also very cost effective, the rapid, unprecedented growth of Tomball College quickly demanded the creation of additional space. The original structure was 166,800 square feet, completed at the cost of $9,540,00,[51] which was also a great boon to the taxpayers in that the college was built at one million dollars under budget.[52] Yet soon Tomball College experienced growing pains; increased enrollment every fall and spring since its opening created the pleasant problem of facing an immediate future without enough classrooms or parking places for its student body. Thus in 1989, Dr. Lazenby began planning for an extension of the South Wing. In 1992 this 53,000 square foot[53] academic wing was completed at a of cost $3,337,000.[54] At the same time, the library was enlarged from 950 square feet to 1300 square feet.[55]

Once the building plans were in the works, the Board of Trustees addressed the challenging task of choosing the founding president of the new college. He had to be a special person, demonstrating a superlative background in community college education while at the same time possessing a deep and abiding commitment to the community and its partnership with the college. That man was Dr. Roy L. Lazenby. Born and raised in Carlsbad, New Mexico, Dr. Lazenby was a man of diverse educational background, with a B.S. in business education, a M.S. in guidance and counseling, and a Ed.D. in administration. Additionally, Dr. Lazenby was a long-standing district employee with a broad range of experience with the district. One of the first ten employees in the entire district (and the fifth administrator), he was hired originally in June 1973 as the Director of Student Services and Registrar for North Harris College. Dr. Lazenby also served as the Dean of Student Services for North Harris College before being named founding president of Tomball College in 1986.[56]

In addition to extensive service to the college district, Dr. Lazenby has been and continues to be an active participant and valued member of the Tomball community. Drawn to Tomball because of the beauty of the area, the quality education provided by Tomball ISD, and the small but friendly sense of community, Dr. Lazenby became a citizen of Tomball in 1978. Since then he has been active in the First Baptist Church of Tomball, the Tomball Rotary Club, the Tomball Area Chamber of Commerce, the Board of Directors for Leadership North Houston, the Cypress-Fairbanks Chamber of Commerce, and the Magnolia Chamber of Commerce.[57] Active in these organizations, he has worked tirelessly to let the community know that Tomball College exists because of and for the community. In his tenure as charter president, he has opened the college's doors for innumerable community events while also touting the quality education that is available at Tomball College. Clearly, Dr. Lazenby, as founding president of the college and as an integral part of the Tomball community, demonstrates

the kind of partnership between college and community that makes the college district a model of excellence in education.

In June of 1988 with a president nonpareil and a beautiful building nearing completion, Tomball College was preparing for its first semester. That summer Tomball ISD continued to show its support for the college by providing office space and classrooms in the library of Tomball Intermediate School. Dr. Lazenby used the back as office space, interviewing faculty and staff and monitoring the college's construction.[58] Meanwhile, a few summer school classes were held in the same building because classes were not scheduled to be held on the campus itself until the beginning of the fall semester. However, the collapse of part of the library ceiling at Tomball Intermediate and the subsequent asbestos removal necessitated that classes during the second summer session be moved to the campus. To accommodate these students, the building partially opened in July when Steve Wooten, district director of construction, came in from the district office and cordoned off which parts of the building could be used: a few classrooms, the front registration area, and Dr. Lazenby's office; the rest of the building was off limits.[59]

Then in August the energy and excitement of the employees of Tomball College became almost tangible. Determined that the building's opening be perfect, employees, their families, and community members pitched in. On Aug. 1 when the furniture started coming in, the entire commons became a furniture assembly area, teeming with people with screwdrivers and drills, putting together desks, tables, armchairs, and faculty desks.[60] As opening day swiftly approached, no job was too menial. Employees pitched in no matter their job title, moving furniture, hauling trash, dusting, polishing windows. The epitome of cooperation and team-spirit was President Lazenby himself, who acted as a jack of all trades: employees remember seeing him pitch in, building furniture, answering questions, and directing students. As one faculty noted, "the attitude overall was we're all in this, all for one and one for all . . . whatever had to be done, we did it because we wanted the building to look absolutely perfect when we opened Day One."[61] Janice Peyton, Director of

*Tomball College, coreopsis in bloom.*

the LRC until 1995, perhaps best described this sense of unity: "Such a team spirit existed that the campus was smilingly referred to as a cult."[62]

The team spirit of the college was also clearly reflected in the first registration. Conducted in late August in the downstairs commons area, registration was hectic because the building had just opened and there had been no opportunity for prior student advising. Yet there was energy, excitement, and hope. United with a sense of purpose, all staff, faculty, and administration were involved. Everyone did everything. For example, the president himself worked the floor, advising students and determining residency.[63] Dr. Carnahan, in addition to her duties as Registrar, also acted as computer technician and a maintenance worker.[64] Moreover, since the entire facility had been open only for a few days, most faculty had not even had an opportunity to locate and move into their offices, and with the frenetic pace of registration, many did not locate their offices until three days after the close of registration.[65] Because of a commitment to meeting predicted enrollment figures, everyone was hanging on the numbers, so at the end of every

day, when the employees would get the count, a huge cheer would ring out through the Commons. There was a great air of celebration because they were proud to be meeting and exceeding goals.[66] On the final night, when the numbers were totaled, it was apparent that Tomball College had smashed all predicted enrollment figures. The final official figures revealed that the excitement of Tomball and the surrounding communities of Magnolia, Montgomery, Waller, Klein, and Cypress-Fairbanks at having quality, affordable education close to home had translated into 1750 students that first semester.[67] So at the close of registration, two faculty members, ebullient about the high enrollment numbers, grabbed their guitars and in celebration began to serenade the employees; the few students remaining soon joined in as did many other faculty and staff members.[68] Thus, the first registration at Tomball College ended in a celebratory songfest that reflected the employees' high spirits and their exhilaration at opening a new college.

After this highly successful beginning, the college held the dedication ceremony on

September 25, 1988.[69] Showing their pride in their college, almost a thousand members of the community attended the ceremony. It was at this time that the Roy C. Hohl Fitness Center was dedicated in memory of one of the main people responsible for bringing the college to the area. To demonstrate its support for the new college, the town even declared the day "North Harris County College Tomball Campus Day" in a resolution read by Lee Tipton, Tomball mayor at the time.[70]

One of the hallmarks of the first year was the sense of camaraderie and unity among employees. Faculty, staff, and administration were all on a first name basis because of mutual respect and unity of purpose. This sense of team building was demonstrated in the "Breakfast Club," an informal gathering of faculty who met early in the morning before classes in order to have coffee and conversation and simply to enjoy each other's company.[71] That sense of connection that started early in the morning continued throughout the day in faculty office suites since the suites were not discipline specific. Faculty had been given the opportunity to choose their own offices, and the first ones chosen were offices with windows. However, the result of the "moth theory"—faculty like moths were attracted to the light—was serendipitous. The college had true interdepartmental officing that built collegiality, made the faculty a community, and created an environment that allowed for healthy exchange of methodology and ideas.[72] In fact, such was the family feeling among the faculty that it refused to single out only three teachers as recipients of a teaching excellence award. Instead, Dr. Lazenby arranged for a dinner in a house among the pine trees at Girls Country to celebrate the faculty's efforts during that first year.

Another hallmark of the first year, and indeed all years, is the contribution of the adjunct or part-time faculty at Tomball College. Adjunct instructors have always been integral to the institution and the quality of instruction that it is able to maintain. As one full-time faculty notes, "If we hadn't had that support of our adjunct faculty, there is no way we would be where we are today...We had absolutely dedicated adjunct faculty that have supported us not just teaching classes but that served on our advi-

*Dr. Roy Lazenby, founding president of Tomball College.*

sory boards. They've been available to students by phone, on weekends... they've just been outstanding."[73] Adjuncts have also started and built programs in areas with no full-time faculty, including music, art, speech, foreign language, and photography. In addition, adjuncts have been very valuable as professional tutors in the Learning Lab,[74] and many are award winners with extensive experience in their fields.[75]

Also especially noteworthy from the beginning has been the college's embrace of technology to make the facility and the education state of the art. In the first year, when the college operated with a streamlined faculty with very little support staff, Tomball College instituted the first voice mail system in the district with registrar Francette Carnahan as the "voice."[76] In addition, to ensure cutting-edge education, Camille Pittman insisted that the two labs be equipped with fifty 286 computers—state of the art at the time—instead of typewriters.[77] Furthermore, Tomball College installed the district's first computer network,[78] and the college's library was the first in the district to test and use CD-ROM products.[79] In subsequent years, computers allowed the college to reach farther out to the community. For example, the college offered its first courses over a bulletin board system in

1992. Then the Internet expanded the college's outreach to the rest of the world by offering the district's first course—English 1301—over the Internet in fall 1994.

Although not a highlight of the first year, one of the memorable events was connected to a nerve-wracking ice storm. The Southern Association of Colleges and Schools (SACS), the organization that extends accreditation to educational institutions, had planned its visit for one day in February. Unfortunately, a rare ice storm hit the area the night before, making the roads treacherous. Dr. Lazenby made it in his car only as far as a ditch near Tomball High School, and few cars could negotiate the ice-covered entrance to the college. The SACS team members experienced a harrowing ride in a van on slick roads before they arrived at the entrance of the college. Since their vehicle was unable to cross the ice-covered entrance, the team had to abandon the van and endure a slippery walk down the entrance way to the campus. Once inside, the team remained only forty-five minutes, perhaps because they were unhappy about having risked life and limb, although most of the employees would assert that the team simply could find little to criticize.[80]

Despite an occasional rough spot, the first year was marked by high spirits, buoyed by a sense of partnership with the community. Local organizations, businesses, and citizens contributed services, time, and materials. For example, the Tomball police department "kept constant vigil" until the college could install an alarm system.[81] IBM loaned software to the college, and one of the company's employees offered his time to install it and provide training.[82] When the college faced a shortage of furniture, local schools loaned furniture. Compaq donated approximately fifty 8086 computers to Tomball College.[83] Michael Richard, now Director of Building and Grounds, remembers that when a hurricane threatened the area, he showed up at Neidigk Lumber Company with his pick-up truck but with no way to pay for the plywood he needed, yet Neidigk allowed him to fill up his pick-up truck on his word as a Tomball College employee.[84] Tom Lovell, Professor of History, donated many of his books to fill out the library's embryonic collection. The geology lab was well-stocked after the contribu-

tions of the Ed Rose Collection, Tom and Rosemary Eckers Collection, and Hulon Madeley Collection.[85] Volunteers worked in the library and Learning Lab since the college had no budget for library aides or tutoring. Part of the Community Volunteer Program [86] created by Professor Sandra Lloyd and LRC Director Janice Peyton, these volunteers filled a great need. One of these volunteers was Miriam Hotard, or "Miss Miriam" as she was known, who offered expertise gained as librarian at the Houston Institute of Religion.[87]

Contributing to the college's success were its premier vocational/technical programs. One of these is the Veterinary Technology (Vet Tech) program headed by Professor George Younger. Utilizing his knowledge of Vet Tech programs throughout the United States, Dr. Younger put together a program for Tomball College that is without peer in the state of Texas. Dr. Younger took an empty, dirt-floored part of the West Wing that had been designated as the Vet Tech area and molded it to fit the students' needs; that area is complemented by the Large Animal Facility along with 4 and 1/2 acres of pasture land. With superior facilities and a carefully formulated 67 credit hour program, Dr. Younger and the other vet tech faculty have created a program that reflects true excellence. Students from Tomball College consistently pass state and national board exams at the rate of 99.7% with their next closest competitor at a rate of 78%. Even more impressive is the placement of students. Each graduate in the program is offered 8 to 10 jobs in the Harris County area alone. Once hired, the new graduates excel, improving the state of veterinary medicine in Texas.[88]

Tomball College's other premier program is Human Services headed by Professor Stephen Haberman. This program, one of the most effective and flexible vocational programs in the entire district, is constantly adjusted to fulfill the frequently changing licensing and accreditation laws, and at the same time it provides custom-tailored training for each student. Connected to this custom tailoring is the creation of a complete clinical practicum with an on-site treatment facility used to train interns in the areas of addictions and mental health services. This facility, called the Tomball College Counseling Institute, offers students and the

community counseling in compulsive gambling, drug addiction, alcohol addiction, and other mental health needs. At the same time, Tomball College counselor-intern, practicum students are able to complete their licensing and accreditation requirements while under supervision of licensed providers. Because of its success, the program receives many referrals from community groups, the state-wide hotlines, and the district's employee assistance program. In short, this program is one that is highly respected by and involved with the community.[89]

Throughout Tomball College's history, the unifying motif of community partnerships has been evident in every facet of college life: academic, intellectual, social, cultural and athletic. In academics the college has partnered with Tomball Regional Hospital since 1990 to bring the nursing program to Tomball College. The college offers the classes, and the hospital generously provides a laboratory, a part-time laboratory instructor, equipment, supplies, and access to the hospital's library and audiovisual materials.[90] In another academic partnership, Professor Larry Clark founded "The Gatsby Project" in fall of 1993. This partnership first paired students from local middle schools and high schools with Clark's college students in an exchange of ideas about F. Scott Fitzgerald's *The Great Gatsby*. The project has continued with other novels and moved to the Internet in 1995.

In intellectual partnership, the Brown Bag Seminars were instituted at Tomball College in 1989 under the leadership of history professor Tom Lovell. The Brown Bag Seminars, scheduled during the lunch hour when there are no classes, allow students, faculty, staff, and community members to have lunch while listening to featured speakers present viewpoints on many and varied topics: politics, business, literature, music, art, and journalism. The speaker could be Mattress Mac discussing theories of management, Neil Frank talking about hurricanes, a syndicated columnist discussing the upcoming election, or a poet reading his or her own works.[91] Additionally, one of the community's most visible connections to the college—Continuing Education (CE)—offers the community classes in computers, foreign-language, and business.[92]

The college has also connected to the community socially with the Christmas Lighting of the Commons ceremony. The Lighting of the Commons was instituted by Founding President Roy Lazenby in order to thank Tomball for its support, and to share with the citizens the beauty of the college in the Christmas season. Every year, at the beginning of the Christmas season, the commons area is elaborately decorated. The evening begins with wassail and gingerbread. A program follows consisting of a holiday narration, carols of the season, and a climactic lighting of the huge Christmas tree as well as the commons area, bathing the darkened Commons in a sea of twinkling lights. The evening ends with the surprise arrival of Santa, long-standing CE instructor Neil McDonald, who provides a photo opportunity for all the children (and their parents). Before he leaves, he collects any donated gifts brought by concerned Tomball citizens and college personnel to later deliver to area hospitals and nursing homes.[93]

Culturally, Tomball College has worked to provide a forum for students, employees, and community through travel and literary and artistic expression. The Travel Abroad Program, developed by Professor Linda Bryan in 1993, allows students to earn credit and community members to experience first-hand, through immersion in foreign cultures, the history, art, architecture of other countries. Participants develop an appreciation, tolerance, and respect for other cultures while visiting locales such as England, Italy, and Greece.[94]

Another opportunity for literary and artistic expression is available in the *Inkling*, the district's only creative arts magazine, which first published the poetry, short stories, and artwork of students, college employees, and community members in 1991.

In athletics, Tomball College has connected with the community both in credit courses and in special events. In order to make physical activity meaningful and to make it part of one's lifestyle, the kinesiology department has created a Venture Dynamics Program. Focusing on outdoor activities such as camping, canoeing, backpacking, and repelling, these courses emphasize teamwork and are actually a combination of interpersonal skills, physical skills, and academics.[95]

On a less serious note, the Veterinarian Technician Student Organization, each year conducts the K-9 Fun Run as their big fund-raiser. This race, one mile around the campus and run by an individual with his dog on a leash, has become a favorite tradition in the community. People from all over the district look forward to the race and call months ahead to make sure that this activity will continue. Especially memorable was the first year when Dr. George Younger used a starter pistol to start the race, which caused the dogs to react in various ways: one charged Dr. Younger while others broke leash and ran into the woods or otherwise scattered.[96]

*Tomball College.*

In short, Tomball College finds its unique identity in the special rapport that exists between it and the Tomball area. The citizens of Tomball have long demonstrated their commitment to higher education. While those living in surrounding school districts have voted down the opportunity to join the college district—sometimes more than once—the people of Tomball fought to become part of the district.

When Tomball was initially thwarted in its bid to become one of the founding ISDs of the district by Klein's withdrawal, Tomball's leaders went all the way to the state legislature for a solution.[97] And so great was the community's support of education that, after having already decided to tax themselves in a bond referendum for Tomball ISD a few months earlier, voters agreed more than three to one to join the college district despite the additional tax burden.[98]

It was only appropriate that the district ultimately designated the new college not "West Campus," as the planners had originally labeled it, but "Tomball Campus," reflecting its identity with the community. With the community displaying that kind of determination and dedication, the faculty and other employees of Tomball College felt a fierce desire to match the community's commitment. Indeed, the college's employees are professionals who work in tandem with each other and with the community to produce quality education in all disciplines and in all facets of life. They are united in the common goals of service to the students, to the community, and to the institution. In short, from its beginnings in a field of bluebonnets to its present day operation, Tomball College has worked hard to fulfill the community's dream of having access to quality education.

# NOTES

[1] The movie "Field of Dreams" is based on W.P. Kinsella, *Shoeless Joe* (Boston: Houghton Mifflin, 1982).

[2] Spring Creek gets its name from the twenty-five hundred springs that feed it; it runs for sixty miles through three counties, starting northwest of the college in Waller County and joining the San Jacinto river a little south of Kingwood College. Lessie Upchurch, *Welcome to Tomball: A History of Tomball, Texas*, ed. O B Lee (Houston: D. Armstrong Co., Inc., 1976), p. 3.

[3] North Harris County Branch of the American Association of University Women, *The Heritage of North Harris County* (1977), p. 6.

[4] Lessie Upchurch, interview by Douglas Boyd, Tomball, 1996.

[5] *The Heritage of North Harris County* , p. 17.

[6] Upchurch, *Welcome to Tomball*, pp. 14-15.

[7] That section of the creek belonged to Abram Roberts, a settler from Kentucky, who had named that area "New Kentucky." Sam Houston supposedly drank from Roberts' well, which is all that remains in the small county park created there. Because of competition with the city of Houston, Roberts' "New Kentucky" disappeared in 1840. *The Heritage of North Harris County*, p. 21.

[8] Ibid., 24-25, 63.

[9] Upchurch, *Welcome to Tomball*, p.16.

[10] *The Heritage of North Harris County*, p. 64.

[11] Shirley Klein Harrington, ed., *A Tribute to Tomball: A Pictorial History of the Tomball Area* (n.p., 1982), p.20.

[12] Upchurch, *Welcome to Tomball*, p. 53.

[13] Ibid., 55-56.

[14] Ibid., 107.

[15] *The Heritage of North Harris County*, p. 65.

[16] Upchurch, *Welcome to Tomball*, p. 152, pp. 200-1

[17] Ibid., 165, 202.

[18] Elmer Beckendorf, interview by Rebecca Tate, Rose Hill, 1996. Carolyn Hohl, interview by Rebecca Tate, Tomball, 1996.

[19] Ibid., Hohl, interview by Tate.

[20] Greater Houston Community College Commission, *Local Survey Report: A Comprehensive Survey in Support of Application to Establish a Public Junior College*, July 15, 1968.

[21] Elmer Beckendorf, interview by Rebecca Tate, Rose Hill, 1996.

[22] Carolyn Hohl, interview by Rebecca Tate, Tomball, 1996.

[23] Roy Lazenby, interview by Rebecca Tate, Tomball, 1996.

[24] Tomball Independent School District, School Board, *Special Minutes*, Jan. 16, 1982.

[25] Elmer Beckendorf, interview by Rebecca Tate, Rose Hill, 1996.

[26] North Harris Montgomery Community College District, Board of Trustees, *Minutes*, Nov. 8, 1984.

[27] Elmer Beckendorf, interview by Rebecca Tate, Rose Hill, 1996.

[28] At one time, Highway 249 consisted of only two lanes. Luckily, the Highway Department finished the expansion of 249 (149 at the time) to six lanes with a center turn lane in time for the college's opening.

[29] "Technical, Vocational Students Are Schools' Lifeblood," *Houston Post*, March 6, 1988.

[30] Elmer Beckendorf, interview by Rebecca Tate, Rose Hill, 1996.

[31] Bruce Wallace, interview by Douglas Boyd, Houston, 1996.

[32] Upchurch, *Welcome to Tomball*, pp.198, 200.

[33] Camille Pittman, interview by Rebecca Tate, Tomball, 1996.

[34] Roy Lazenby, interview by Rebecca Tate, Tomball, 1996.

[35] Ibid.

[36] Debbie Bell, interview by Douglas Boyd, Tomball, 1996; Michael Richard, interview by Douglas Boyd, Tomball, 1996.

[37] Michael Richard, interview by Douglas Boyd, Tomball, 1996.

[38] Lessie Upchurch, interview by Douglas Boyd, Tomball, 1996.

[39] Tomball College, Groundbreaking Program.

[40] North Harris Montgomery Community College District, Board of Trustees, *Minutes*, Dec. 11, 1986.

[41] Bruce Wallace, interview by Douglas Boyd, Houston, 1996.

[42] Ibid.

[43] Ibid.

[44] Ibid.

[45] Ibid.

[46] Ed Albracht, interview by Rebecca Tate, Tomball, 1996.

[47] Anna Stafford, interview by Douglas Boyd, Tomball, 1996.

[48] At one time tile lined many of the walkways, but because lawnmowers continually chipped it, it was removed. Camille Pittman, interview by Rebecca Tate, Tomball, 1996.

[49] Bruce Wallace, interview by Douglas Boyd, Houston, 1996.

[50] Francette Carnahan, interview by Rebecca Tate, Tomball, 1996.

[51] Tomball College Dedication program

[52] Roy Lazenby, interview by Rebecca Tate, Tomball, 1996.

[53] Ibid.

[54] Bruce Wallace, interview by Douglas Boyd, Houston, 1996.

[55] Janice Peyton, interview by Douglas Boyd, 1996.

[56] Roy Lazenby, interview by Rebecca Tate, Tomball, 1996.

[57] Ibid.

[58] Hap Harrington, interview by Douglas Boyd, Tomball, 1996.

[59] Francette Carnahan, interview by Rebecca Tate, Tomball, 1996.

[60] Ibid.

[61] Camille Pittman, interview by Rebecca Tate, Tomball, 1996.

[62] Janice Peyton, interview by Douglas Boyd, 1996.

[63] Roy Lazenby, interview by Rebecca Tate, Tomball, 1996.

[64] Francette Carnahan, interview by Rebecca Tate, Tomball, 1996.

[65] George Younger, interview by Rebecca Tate, Tomball, 1996.

[66] Sandra Lloyd, interview by Rebecca Tate, Tomball, 1996.

[67] Francette Carnahan, interview by Rebecca Tate, Tomball, 1996.

[68] Tom Lovell, interview by Rebecca Tate, Tomball, 1996; Ed Albracht, interview by Rebecca Tate, Tomball, 1996.

[69] Tomball College Dedication program

[70] "NHCC Dedicates New Tomball Campus," *Tomball* (Texas) *Potpourri Newspaper*, Oct. 12, 1988, p. 2.

[71] Sandra Lloyd, interview by Rebecca Tate, Tomball, 1996.

[72] Francette Carnahan, interview by Rebecca Tate, Tomball, 1996.

[73] Camille Pittman, interview by Rebecca Tate, Tomball, 1996.

[74] Sandra Lloyd, interview by Rebecca Tate, Tomball, 1996.

[75] Steve Haberman, interview by Rebecca Tate, Tomball, 1996.

[76] Francette Carnahan, interview by Rebecca Tate, Tomball, 1996.

[77] Camille Pittman, interview by Rebecca Tate, Tomball, 1996.

[78] Mark Dial, interview by Douglas Boyd, 1996.

[79] Janice Peyton, interview by Douglas Boyd, 1996.

[80] Ibid.

[81] Michael Richard, interview by Douglas Boyd, Tomball, 1996.

[82] Camille Pittman, interview by Rebecca Tate, Tomball, 1996.

[83] Mark Dial, interview by Doug Boyd, 1996.

[84] Michael Richard, interview by Douglas Boyd, Tomball, 1996.

[85] Hulon Madeley, interview by Rebecca Tate, Tomball, 1996.

[86] Sandra Lloyd, interview by Rebecca Tate, Tomball, 1996.

[87] Janice Peyton, interview by Douglas Boyd, The Woodlands, 1996.

[88] George Younger, interview by Rebecca Tate, Tomball, 1996.

[89] Steve Haberman, interview by Rebecca Tate, Tomball, 1996.

[90] Nockie Zizelmann, interview by Douglas Boyd, 1996.

[91] Tom Lovell, interview by Rebecca Tate, Tomball, 1996.

[92] Debbie Bell, interview by Douglas Boyd, Tomball, 1996.

[93] Roy Lazenby, interview by Rebecca Tate, Tomball, 1996.

[94] Linda Bryan, interview by Rebecca Tate, Tomball, 1996.

[95] Rick Grimes, interview by Rebecca Tate, Tomball, 1996.

[96] George Younger, interview by Rebecca Tate, Tomball, 1996.

[97] Diane Holland, interview by Douglas Boyd, Tomball, 1996.

[98] Hap Harrington, interview by Douglas Boyd, Tomball, 1996.

# MONTGOMERY COLLEGE

by William D. Law, Jr.

*Montgomery College,*
*The Woodlands, Texas.*

Because their very nature is tied to the area they serve, community colleges are often the creatures of geography, indeed more often than not a political geography. It is a rare situation to find that the creation of a community college does not represent the prevailing politics of the time and the best compromise of civic leaders in their attempts to meet the needs of the broader community. The North Harris Montgomery Community College District is no exception to this phenomenon. Indeed, the creation of Montgomery College, is nearly a textbook case of how a community comes to create a vision of itself and its future and how it struggles with the best means to incorporate educational opportunity into that vision.

From its very creation, Montgomery County (and Conroe in particular) had a political geography by which it was related to, but distant from, the city of Houston. Montgomery County traces its formal beginning to its charter granted by Governor Sam Houston on December 14, 1837. The county was the third to be chartered in the new Republic and it took its name from Andrew Montgomery who built the first permanent trading post in the area in 1823, in the community that still bears his name.[1] The city of Conroe evolved from the sawmill established by Isaac Conroe in

*Dr. William D. Law, Jr. is the founding president of Montgomery College.*

1881. Its "distance relationship" reflected the fact that Conroe had built a four mile rail spur to join his holding to railroad lines that crossed the county on their way to Houston. In fact, Isaac Conroe lived in Houston and would flag down a passing train when he wished to return home. In 1886, he was able to convince the rail company to make a scheduled stop at "Conroe's switch" giving permanence to the site that quickly grew in scope and importance to become the county seat.[2]

The notion of both distance and relationship to Houston continued to describe much of the development of Conroe and Montgomery County, through the expansion of the ranching, timber, and eventually oil industries in the 20th century. Indeed, even today, Conroe markets its attractiveness as "Houston's Playground" to emphasize the natural resources available to city residents.

Clearly, as the suburbanization of Houston was occurring in the years following the Second World War, civic leaders in emergent communities beyond the city limits sought to provide educational opportunity closer and more responsive to local needs. As Americans (in numbers that could only be imagined decades previously) achieved the dream of owning their own home, they sought also to create opportunities for themselves and their children to go beyond high school, historically the educational level of attainment that supported most employment.

The most notable response to these aspirations was the emergence of the community college movement in America. This uniquely American education innovation which was spawned in the United States following the Second World War was riding the crest of the wave of the creation of new suburbs throughout the country. North Houston/Harris County was no different from hundreds (now thousands) of similar towns and counties throughout the country.

In the early 1970s, residents of expanding communities on the north border of the city of Houston, agreed to create their own community college district. They would tax themselves and elect fellow citizens to structure the North Harris County College to provide a means for supporting their hopes of prosperity through

education. The college began operations in 1973.

The post-war suburbanization of American cities had an impact on the socialization of families and communities that was not fully understood or anticipated. As a result, policy analysts, academics, politicians and civic leaders devoted (and continue to devote) large amounts of time and talent in studying the impacts—positive and negative—of the migration of citizens to new communities away from the cities. The results of such introspection led to a number of serious concerns regarding the problems caused by the creation of tasteless, "cookie-cutter" tracts of homes that often appeared to foster social disintegration, as the traditional city neighborhoods were left behind. The loss of social contact, of the permanence of neighborhoods, of some communal values were phenomena that offset the obvious benefits of new homes, open spaces, and greater mobility of workers and their families.

In retrospect, these changes—positive and negative—did not fully impact Conroe and Montgomery County as much as other communities in the 1950s and 1960s. Quite simply, the "distance" aspect of the relationship to Houston was yet the predominant factor. Expanding communities between Houston and Conroe along the joining highway (Interstate 45) were still attractive enough to those moving from the city to make travel further out to Conroe and its environs less logical.

The continued study of problems associated with the suburbanization of America in the 1950s and 1960s gave rise to several notable attempts to create communities that addressed both the strengths and weaknesses of the migrations. Across the country, there emerged the creation of a number of "planned communities" as pilot projects intended to capture the best of the historical neighborhood roots and the obvious benefit of home ownership and quality of life issues associated with less congestion. The establishment of one such community in Montgomery County was to alter the "distance relationship" in a way that was to lead directly to the creation of Montgomery College.

In a series of related events from 1964 through 1972, George Mitchell, an independent Texas oil and gas operator, put into place a plan for a highly planned community 27 miles north of Houston. The Woodlands, as the community was to be named, was located by Mitchell on some 25,000 acres of land on the southern edge of Montgomery County running north to nearly the San Jacinto River, whose winding path bisects the county.

The land acquisition, planning and financing built upon experiences of other such communities—Columbia (Maryland), Irvine (California), Reston (Virginia). The first homes in the community were sold in 1974 and through the ensuing decades, the five towns that comprise The Woodlands had grown to some 45,000 citizens by the mid 1990's. The careful planning, tight building restrictions, high esthetics and emphasis on security allowed, over time, for continued growth in high priced homes and the resultant commercial economic impact such home owners generate.[3]

The growth and development of this community was to change the political geography of the county almost overnight. Where previously the "distance relationship" to the city of Houston commanded the attention of local citizens, now a much greater attention sprung forth on community and social issues and the potential impact "north of the river" (where families had lived for many years) or "south of the river," home to increasing numbers of newcomers, at times characterized as unconcerned with the issues their relocation created.

As part of the development for The Woodlands, Mitchell (through the development company he formed, The Woodlands Corporation) had made a number of overtures to incorporate education into the fabric of the community. Executives of The Woodlands Corporation sought election (and were successful) to the school board of the Conroe Independent School District. Indeed, Woodlands corporation President Roger Galatas served on the school board from 1973 until 1979. He was followed by Coulson Tough, a vice president of the corporation, and later by Gerald Irons, another senior executive. Relatedly, Mitchell, through The Woodlands Corporation strongly supported the establishment of an independent school, the John Cooper School, as an alternative to the public education process.

The success of The Woodlands Corporation in supporting the timely expansion of elementary and secondary education to the rapidly growing Woodlands community came at a price. Financing new school buildings and the attendant operational expenses meant that taxes increased for all citizens of the school district. Such increases were poorly received by many citizens in the communities north of the river where the feeling was that their tax dollars supported growth and development for newly arrived residents of the county at the expense of needed improvements in all schools. Compound such sentiments in other aspects of everyday life—roads, social services, security, and other governmental services—and the resultant friction between "north county" and "south county" is understandable.

The accomplishments of Mitchell and others to provide a full range of services for the carefully planned Woodlands community were not in one critical area—post-secondary education. In retrospect, a series of initiatives that proved to be "dry holes" to the oil and gas wildcatter, eventually became the basis upon which Montgomery College was created.

In the early 1970s Mitchell worked in partnership with leaders of the University of Houston to gain support for the approval of a "north" campus of the university. In 1974, the Texas Higher Education Coordinating Board in a white paper report recognized the recent and future growth of the county as suitable to support the expansion of the University of Houston into Montgomery County. Such possible expansion was not imminent, however, as the Coordinating Board sought to protect the legitimate interests of Sam Houston State University (SHSU) in Huntsville. In their deliberations, the Coordinating Board indicated that no expansion would take place until SHSU exceeded 10,000 students and the general population of the area to be served exceeded 750,000 persons.

The forward motion to create a campus for the University of Houston was stopped, however, in 1977 when University of Houston officials acquired facilities on the north edge of the city and created the University of Houston Downtown Campus. This acquisition, undertaken as part of an effort to expand opportunities for residents of the City of Houston, was determined by the Coordinating Board to be the expansion permitted under its earlier report. Despite strong lobbying by Mitchell, the Coordinating Board maintained its position and resisted additional expansion plans. Indeed, in subsequent years, a $250,000 planning grant approved by the Texas legislature to determine the feasibility of expansion of higher education to Montgomery County was vetoed by Governor Mark White at the urging of other university interests, specifically those at Prairie View A&M University.

The inherent need for access to post-secondary education to meet the needs of The Woodlands residents gave rise to another Mitchell-supported venture with the University of Houston. In the spring of 1980, the University of Houston initiated a Woodlands Institute in space provided by The Woodlands Corporation on Grogan's Mill Road in the very center of the Woodlands. Although limited in the number of courses offered, The Woodlands Institute was seen as a means of providing coursework for those in the growing population who sought to pursue a baccalaureate degree. This effort was short lived, however, ceasing operation in 1988. The general consensus on the failure of the operation reflected a narrow scope of course offerings and a corresponding reticence on the part of citizens to make a commitment to an apparently tenuous program.[4]

A final initiative on the part of Mitchell to entice the University of Houston to commit to an expanded presence in The Woodlands occurred in 1986. By this time, the University of Houston had established a small branch campus operation in a new development, Cinco Ranch, west of Houston. Mitchell offered the university 10 acres of land on the north edge of The Woodlands and a start-up grant of $2 million if the university would match its commitments to programs and courses that were in place at Cinco Ranch. No progress was ever made in response to this offer.

While it is clear that George Mitchell was personally leading the efforts to secure a presence of the University of Houston in The Woodlands, these efforts were in no means being undertaken individually. A group of civic leaders, many with ties to the University of Houston, had formed a loose-knit organization,

generally referred to as the University of Houston "support group," under the general auspices of the South Montgomery Woodlands Chamber of Commerce. Dan Hauser, then president of the local office of the Bank of the Southwest, assumed a leadership role in the group. While Mitchell's efforts utilized his business and civic contacts to garner support from University of Houston trustees and financial backers, the support group's efforts were largely focused on raising "grass roots" support for some University of Houston presence.

In a watershed event, members of the support group were successful in finally establishing a meeting with Dr. Kenneth Ashworth, the Commissioner of Higher Education for the State of Texas in early 1986. At that meeting, Ashworth left little doubt that the increasing stress on state resources for colleges and universities, as well as the demands for expansion in other areas of the state, left little hope that the Coordinating Board would support an effort to create a branch of the University of Houston in The Woodlands. Despite the disappointment of this harsh reality, the support group began to explore a wide variety of options to secure some post-secondary education in Montgomery County. In short order, joining the community college district emerged as a potential "first step."[5]

Expanding their efforts after a series of meetings with Chancellor Joe Airola of the North Harris County College District, and encouraged by the fact that the New Caney Independent School District (just east of the Conroe Independent School District) had recently been able to run a successful campaign to become a member of the college district, the support group eventually organized a petition drive to secure a sufficient number of signatures to cause a referendum to be called for the purpose of joining the North Harris County College District. Hauser was able to use his professional contacts to gather the support of civic leaders from Conroe as well as from The Woodlands to form a support group, Citizens for Higher Education, to raise both money and public support for the annexation initiative. John Wiesner, a civic leader and prominent member of the Greater Conroe Chamber of Commerce provided leadership to the group from the Conroe community. Wiesner and Hauser served as co-chairman of the Citizens for Higher Education committee.

The campaign, which was eventually to prove unsuccessful, developed along several major themes. First, there existed in Montgomery County at the time a well organized anti-taxation group, Montgomery County Association of Concerned Taxpayers that reflected a strong public concern regarding increased taxes; second, the college district was not prepared to address the key issue relating to the commitment to construct a campus facility in the county.

The chairman of the college district board at the time, Brad York, represented the limited extent of the board's commitment in a letter to the editor of the *Conroe Courier*, published the day before the annexation vote in January 1987. York indicated that should the citizens of the Conroe Independent School District vote to join the college district, "we would immediately expand our services into existing CISD facilities until studies show a campus is needed." York further noted that the strong financial record of the district would allow for a campus to be built "on a timely basis" upon documentation of the need.[6]

The concern over the impact of taxes, the inability to assure a campus (and a suspicion on the part of some evidenced in letters to the editor and in public forums that any campus to be approved would be located within The Woodlands) appeared to have the effect that private expressions of support from some elected leaders and local officials were not translated into the necessary strong public support that would assist in gaining a successful vote. Referendum organizers note particularly that even beyond the "watchdog" scrutiny of the Concerned Taxpayers some county officials at times appeared to be raising mundane technical issues regarding the forms used to secure voter signatures or the form of the signatures themselves. In fact, two series of petitions had to be collected

In the final analysis, the Citizens for Higher Education and the college district board were not able to satisfy concerns from voters at a level that allowed for a sufficient support to emerge. The vote took place on January 17, 1987 and failed by a vote of 3,444 (64%) to 1,999 (36%).

The defeat of the annexation initiative diffused the issue of post-secondary education for Montgomery County. Elected officials and many civic leaders who supported the annexation recognized that overcoming the defeat would require an energy and strategy that was not readily apparent. The anti-tax fervor of communities everywhere—Montgomery County being no exception—appeared to be much stronger than the well-intentioned desire to lower the cost of community college education to those individuals who were attending North Harris County College.

An effort to revive the issue emerged, however, in the early months of 1990. In discussions regarding the priorities of the South Montgomery Woodlands Chamber of Commerce, the newly installed chairman of the Board of Directors, Mary Matteson and Chamber president Kevin Brady determined that a second annexation vote might be successfully waged if a more focused, better financed information campaign could build on the successful components of the earlier failed campaign. Brady and Matteson were pleased to find that the leadership of the Greater Conroe Chamber of Commerce had likewise considered the annexation issue on its priorities. The decision was made to join forces and to once again attempt to convince voters that joining the college district was in the best interests of the community.[7]

The Citizens for Higher Education was reformed, reflecting very strong civic leadership from the communities both north and south of the San Jacinto River. John Wiesner once again agreed to lead the effort, this time with Matteson serving as the other co-chair. Other business leaders including Don Buckalew, Numsen Hail Curtis Williams, Marcia George joined with civic leaders including attorneys Steven McLain, Larry Forester, and David Crews to lend strong support from the Conroe community for the second effort. Joining the group from the community south of the river included Dr. David Gottlieb, vice president of the Woodlands Corporation (and former dean at the University of Houston), Julie Martineau, Ann Friend, and Dan Hauser.[8]

Working with Chancellor Dr. Joe Airola, the committee worked to address the key factor of a commitment to a campus upon the occurrence of a successful vote. Additionally, to address the issue of taxation concerns, a plan had begun to formulate to expand the size of the North Harris County College Board to allow for one or more members from CISD to be members of the board.

As might be expected, the issue of where a facility might be constructed in Montgomery County was problematic. At face value, any decision to locate north or south of the San Jacinto River could be construed as favoritism or capitulation to the pressures and desires of either part of the larger CISD community. Despite anti-tax sentiments that appeared to dominate most public discourse, in those referenda where voters could express a specific vote for a specific project, success was not uncommon. Unlike the earlier vote for joining the college district, it was felt by all those who were leading the second initiative that the identification of a specific campus location would foster a much higher level of support among voters.

Changing their stance from the previous election, the college district board authorized Airola to determine the best location for a future campus in Montgomery County. A second, smaller community group was appointed in late fall 1991 to assist Dr. Airola in identifying potential sites.

The work of the group was guided by three central parameters:

- the site needed to be large enough to accommodate current and future enrollment demands, not less than 100 acres in total;

- the site needed to be easily accessible to the commuter students who would comprise the student population of the college;

- the site needed to be centrally located within the district.

In a move that was to reflect on the very foundation of the college, the review committee undertook its work by taking a map of the county and drawing a circle with its center at the intersecting point of Interstate 45 and County Road 1488, just north of the San Jacinto River. Analysis by the Director of Institution Research,

Dr. Mike Green, had determined that this point represented the demographic center of the new district. It also represented the geographic center between the southern edge of the Woodlands (Rayford/Sawdust Roads) and the northern edge of Conroe (Interstate 45 and Loop 336 North) Sites within a three mile radius of this point would be given first consideration for the location of a new campus. This general area was largely undeveloped and was seen as the most likely "common ground" for a joining of the interests of the two communities.

Airola reserved to himself the responsibility for making the final recommendation to the college district trustees. He did extract a commitment, however, from the citizens agreeing to serve in the screening committee that they would support his recommendation from the sites that they identified meeting the criteria.

At final analysis, three sites were identified with two sites emerging as preferable. The first was located at Interstate 45 and the South Loop 336 at the southern edge of the city of Conroe. This particular tract was owned by the Friendswood Development Corporation and was part of an extensive 3,600 acre site acquired for future development. The second parcel was located 1000' west of Interstate 45 on a planned but not yet constructed portion of Highway 242, bisecting Montgomery County on an east-west axis. This property was owned by The Woodlands Corporation (and was in the same general area as the land previously offered to the University of Houston).

The Friendswood tract was eventually eliminated from consideration in light of the fact that no infrastructure improvements had been made and none were currently planned. To develop the campus, the college district would have to incur expenses relating to utilities, drainage, and some roadways.

The site proposed by The Woodlands Corporation did not have these limitations. However, some concerns regarding access were identified. That part of Highway 242 running west from Interstate 45, eventually swinging to the north to intersect with the east/west County Road 1488, was yet in very preliminary planning stages at this time. Funding for the divided four-lane highway had been identified by the state but the necessary right-of-ways had not been secured and engineering studies completed. These concerns were removed when The Woodlands Corporation committed sufficient funding to complete the engineering for the Highway 242 construction and agreed to provide all necessary land for necessary right-of-ways for the portion of the new road west of Interstate 45.[9]

In establishing the sale price of the 100 acres of land, Mitchell and The Woodlands Corporation crafted an agreement by which the college district would purchase 80 acres at a price of $3 million and the adjacent 20 acres would be donated to bring the parcel to the minimum acceptable size.[10]

In February of 1991, the college district board signed a no cost option on the Highway 242 property with The Woodlands Corporation. The option obligated the college district to purchase the site contingent upon a successful vote of the taxpayers to join the college district. The vote was scheduled for May 9, 1991.

In this second attempt at annexation, supporters were able to develop a more organized, informative campaign in conjunction with the college district trustees and the district staff. This grassroots effort combined with the policy decisions to both build a campus and to expand the board to include representatives from CISD proved to be the means by which voters of the school district were persuaded to join the college district. In its review of the coming annexation election, The Conroe Courier noted that "there has been little public opposition to the community college proposal. The Courier has endorsed the issue."

The final result proved to be in accordance with the Courier's earlier assessment. The final vote showed a massive increase in the number of persons voting (9,361 compared to 5,443 previously), and a vote total of 5,714 (61%) votes for the annexation with 3,647 (39%) voting against. Yet the generally strong support masked the reality of the political geography: the annexation vote failed in every district north of the river garnering an average of 44% positive vote. At the poll south of the San Jacinto River, the positive vote averaged 78%. Nevertheless, the fact that the initiative had passed based on the combined efforts of leaders from both areas of the district established a sense of accomplishment that the divisive nature of the "north and south" had been overcome on an issue of importance to all citizens.

Prior to the formal initiation of the annexation campaign, Chancellor Airola had announced his retirement from that position, effective with the selection and appointment of a successor. In December 1990, Dr. John E. Pickelman was selected as the Chancellor of the North Harris County College District, with his employment to commence on March 1, 1991. Airola's strong record of leadership had fostered the expansion of the North Harris County Community College District to emergent communities both east and west of the original campus on Aldine-Westfield. The reputation for strong academic coursework of the college district had led to more than 1,100 students from the Conroe Independent School District to enroll in the college district by this time, despite the cost of out-of-district fees and the problems associated with commuting long distances to attend classes. In both the earlier (1987) campaign as well as the present annexation initiative, both supporters and opponents recognized the impact and benefit of the district to citizens.

The appointment of Pickelman as Chancellor of the North Harris County College District was to prove to be among the most important determinants in the creation of Montgomery College in the succeeding years. Although coming to the chancellor's position from the presidency of the single campus Galveston College, Pickelman had significant background in the multi-campus Dallas Community College District. From that experience, Pickelman possessed a strong belief that the colleges could increase their impact in their communities if they had an individual identity within the larger framework of the identity of the district. The immediate result of this philosophical belief was that the previously named East Campus and West Campus became Kingwood College and Tomball College. Central to these identities of a "multi-college district" was a commitment to expand the scope of programs and services at these former branch campuses to more fully meet the needs of the students and communities being served.

This philosophical shift from branch campuses to a multi-college district with individual identities for the member colleges was a central tenet to the creation and planning of Montgomery College. From the earliest discussions with civic leaders, Pickelman described the creation of a comprehensive community college that would be able to meet a full range of educational needs of the communities it would serve. This commitment included both the very strong tradition of preparing students for transfer to baccalaureate-level colleges and universities as well as the identification and establishment of one and two year occupational programs designed to prepare adults for employment. Equally important, the commitment also included the full range of student support services to be available locally—advisement, counseling, and financial aid.

In December of 1991, a national search was initiated to identify the person who would serve as president of the college and who would plan the programs and services, oversee the construction of the facilities, and select the faculty and staff. This early identification of the chief officer was a second significant departure from prior practice and reflected the change in district philosophy from a branch campus system to a multi-college system.

In response to the national advertising for the position, some 92 applications were filed. From this group, five finalists were identified and invited to visit for extensive interviews. Again reflecting both the genesis of the college from its local roots and the leadership philosophy of chancellor Pickelman to foster local identities for the colleges, an important part of the selection process included an interview luncheon of the candidate by a group of approximately 15 leading citizens. The insights and comments of these individuals were solicited by Pickelman as part of his decision making process.

On May, 1992 the Board of Trustees of the college district selected Dr. William D. Law, Jr. as the founding president of Montgomery College. At the time of his selection, Law was serving as the president of Lincoln Land Community College in Springfield, Illinois. He had previously served as vice president for Institutional and Program Planning for the St. Petersburg Junior College District in Florida as well as the Staff Director for the Committee on Higher Education in the Florida House of Representatives. His Ph.D. degree had been

awarded in the area of Design and Management of Post-secondary Education Systems from Florida State University in 1978.

The first and immediate challenge presented to the new president was to obtain suitable space for classes to be offered while the permanent campus was being designed and constructed. Initiating an interim instructional plan had been part of the commitments made during the annexation referendum. Reflective of the commitment to construct a comprehensive college from the outset rather than a phased-in branch campus, the plans anticipated that the interim facility would be needed until the Fall 1995 semester.

Preliminary efforts by Vice Chancellor H. Pat Pate and Staff Architect Steve Wooten had identified a highly desirable space in an easily accessible shopping center in Conroe. The Pinehollow Shopping Plaza was located adjacent to Interstate 45 and the major arterial Loop 336 at the north edge of the city. The desirability of the property reflected this accessibility, its size—21,000 square feet—and most importantly, its location in the city of Conroe. The trustees, as well as the chancellor, discerned that the most appropriate way to consolidate community support where the vote had failed was to demonstrate a strong commitment to the citizens north of the river.

The context of this last factor reflects the important thread of the founding of Montgomery College—the commitment to serve the entire community and to span the divide of the San Jacinto River. The stunning development of The Woodlands and the peripheral areas adjacent to Interstate 45 created a constant pressure on elected and civic leaders to assure that all parts of the county received equitable services and considerations. The fact that the referendum annexing the Conroe Independent School District had twice in those precincts north of the river argued for a strong statement on the part of the college district that every effort would be made to assure access for all citizens to the college.

The commitment was logical and supportable to make, but proved to require some diligence to carry out. In 1992, Texas was in the midst of a major recession that reflected both a global dampening of the oil industry and a real estate bust resultant from the near collapse of the savings and loan industry. As a result of these factors an inordinate amount of commercial property was in default and under the control of the Resolution Trust Corporation (RTC), a federal agency created to arrange for the sale and disposition of property held by distressed or failed savings and loan institutions. The Pinehollow Shopping Plaza was one such property.

In anticipation of being able to lease the vacant property, the college district had acquired the services of the architectural firm of Joiner and Associates to design the interior space for necessary classrooms, study areas, registration and support, and administrative offices. The plan developed by Joiner and Associates carved out 15 classrooms, including two computer laboratories, three administrative offices, and a large general purpose area whose primary function was to serve as a place to support the needs of faculty to prepare for their courses.

Operations of the RTC, however, were not able to support the enthusiastic timeframe of the college. What, to all appearances, should have been a routine commercial lease agreement became a major undertaking in the unsettled financial environment of the time. By mid-June, it was apparent that the Resolution Trust Corporation was not appropriately staffed to execute operational agreements, its attention being devoted to the sale of property instead. At its June meeting, the District Board of Trustees was advised that efforts to acquire permanent space would continue, but that the decision had been made to offer the fall semester at night in the high schools of the Conroe Independent School District.

Upon arriving in Houston in July of 1991, President Law had been joined by two senior administrators from the district, appointed by Chancellor Pickelman. Dr. Kenne Turner was named Dean of Educational Programs for Montgomery College. At the time of his appointment he was serving as Executive Director of Resource Development and Career Education and had 8 years experience in the North Harris district.

Marie Bayard was appointed to the position of Assistant to the President. Bayard had been serving as the Director of the Licensed Vocational Nursing program at Kingwood College. Moreover, Bayard was one of the most experienced administrators in the district, having been a charter member at both North Harris and Kingwood College.

In operational terms, Turner was assigned responsibility for the organization and delivery of the courses (including the selection of adjunct faculty); Bayard was given the responsibility for the support services (registration, advisement, reporting) as well as general administrative duties. Calling on their experience, Bayard and Turner were able to organize a night semester with 25 courses offered at both Conroe High School and McCullough High School in The Woodlands. Registration, textbook, and other necessary instructional support were put in place to support an initial enrollment of some 376 students in this first semester.

The enthusiasm of getting started by using local high schools at night deflected some concern regarding the unavailability of a more permanent site. While still attempting to engage the RTC, President Law began to explore possible alternatives to the Pinehollow location. Alternative sites in Conroe and in strip mall locations along Interstate 45 south of the river were explored but rejected. The initial strong response in the high schools reaffirmed that the potential student population could exceed 1,000 students prior to the opening of the new campus. Any site significantly smaller than the 21,000 square foot Pinehollow site (which had the additional benefit of nearly unlimited parking for students) was considered inadequate.

In early September, however, Law received word that the Pinehollow Shopping Plaza was scheduled to be sold by the RTC to an investment corporation in Chicago. Upon confirmation of this information, Vice Chancellor Pate proceeded to negotiate a contract for the necessary space and in early October, immediately upon the sale of the shopping center, a lease for the "Conroe Center" of Montgomery College was signed. Modifications to the facility were completed as planned by early December and on December 12, 1992 the formal ribbon cutting ceremony was held. Some 250 citizens, including some who had worked for as long as six years in bringing North Harris County

College—now renamed as the North Harris Montgomery Community College District—to Montgomery County.

As part of the short ceremony surrounding the ribbon cutting, President Law's comments included a short phrase that would later be repeated in every public ceremony at which the college was featured. He told the supporters that from his perspective—and he hoped from theirs—"the sun is always shining at Montgomery College, because we have the opportunity to help people change their lives." As the college continued to develop, and as the community supporters continued to grow and to participate in the public celebrations and ceremonies, this catch phrase—"the sun is always shining at Montgomery College"—appeared to serve its intended purpose of reminding people of what the role of the college would be in their community.

The success of the Conroe Center in establishing the roots of Montgomery College in the county and in Conroe, particularly, were reflected in its enrollment growth prior to the opening of the permanent campus. In successive semester (excluding summers) the campus headcount enrollment for credit courses was 782, 1059, 1034, 1458, 1849.

Prior to the selection of Bill Law as the founding president of Montgomery College,

Chancellor Pickelman and the Board of Trustees undertook a number of decisions regarding the scope of the new college in order to expedite the construction processes. Key staff members of the college district's central office provided early planning and guidance to the project. In particular, Vice Chancellor Dr. Nellie Thorogood and Director of Institutional Research, Dr. Mike Green analyzed the potential student enrollment and provided estimates upon which the facilities plan could be based. Thorogood also provided a preliminary program plan detailing the types of transfer and occupation programs that might characterize the offerings of the new Montgomery College.

In October, 1991 the Board of Trustees also selected RWS Incorporated as the architects for the Montgomery College project. Mr. Bruce Wallace, a partner in the RWS firm, was identified as the Project Architect. Wallace and RWS had extensive background with the North Harris Montgomery Community College District, having been the principal design firm for both the Kingwood and Tomball College projects.

The plan presented to the board for its approval envisioned a campus of five two-story buildings, totaling some 240,000 square feet of space. The centerpiece of the campus was to be a learning center/library appropriate to support the comprehensive nature of the programs to be offered.

In keeping with the comprehensive college philosophy of Chancellor Pickelman, the plans for Montgomery College included a commitment to the fine and performing arts. A small theater of approximately 350 seats for student and community productions was included in the preliminary plans, as well as classrooms and labs to support art and music instruction. The educational specifications approved by the Board of Trustees contained a large student commons (cafeteria) that would allow for both food service to support student needs as well as flexible space to support use of college facilities by community groups. The board in its review urged the inclusion of two-level walkways to join the buildings allowing comfortable passage to students even on days of inclement weather.

Upon resolution of the Conroe Center lease issue, Law proceeded to meet with the architects two days each week for the September through January period. Much of the time was devoted to the normal range of issues attendant to the construction of a major educational facility— number, size, and location of classroom, labs, offices, specialized facilities. In the absence of faculty and staff, Law called upon a large num-

ber of faculty from the existing colleges to assist in focusing on the specific details of construction that would permit the best possible classroom and learning environment. During these months leading up to the issuance of the general construction contract, two issues that would prove to be central to the "personality" of Montgomery College proved to take the most time and thought.

The first of these issues related to the environmental concerns of the 100 acre site itself. In laying out the plans for the approved facilities, as well as planning for eventual expansion, the need to focus on the protection of the heavily wooded site became critical. Central to the discussions was the fact that a significant portion of the site was known to be wetlands, protected from development under the federal Environmental Protection Act. At one point in the Fall of 1992, a preliminary estimate that as much as 20.6 acres of the site would be classified as wetlands threatened the continuity of the project. It was clear that an area of that size excluded from development at any future date would for all practical purposes render the site unsuitable.[11] The issue was finally resolved with the Army Corps of Engineers, the agency responsible for EPA technical assessments. After more detailed

*Montgomery College Entrance.*
COURTESY: TIM SADLON/TGS PHOTO

assessment and analysis of the site, it was determined that less than 11 acres in the northwest corner of the property would be classified as protected. This area was able to be lined out such that no present or future construction would be restricted.

A second environmental issue also emerged. The 100 acre tract of the college campus lies within a few thousand feet of the Jones State Forest, an area that is home to a protected species, the red-cockaded woodpecker. Prior to the identification of the tract for the purposes of the college campus, environmental studies had been conducted to determine that the site and the adjoining areas outside the Jones Forest were not nesting habitats of the protected species. Despite these earlier studies demonstrating no habitat concerns, the college district was forced to reevaluate the college site and to reaffirm the absence of woodpecker habitats. The study conducted some five years earlier was subsequently updated and all necessary environmental approvals were given in a timely basis.

Another issue was less threatening to the timetable of the construction project, but more significant in long term impact: planning for the use of instructional technologies throughout the college. Stunning technological achievements had emerged in the use of computer-based tech-

nologies since the planning and construction of the college district's last campus in Tomball. New and emergent potential for information sharing through the global Internet was the most perplexing issue. At the same time, distributing information in many forms—not just text—characterized much of the development of new software applications as well as support hardware. Lastly, the means of distribution—cable, digital broadcast, infrared signals—challenged existing concepts of communicating over copper wires.

The technology issue was paramount to the creation of a library and learning resource center. Again, technological developments in access to remote information data bases or sources challenged basic concepts of the nature of a community college library. How much space would be needed for print volumes and resource materials? How much for computer terminals and network devices? How much for research work areas? How much for casual reading space?

In the matter of an open access learning support center, once again the need to discern the changes in student learning activities that would be a function of the adoption of new and future technologies became paramount. How much activity and in what form would students need out of class support? When and in what forms would students access instructional support from home or work? When and in what form would faculty be able to communicate with and support students via technology? How would the college keep current in this rapidly developing environment?

Clearly, some aspects of these issues would require immediate decisions. Other aspects, however, were clearly more enduring and more dependent on future developments both within and without the college. In the end, Law's choices reflected the fact that the pace of technological change would remain too rapid to allow for enduring decisions. The more important factors would be to establish a campus where such technological developments could be incorporated into the instructional plan if they improved student learning.

The centerpiece of the campus architecturally, philosophically, and organizationally would be the Extended Learning Center. This building would be the signature design and would support the following instructional concepts:

- Students would be challenged to extend their learning beyond the classroom time and location in each course offered by the college; the college would support the use of technology as a central component in every course;

- Students would take a more active role in their learning; classroom lectures would be reduced in favor of more active processes;

- The Extended Learning Center would be open 85-100 hours per week to assist students in their learning on a schedule convenient to the student.

To prepare for future technological developments that might occur, the campus design called for every classroom to be outfitted from the very beginning with the necessary wiring to permit access to local and remote information networks. Further, each classroom was constructed with sufficient capacity to permit as many as 24 computers to be located in the room should future events warrant such change.

*Governor George W. Bush dedicates Montgomery College in August, 1995.*

COURTESY: TIM SADLON/TGS PHOTO

Construction of the college began in early July of 1993 following the selection of Dal-Mac Construction of Dallas as the general contractor. The low bid accepted by the Board of Trustees called for a contract of $23.8 million dollars for college construction. The construction timetable envisioned a project length of just under two years, allowing for the college to begin classes at the new facility in the Fall, 1995 semester.

In response to the environmental concerns, the construction contract called for a careful plan that would allow for the maximum retention of trees on the heavily wooded site. Specific language of the contract required that Law or his designee would have to review and approve all plans for clearing or removing any trees during the construction.

As construction continued, Law began to assemble his administrative team. In August of 1993, Dr. H. Pat Pate moved from the college district office to assume the role of Vice President for Support Services. Day-to-day activities in the construction of the campus were assigned to Pate. In September of 1994, Dr. Mary O'Neil-Garrett was hired as the college's Vice President for Educational and Student Programs. Responsibility for the program plan in both student development as well as the transfer, occupational, and non-credit coursework was assigned to her. To assist in the refinement of a technology plan for the campus and the programs, Law hired Mr. George Crossland as the Dean of Technology for Montgomery College. Crossland was assigned responsibility for all areas relating to technological support including administrative as well as instructional applications. Crossland joined the staff in June, 1994.

In September of 1994, Law began the process of hiring faculty who would be the founders of Montgomery College. To accomplish this, a professionally-prepared viewbook was created as a means of communicating the essential information regarding Montgomery College, the communities it was to serve, and the history of the college district. The viewbook also contained information on the manner in which faculty would be selected.

The centerpiece of the faculty selection process was the requirement that those interested in teaching at Montgomery College prepare a portfolio addressing a number of areas central to the nature of teaching in the community college environment. This process was in marked contrast to the more common resume submissions exclusively outlining educational credentials and publications.

Specifically, the areas that candidates would need to address included evidence of how your students are challenged and nurtured beyond the classroom, and how you use technology to supplement and enhance the instructional environment.[12]

In an effort to determine the impact that technology was having on the hiring process, the first national announcement of openings for the founding faculty appeared in the *Chronicle of Higher Education* on October 3, 1994 and indicated that those interested in receiving the informational viewbook should request that information via e-mail. The college's e-mail address was listed, but a street address was not given. By early December, more than 1,000 persons had requested the information through this means.

A second national announcement ran in *The Chronicle* in early January of 1995, this time including street as well as e-mail addresses. In the end nearly 1,800 persons requested information on the founding faculty positions. From the 1,800 requests, the college received nearly 800 completed portfolios for the 45 founding faculty positions. By Spring of 1995, O'Neil-Garrett, joined now by the academic administrators who would supervise each instructional division in the college, had reviewed all portfolios and initiated the interviewing process for candidates. Through the February to May time period, some 211 persons were interviewed for faculty positions at the college.

Planning for the college indicated that an operating budget of some $7.5 million dollars would be needed. This figure reflected projections of an initial enrollment of approximately 3,200 students. Funding for post-secondary education in Texas provides resources based on demonstrated enrollment levels in one completed "base year" period as the basis for resources in the subsequent years. With the prior base year being held at the Conroe Center, and being just a fraction of the anticipated enrollments for the 1995-96 year at the new campus, the college district would be in a position of having to pay for the initial operating budget of the college entirely from its own resources for all growth beyond the base year levels. To alleviate this situation, Chancellor Pickelman undertook a year-long effort to lobby the Texas Legislature for special start-up funding for Montgomery College. In essence, the legislature was asked to treat the projected enrollment levels as if they had already occurred.

Pickelman was able to garner the support of every legislator who represented part of the college district to support the request. This unified approach, spearheaded by Representative Sylvester Turner of Aldine and Representative Kevin Brady of The Woodlands proved success-

*Founding president, Dr. William Law, with George P. Mitchell, chairman and CEO of Mitchell Energy & Development Corp.*

ful, with the legislature providing a special appropriation of $7.6 million dollars for the 1995-97 biennium.

On Tuesday, August 1, 1995 Montgomery College opened its doors for student registration and support services. While classrooms, labs, the Extended Learning Center and other instructional space were generally ready for use, construction delays left many exterior tasks unfinished. Additionally, the Theater and Fine Arts Building was unavailable for use, having fallen seriously behind in its construction schedule. Indeed, persistent problems relating to subsoil conditions early in the construction process and water seepage into the excavated orchestra pit later in construction caused this particular building to be delayed in opening until January, 1996.

On Monday, August 14, 1995 Governor George W. Bush joined the Board of Trustees of the North Harris Montgomery Community College District in the official dedication of Montgomery College. More than 1,000 citizens attended the ceremony, held on the second floor of the Extended Learning Center. In his remarks,

Bush noted the strong, cohesive, local support that led to the creation of the college. He went on to reflect: "The community college is a vital link between education and jobs. The colleges help bridge the gap. Texas' community colleges are vibrant and vital to our future. They serve a diverse population, and that's healthy for Texas."

Indeed, at the ceremony, many citizens noted that the annexation vote and the subsequent creation of Montgomery College had become the central event in the change once again of the political geography of the county. The north-south rifts of past years had been largely meliorated with the continued cooperation demonstrated by all parts of the county in the creation of the college.

For his part, Law's comments promised that faculty and staff would not "cease our efforts until we have become the finest community college in the nation." And, once again, Law reminded family, friends, supporters, staff and all assembled that "the sun is always shining at Montgomery College, because we have the opportunity to help people change their lives."

# NOTES

[1] Robin Montgomery, *The History of Montgomery County* ( Jenkins Publishing Company, Austin and New York, 1975), p.285.

[2] William Harley Grandy, *A History of Montgomery County, Texas.* Master's Thesis, University of Houston, August 1952.

[3] Richard Payne and Drexel Turner, *The Woodlands* (The Woodlands Corporation, 1995), pp.93-95.

[4] Interview with Dr. David Gottlieb.

[5] Interview with Dan Hauser.

[6] *Conroe Courier*, Letter to the editor, January 16, 1987, p. 4.

[7] Interview with Rep. Kevin Brady.

[8] Interview with Mary Matteson.

[9] Interview with Roger Galatas.

[10] Interview with Dr. Joe Airola.

[11] The Board of Trustees had anticipated that some reserve for wetlands would be needed and had negotiated in the acquisition of the tract that if the amount exceeded 15 acres, replacement land would need to be provided by the Woodlands Corporation.

[12] *Montgomery College Program Plan* (pamphlet), September, 1994.

# NORTH HARRIS COLLEGE'S JOURNEY TO BUILD BRIDGES TO THE ALDINE COMMUNITY:

*A victorious homecoming*

by Geraldine Gallagher

*George Washington Carver Center, Aldine, Texas.*

Carl Sandburg wrote: "Nothing happens unless first a dream." That dream began in 1972 when voters of Aldine, Humble and Spring Independent School Districts voted to create a new community college, North Harris County College. The first students and teachers gathered in the borrowed classrooms of Aldine High School. There were over 600 eager learners in the first semester, which began in August 1973 before much of north Harris County was developed. In August 1976, the college moved from those temporary quarters to the newly constructed, permanent buildings on a sprawling campus north of the Houston's Intercontinental Airport.

*Geraldine Gallagher is the Executive Director of External Affairs for North Harris College.*

As the college district expanded, breaking new ground and increasing its size to include six school districts, some 1,000 square miles and more than one million residents, its attention began to focus on prospective students who lived further north in the district. Tomball College, Kingwood College and Montgomery College were built in the far northern portions of the district's service area. North Harris College's enrollment of 613 students in fall 1973 increased to 7,591 in just eight years. What's more, North Harris College had the greatest geographic reach of the four colleges, drawing students from a 30-mile radius of the campus, including a significant number from Montgomery County.[1]

The district was growing up. It had evolved from its origin as a single college to a multi-campus college and then to a district of comprehensive community colleges. The district was renamed North Harris Montgomery Community College District in 1991.

One result of creating these new full-service colleges was the predictable loss of enrollment at the first campus, North Harris College. In 1992, North Harris College's student body was larger than that of the other two colleges put together. The district was recognized by the Texas Higher Education Coordinating Board as being among the fastest growing in the state of Texas. This was hardly surprising since census statistics provided by the NHMCCD Office of Institutional Research in the early 1990s showed that the district service area was also among the fastest growing in the state, with more than one million residents living in the six school districts that formed the college district.[2]

Three years later, after the construction of the Montgomery College campus just north of The Woodlands, North Harris College's size was just about equal to the enrollment of the other three colleges combined.[3]

In fall 1992, North Harris College enrollment had peaked at an unprecedented level of more than 12,000 students enrolled in credit courses. Another 19,000 students took non-credit classes.[4] But a couple of years later, as Montgomery College began drawing students from north Spring and The Woodlands to, first, its Conroe Center, and then in 1995, its brand new college, North Harris College began to face a steady loss of student enrollment.

This was not a miscalculation, but rather it was part of a strategic decision made by the college district's board of trustees. With the annexation of Conroe Independent School District and the subsequent birth of Montgomery College, North Harris College's renewed mission was to return to its roots in Aldine ISD. While the other three NHMCCD colleges tended to serve the northern residents because of their proximity, North Harris College was given the opportunity to focus its resources and energy on the southern portion of the district.[5]

At the time, the number of students attending the college from the south—within Aldine ISD zip codes—was roughly half that of students who lived north in Spring ISD zip codes, despite the fact that the more densely populated Aldine community boasted nearly double the number of residents.[6] It was clear to district trustees and college administrators that the southern sector of the college's service area was under-served.

Dr. Nellie Carr Thorogood was an early visionary and champion of outreach to the Aldine community. Previously president of Kingwood College, Dr. Thorogood began serving under the chancellor as vice chancellor for external affairs. Newly hired chancellor Dr. Pickelman and the college board of trustees brainstormed ways to more effectively serve south Aldine. In fact, the board put its commitment to paper, proposing to expand services in Aldine as part of an initiative to "develop programs to ensure access to comprehensive educational programs and services to all residents of the district."[7]

Under the direction of the new chancellor and North Harris College's even newer president, Dr. Sanford C. Shugart, the board urged college officials to move forward in serving Aldine. Dr. Shugart recalled driving through the Acres Homes area with Dr. Thorogood when he was interviewing for his position during the summer of 1991 and recognizing the grand opportunity to provide learning and training to a community in need.[8]

"Carver High School in Acres Homes was a satellite location for us in 1973, but our locations drifted for the first three or four years, mostly operating out of Aldine High School. We migrated more to MacArthur and Eisenhower High School because they had more comprehensive labs and room to accommodate us, plus police, custodians and services." Dr. Thorogood explained.[9]

Dr. Shugart, hired in fall 1991, hit the ground running. In the next year, he and a team of administrators met in more than a dozen meetings with Aldine ISD officials and business and community leaders to discuss educational needs and to brainstorm solutions. The administrative team then worked with college faculty and staff to respond to demographic data and the information gathered from Aldine leaders. The center's founding director, Dr. Rosario Martinez, began work in December 1992.[10]

Thus, the year 1992 marked the true beginning of North Harris College's homecoming to the Aldine community. Three years later, as the college prepared for the ground-breaking of a free-standing facility that grew from this initiative, Dr. Shugart told Mike Keeney, editor of the *Northeast News*: "Aldine ISD gave birth to the college. Not only were the first North Harris College classes offered in AISD classrooms, but W.W. Thorne was superintendent of Aldine ISD before he took the job as the college's first president. And current AISD superintendent, Sonny Donaldson, is my best partner in the community."[11]

In November of that year, North Harris College President Shugart presented to the board of trustees a preliminary plan for the new center. The Aldine Center, he explained, was established by North Harris College, in conjunction with community leaders, to serve the various communities in Aldine ISD. "The center will not be a single location, but a series of outreach campus sites, designed to offer educational programs and services which the communities need and desire. Each will also be expanded over time as further needs are identified through community and college collaboration. In a very real sense, The Aldine Center is truly that – a centering and focusing on the specific educational and service needs of the community," Dr. Shugart reported to the college district's board of trustees on Nov. 19, 1992. "The Aldine Center's purpose is to engage the members of the various communities in the Aldine ISD and to meet their educational needs, encouraging them to return to the classroom or continue with their studies. Those returning to the classroom at the alter-

native campus sites will be encouraged to make the transition to the NHC campus. By using the multiple-site approach, the college will be avoiding the image of locating a single, large center at one site. Rather, by establishing a series of sites throughout the Aldine ISD, The Aldine Center will be better equipped to serve citizens through the Aldine school district's various communities in their individual neighborhoods."[12]

In December of 1992, the college announced through the local weekly newspapers the launch of its new outreach initiative. A concept, rather than a place, The Aldine Center program began to make educational inroads into the community south of the Beltway. On New Year's Eve, the *North Freeway Leader* reported that the new Aldine Center would improve services to the Aldine area.[13]

National statistics supported the need for education. At the time, the U.S. Census Bureau reported that the work force of the year 2000 would be a dramatic change from employee pools of the past. What's more, survey after survey indicated that future workers would be ill-prepared to meet the demands of a competitive job market.[14]

The answer? A 1992 report by The College Board in New York pointed out that technical training and literacy education were required to help bring young people up to speed and prepare them to be the skilled workers of the next decade. The timing was especially good for North Harris College administrators, who planned to take the first step to address the issue by bringing education to people who might not otherwise be able to take advantage of traditional higher education opportunities because of family, work or financial responsibilities.

"The role of the community college is to serve the needs of the community, whatever they might be," Martinez explained. "In the North Harris College community, there are pockets of prospective students who have chosen not to attend college because they were not aware of their options or because they believe it was impossible for them. But as many of North Harris College's current and past students can tell you, it is possible to work full-time, handle family responsibilities and attend college."[15]

While juggling myriad responsibilities, the students could attend the new center to get the training they needed to start a new career or move up the job ladder. "We are offering courses that students can take for college credit—to transfer to a university, enhance their workplace marketability or to learn a new skill to begin or change careers," Martinez said in preparing for the first semester. "The job market continues to be extremely competitive and the only way to succeed is to obtain training and education."[16]

On January 15, 1993 the community celebrated the symbolic ribbon-cutting for The Aldine Center at the Aldine ISD alternative high school which was then called the Aldine Contemporary Education (ACE) Center. In addition to trustees of NHMCCD and AISD, several local leaders were on hand, including U.S. Rep. Gene Green, state Reps. Kevin Bailey and Sylvester Turner, and Acres Homes Chamber of Commerce chairman, Roy Douglas Malonson. Afterward, neighborhood children collected red-and-white helium balloons from a clown and gobbled down hot dogs, while FM 102-JAMZ DJs provided a live radio remote just outside.[17]

In early 1993, the college district's board of trustees approved a revised budget of $155,330 to support the work of the new center.[18] The first classes met on January 18th, three days after the ribbon-cutting ceremony. "This is an important first step for us," Martinez said. "North Harris College is committed to breaking down barriers that have traditionally kept members of the community from attending college. We are opening up access by providing college-credit courses right in the neighborhood—to make attending class more convenient for people who are juggling family and work responsibilities."[19]

Implemented as an outreach program of North Harris College in joint partnership with the Aldine Independent School District, The Aldine Center officially opened its doors in spring 1993 with the offering of credit and non-credit classes at the Aldine Contemporary Education Center. An innovative, alternative high school, the ACE Center was a natural site for those first classes for several reasons.

First, ACE Principal Clarence Johnson had created a safe, nurturing and creative environment that fostered student growth, learning, self-discipline and achievement. Though overall student success was high, the ACE art students, in particular, were nationally recognized for their skill and talent. The ACE Center was an educational model—a bright star tucked in a neighborhood of predominantly African-American, lower-income residents. Additionally, the school was built near the corner of West Little York and West Montgomery Road in the Acres Homes community—which was experiencing an economic development renewal under the direction of Roy Douglas Malonson and other business leaders. The timing was right for partnership between the college district and the Acres Homes business community to help boost quality of life in the neighborhood.

Finally, the ACE Center was located on Victory Street, which in 1991 was still an unpaved road just minutes from where Interstate 45 crossed West Little York. Further, road construction to open Victory through to Shepherd Road was incomplete, making the road impassable to the east. "Victory Street became a symbol," says Dr. Nellie Carr Thorogood, NHMCCD vice chancellor for external affairs. "The road itself is of major significance. In 1973, it was unpaved. In 1991 or '92, we were looking around – and the road was *still* unpaved. In front of the high school was unpaved. Victory Street then took on a meaning in my mind. Here the kids from ACE were getting great scholarships. Representatives from really major art institutes and big universities were coming to give them money to advance their education, and they were driving to the school on a dirt road. It became a symbol," Thorogood explained.[20]

Randy Bates, a member of NHMCCD's Board of Trustees, summed up the vision of the board as "The victory on Victory Street," a phrase that would come to symbolize the bridge to new opportunities in Acres Homes.[21] On Nov. 15, 1995, Bates would say in the *Houston Chronicle*: "Victories are a big deal in the Aldine Community, especially when it comes to education."[22]

The reasoning was simple: Higher education levels translated into greater literacy, a prepared work force, lower crime rates and increased household incomes. Forty-seven students enrolled in credit classes that first semester on Victory Street. The typical college student at ACE was a single, African-American woman, 20 to 29 years old. Ninety-six percent of those students successfully completed their first semester. Dr. Martinez noted that most of these first-generation college students would not have been able to attend college without the scholarship funds North Harris College provided.[23]

Stephanie Carter, along with her husband Cassius, attended Carver Center from its first semester and continued to earn associate's degrees. Carter, whose dream was to enter the teaching profession, said Carver was "her road out of poverty... her answer to prayer."[24]

In collaboration with the Aldine Youth Program, which was directed by Aldine's best-known humanitarian and child advocate Sylvia Bolling, The Aldine Center offered transportation and scholarships for 20 high school dropouts to prepare for GED training; 80 percent passed their tests.[25]

In March 1993, North Harris College president, Dr. Sanford Shugart announced to the trustees that The Aldine Center would begin offering both credit and non-credit summer '93 classes throughout the community at several Aldine ISD sites, as well as St. Leo's Church and the NHMCCD District Office. Previously, the college had only offered non-credit courses through the community outreach sites. Academic and technical courses allowed students to study business, English, government, history, math, psychology, sociology, criminal justice and child care. Non-credit offerings included health careers exploration, English for child care workers and introduction to office skills.[26]

The success of the outreach approach became evident: small classes, personal attention and one-on-one assistance helped students to learn. During summer semester, 40 students were enrolled in credit classes; 95 percent passed their courses.[27]

That summer the new center also expanded its scope, providing its first camp for students in the fifth to eighth grades. In addition to providing an entertaining, constructive experience, more than two dozen youngsters who might otherwise have been home alone while their parents worked had a safe place to go and to learn. MacArthur High School, in the east-

ern part of Aldine, served as the hub for the enrichment program in which students were immersed for two weeks in art, music drama and sign language. College staff raised $3,500 to enable these economically disadvantaged children to attend. Members of the community contributed, and college administrators took part in a good-spirited auction of their services to college faculty and staff, raising nearly $2,000.[28]

Field trips took 28 youngsters to see exhibits in area museums, observe arts professionals at work and check out the critters at the zoo. The children also got to play college student, participating in hands-on teaching demonstrations at the college. The campers wrapped up the program with an evening performance in which they showcased for parents what they learned.[29]

Director, Dr. Rosario Martinez, told the *Northeast News* in May 1993, "I want to involve the children as much as possible in the learning process. I want them to participate—to be part of a play, help with stage makeup, put their hands in the clay of a sculpture. I want to expose the children to the arts. I'm hoping that they have artistic talent or that they will become appreciators of the arts."[30]

Martinez added that after the camp, "It was exciting to see the increase in self-confidence. Some who were very shy or reluctant in the beginning really got into the theatrical performance—using Rock n' Roll music—that the children staged for their parents." The campers acted, created their own costumes and produced the backdrop. "The idea is to tap into the talents that might lead to careers and avocations for these children," Dr. Martinez said.[31]

When a little problem became evident to staff members, the spirit of partnership that illustrated The Aldine Center sprung into action. Because many of the campers showed up hungry, the center staff quickly arranged for breakfast and lunch, which was donated by Michelangelo's, McDonald's, and the University of Houston Downtown.[32]

The Aldine Center also hosted basketball campus at Aldine High School, just east of Interstate 45, providing recreational opportunities for neighborhood children. Dr. Martinez reported to the *North Freeway Leader* that June that she hoped the college tour, field trips and other activities would spark an interest in eventually attending college.[33]

The summer camp became something of a tradition. In 1994, the center offered another headstart through the Aldine Youth Career Camp, funded by a grant through the Harris County Private Industry Council. "The camp takes at-risk high school youth (those in low-income families), helps them identify and explore possible careers and emphasizes the importance of education as the pathway to get to that career," said Gayle Noll, North Harris College dean of community education in the *Houston Chronicle*. "We want to make sure we're doing everything we can to provide access to North Harris College. This program is a way for us to build a bridge to these students and show them how to cross that bridge."[34]

Eisenhower High School student Elisea Johnson explained in the July 20, 1994 article, "The camp has shown me how to pursue a career. College looks exciting." After the camp, the 16-year-old pledged to start her education at North Harris College in preparation for her education and career as a gynecologist.[35]

That summer, 15 teens also learned to survive in the high-tech world. From the Acres Homes community, the children worked on state-of-the-art 486 IBM-compatible computers, learning keyboarding, Windows and Word Perfect. "It is important that children find out that computers are friends," said Dr. Martinez. "The students are going to see computers for the rest of their lives, so the sooner they learn how to use them, the better they'll be prepared for the future." John Coe, microcomputer applications instructor for Scarborough High School, taught the eager campers. "When they hit high school, they'll be ahead in keyboarding skills."[36]

The kids agreed. Dakota Weatherby, a 14-year-old student who was going to be a freshman at Waltrip High School, said the camp was useful because "you should start off early [using computers] so you can get a good job." Ten-year-old Kelvin Wiseman, a student at Inwood Baptist, learned to make his own greeting cards. "It's more fun to make my own birthday cards and send them. In this camp, you can have fun while you're learning. If you want to write something, there are different ways you can do

it. I write letters to my mom and other people." Melissa Spano, 10, hoped to follow in her mother's footsteps, getting a good job because of excellent typing skills.[37]

Most of the students attended camp on scholarships provided through community donations and a fund-raising Gospel music event in March. During lunches contributed by Michelangelo's, James Coney Island and Marco's restaurants, the children learned to mind their Ps and Qs through lessons from Etiquette Inc.[38]

Child care expenses continued to be a barrier for many students. In the center's second semester, a $20,000 grant from the Swalm Foundation provided funding for mothers to obtain quality care for their children.[39] The relationship was ongoing, helping more students each year. "We show them that there is a way to go to college," Martinez explained. Pamela Giles, a Swalm scholarship recipient, found the assistance made a difference, covering tuition, fees, books and care for one child. "I love the fact that I had the chance to choose the day care," said the young woman who was studying child care and development. "I am very grateful for the scholarship. It helped me out a lot."[40]

The projects expanded from semester to semester. The growth of The Aldine Center was slow, but steady. One of the challenges that North Harris College staff faced was the recruitment of adults who were more culturally diverse and faced more barriers to college attendance than the traditional student the college had served for two decades. Aldine was the most culturally diverse area that the district served. By the early 1990s, the Aldine community's population was roughly equally divided into thirds: black, white and Hispanic, with a smaller but rapidly growing Asian-American community. What's more, they had lower household incomes than the population north of the college. Aldine students who opted to pursue higher education were typically first-generation college students. This contrasted sharply with the demographic profile of the college's students whose characteristics still reflected the Spring community—overwhelmingly white and middle-class.[41]

This diversity became evident early in the college's history when credit classes were still being held at Aldine High School. Dr. Thorogood told a story of racial polarization and the naivete and color-blindness of North Harris College's first faculty and staff. One evening, Ku Klux Klan members trampled onto the high school campus, burning a fiery cross and staging a loud, violent protest. "Dr. Airola, bless his heart, looked out and decided it must be a sociology class role playing," Thorogood said. "But sure enough, it was the real thing. We spent weeks explaining to new students that their life was not in danger. There are lots of stories around like that. The funny part was, because we were higher education, we assumed that, in the latter part of this century, this kind of display must be role playing."[42]

As the college's commitment to recruiting, serving and retaining a diverse student body became integral parts of North Harris College's strategic goals, the face of the typical student began to change. In 1992, minority students accounted for 28 percent of the college's enrollment, and their presence on campus had more than doubled since the college opened 19 years earlier. What's more, fall 1992 students were born in 76 different nations.[43]

The demographic differences between the college's traditional student and the "new" student posed several challenges, including adapting teaching and learning methods to more effectively reach non-traditional students. An interview with Dr. Shugart, conducted by Alan Hall, NHC professor and a founding faculty member at the center, explored the hot, long-discussed issue of modifying instruction in the May/June 1996 issue of The Advocate, the college union newsletter. "I don't think it is arguable that much about our student has changed over the past 10 years. This, by the way, seems to be true of students throughout the higher education enterprise, at every kind of institution and at every level. Many of our students come to us with very little preparation for college-level academic work, and we have programs to address this. But the difference seems to run deeper. It has something to do with what happens between classes, what kind of learning occurs or doesn't occur independently... I can only speculate on the causes [of differences in outside-the-classroom study habits], but leading my list is a loss of discre-

tionary time to commit to studies. This is no accident. In fact, it has been the objective of national policy [the] past decade and a half to expect students to support more of their costs of their own education by working. They are certainly doing this! And along with other choices and responsibilities, the result is that much of what we used to expect to occur on the students' time just isn't happening. The result is great frustration with what can and cannot happen in the classroom. I think the students' needs vary greatly, but many need a more richly supported learning environment— tutoring, learning labs, problem sets on videotape, new, extended classroom formats, instruction in reading and study strategies, peer tutoring and many other responses. In fact, most of this is well into development at the college," Shugart explained.[44]

Dr. Shugart pointed to several ongoing college initiatives that supported student learning, including developmental math and writing programs, a multi-million-dollar Title III grant, the five-fold increase in professional development over as many years, and release time for development of curriculum and instructional strategies. "The key," Dr. Shugart concluded, "is to be flexible and responsive, and focused on results."[45]

As faculty responded to differing student needs, the program grew. During its first fall semester, classes were offered at both ACE and MacArthur. One-hundred and twenty-four students enrolled in credit courses, while 94 enrolled in non-credit classes. The community outreach was drawing new students to the college: 85 percent of fall 1993 students had never attended classes in the college district before. One in every six students were scholarship recipients.[46]

By spring of 1994, the first anniversary of The Aldine Center, students could take classes in accounting, art, computer information systems, economics, English, government, history, human development, math, physical education, psychology, real estate, sociology and speech. The number of students grew steadily, and the small but dedicated staff continued to work out of borrowed classrooms to give Aldine residents the opportunity to build a better life for themselves and their families. [47]

Attending college was a struggle for many of the students who found their way to The Aldine

Center. Rosalinda Hernandez dropped out of high school during her sophomore year. She earned a GED and 13 years later began pursuing a college degree through the new outreach program. What's even more remarkable is that at the time she was the single mother of nine children; they were 4, 5, 7, 8, a set of twins age 9, 11, 12 and 13. She had been a single parent for three years and faced a multitude of challenges, yet her desire to provide a better way of life for her family prompted her return to school. She juggled her school work and her parenting by studying and doing homework during the day, with her toddler in tow and her other eight youngsters in school. The children pitched in to help their mom succeed, sharing chores and baby-sitting, and completing their own homework while their mom attended classes. In the Aldine Center Agenda newsletter, Rosalinda credited the Aldine Center with having teachers who took the time to provide individual attention, which she believed was crucial for students who have been out of the educational arena for many years. A success story herself with boosted self-confidence, she even provided advice for other high school dropouts: "Don't put things off. Get your GED and go straight to college."[48]

Personal stories such as Rosalinda's prompted NHMCCD trustee Randy Bates to call the Aldine Carver Center, "The victory on Victory Street." By now, the road was paved and opened through Shepherd. "That's what it's all about—individual victories which translate into community victories," Bates explained. "As a board member, there is no greater reward than witnessing these victories firsthand."[49]

The victories in Aldine prompted the Acres Homes Chamber of Commerce to bestow its 1994-95 Partnership on district vice chancellor, Dr. Nellie Thorogood in April 1995. "Under her leadership, and that of college district trustee Randy Bates and the other college district board members, a number of initiatives have begun, including the Aldine Center and the young entrepreneur program for high school students," chamber chairman Roy Douglas Malonson told the Houston Chronicle. "This is just the beginning of what we are looking for in a long-term relationship with the college district. I believe this partnership will be in the best interest of the

Acres Homes community, the chamber of commerce and the college district."[50]

During spring 1995, college officials decided to rename the center George Washington Carver Center. This was consistent with AISD's return to the original name of ACE Center, which previously had been called Carver High School. The first ads reflecting the transition to the official name change appeared in May 1995.[51] But the Aldine initiative was still moving quickly. More quickly, perhaps, than college administrators could have planned.

In fact, the outreach to Aldine expanded rapidly after a prime lease property in Greenspoint hit the market at a discounted rate. A 14-classroom facility became available at reduced cost when the National Education Center had to break its lease. From early 1995, when the space became available to the start of classes on June 5 of that year, the college staff moved at breakneck speed. Dr. Shugart appointed Dr. Gayle Noll, college dean of community education, to serve as executive director of the new site, which was christened North Harris College's Sam Houston Parkway Center.[52]

Located on the top floor of the three-story office building at 16416 Northchase Drive, the Parkway Center was across the parkway from Greenspoint Mall, southeast of I-45 and the Beltway. "Our students come to us because our location is convenient to where they live and work," Dr. Noll explained. In fact, the new center was created to expand service to the 20,000 people who work in the Greater Greenspoint area. At the time, 18 companies had national or world headquarters in the vicinity. More than 50 multinational corporate tenants were housed there, too. What's more, hundreds of small businesses—principally retail trade, services and small manufacturers—peppered the area. "This new center will act as another bridge to the college for the 67,000 residents who live just south of the Beltway. We want to serve the culturally diverse Aldine population, as well as the employees working in Greenspoint," Dr. Shugart said when the new center was opening.[53]

Assistant U.S. Secretary of Labor Doug Ross, in early 1995, underscored the need for post-secondary training. "We have too many workers qualified for yesterday's jobs and too few qualified for today's and tomorrow's jobs. Now and for the foreseeable future, those who succeed will have to be not only highly skilled, but also so broadly skilled that they can change jobs and occupations without missing a beat."[54]

It was a tall order, but one that Parkway's executive director was determined to meet. In its first semester, the Parkway Center offered college-preparation courses in math, reading and writing, as well as university-transfer courses in anthropology, biology, business, economics, English, government, history, human services, math, physical education, psychology, sociology, Spanish and speech. Small business employees were drawn to technical courses in accounting, management, Lotus, Word Perfect, desktop publishing, multimedia, computer graphic arts, office administration, information management, business writing, medical transcription, computer science, legal terminology, CAD drafting, electronics, and child care and development. What's more, students were able to obtain complete course work in law enforcement and emergency medical services.

The American Association of Community Colleges (AACC) reported in 1995 that as much as 75 percent of the existing workforce would require retraining with the next decade. AACC also reported that American corporate training budgets would need to triple to keep up with the increasing demand for technically skilled workers.[55]

"Constant training and retraining are not only the keys to obtaining a better job. In many cases, they are essential for maintaining one's current job," said Dr. Bill Richards, former NHC vice president. Parkway Center "will add a workplace development center to the college's inventory, providing an entire gamut of services." U.S. Secretary of Labor, Robert Reich, supported the value of two-year technical education. "Technical jobs will be the new gateway to the middle class," Reich reported in a 1995 *Money* magazine article. "Though post-secondary education is the route to becoming a 'have' rather than a 'have-not' in the new America, a bachelor's or advanced degree isn't the only ticket. Those who train at two-year community colleges or technical institutes... also stand to prosper."[56]

Dr. Sanford Shugart pointed out that colleges had long remained removed from the reality of the workplace. The Parkway Center, he said, would help bring North Harris College closer to the real world of work. "We see work and learning as interconnected," he explained. "Community colleges like North Harris College are now emerging as major providers of work force training." The career-building programs the college planned to offer at Parkway Center would be adaptable and responsive to the needs of business and individuals in Greenspoint and Aldine. "We're ready to work with the community to design programs as needed."[57]

The 21,000-square-foot Parkway Center had 14 classrooms, as well as labs for computer, child care and the sciences. Initial offerings included course work in 28 majors. The initial operating budget was $600,000.[58] "This will be a full-service outreach center of North Harris College," Dr. Gayle Noll, Parkway Center executive director, explained to Jocklynn Keville, editor of the *North Freeway Leader* and *The Greater Greenspoint Reporter*. "Students often face problems juggling responsibilities. We will take a proactive approach to deal with the problems up front so the students can stay in school. We are placing a lot of emphasis on services for students."[59]

The focus on students was obvious to those who took classes at the Parkway Center. "I like Parkway Center because it is convenient for work and school. And the people are really friendly," said student Don Le. "At Parkway Center, I can really focus on my studies more than at a big college or university. And besides, Parkway Center is small and everybody is friendly," added Martha Martinez. "Parkway Center is convenient to home and easily accessible. There is genuine caring, and the instructors are willing to work with you," reported student Susan Skalak.[60]

Parkway's outreach into the community expanded, particularly among business people who worked in Greater Greenspoint. Student surveys continued to show that Parkway was first choice because of its convenient location. This finding prompted Dr. Gayle Noll to adopt the theme, "Your college degree is just blocks away," which supported the district-wide advertising campaigns themes, "Your star is within reach" and "College is within your reach."[61]

North Harris College's two outreach sites were part of a movement across the country.

"We know from research that taking the college to the community is the most effective means of ensuring the services of the college are getting to all the service area," explained Dr. Bill Richards, North Harris College vice president. In summer 1995, Dr. Richards explained to the board of trustees that Parkway staff had completed a creative project to personally call all 400 graduating seniors from Aldine to share with them information about the new center.[62]

It was that personal touch that supported the success of the center. On Aug. 22, 1995, the *Northeast News* quoted Dr. Noll as she described the Parkway Center's mission: "North Harris [College]'s Parkway Center is a new neighbor dedicated to serving the folks who live and work in the Greenspoint and Aldine communities. We want to assist students in meeting individual career goals by providing friends, professional services to students so students can learn in an environment where they know they are cared about as individuals."[63]

Additionally, partnerships continued to form the foundation of the North Harris College outreach initiative. The Parkway Center formed a special careers coalition with Greater Greenspoint personnel agencies to provide free employment-preparation workshops, interviews and a job bank. The Careers program offered free workshops on resume writing, self-esteem, interviewing and other career topics. In early 1996, more than 65 people had taken advantage of these helpful seminars conducted by local experts in each field. Additionally, Parkway partnered with Aldine High School to bus a group of graduating seniors to the satellite center for early admissions credit instruction. The pilot program set the stage for future expansion.[64]

"At Parkway Center, you actually learn the *real* meaning of the word 'community' in the phrase 'community college,'" explained Kim Monroe, Parkway employee and former North Harris College student.[65]

The Aldine outreach initiative continued to pick up steam. In April 1995, NHMCCD and AISD officials agreed on a preliminary proposal to create a new facility to house the Carver Center. By summer, the boards of both districts were ready to move on the project, with initial discussions among administrators and the architect occurring on July 17.[66]

On September 20th of that year, the college presented its specifications to Aldine ISD, and on October 14th, NHC and AISD approved the lease agreement. At the November 1995 board meeting, NHMCCD trustees approved an interlocal agreement with Aldine ISD to lease the facilities that would ultimately house the Carver Center. Aldine ISD financed the building construction, with the guarantee of shared usage of 4,000 square feet of the 31,000-square-foot facility.

The rationale for the request, which was supported by Chancellor Pickelman, was that "The Carver Center is an integral part of the district's Aldine initiative to provide community-based educational and job training instruction. Aldine Independent School District desires to add an applied technology program to its instructional offerings at Carver High School, offering challenging courses designed to encourage greater enrollment in higher education for its students, and [to] promote continuing education for members of the Acres Homes community. The district desires to build a detached academic facility at Carver High School which it will use to broaden its service to the Acres Homes community and to diversify its instructional program. The sharing of a facility and the related costs of operation is an efficient use of public funds."[67]

By March 1996, Aldine ISD had orchestrated the site demolition for the new building and the adjacent parking lot. By May, the slab was poured and the frame and heavy, structural steel were erected.[68]

Meanwhile, on June 6, 1996, North Harris College's Parkway Center celebrated its first birthday with a warm ceremony featuring Dr. Gayle Noll and her staff and students sharing their experiences of the past year. More than 100 faculty members, students and business leaders attended the event.[69] There was much to celebrate. The year before, college administrators had projected that the center would serve 1,000 students. The Parkway Center's careful attention to students resulted in service more than twice the original projection. The staff had also just offered its first college-credit minimester between spring and summer semesters, offering a two-week, compressed semester in university-transfer courses. Parkway also initiated one-stop student services and extended registration periods. The STAR program provided each student with a career plan and an individual mentor. And the center's expansive outreach efforts included a festive, informative college day event at Greenspoint Mall and the area's first Cinco de Mayo gala. Child care, an issue for students at all three college locations, was supported by a Carl Perkins grant. Parkway also piloted with local personnel agencies a unique set series of four-day, 16-hour comprehensive computer classes to help employees build their skills.[70]

Dr. Sandy Shugart, North Harris college president, told faculty and staff at the celebration how he proud he was of the reciprocal relationship they had built with the surrounding community. "It does feel like a birthday party in here today," he was quoted as saying in an article by editor Mike Keeney of the *Northeast News*. "Some time ago, we developed a strategic plan and one of the goals was to serve the south. We wanted to make a bigger impact in south Aldine to serve more of the market. In many instances, performance lags behind vision, but in this instance, you have outperformed everything we've imagined." Dr. Gayle Noll commented on the impact of the center on the people it serves. "We're building a place that changes individual lives and families forever."[71]

Seventy-six percent of the students that first year lived nearby the center, and 41 percent worked in the area. Eighty-six percent of Parkway's students worked outside the home; 70 percent were women. The student body also reflected the diversity of the neighborhood it served: nearly two-third of them are Hispanic, African-American or Asian-American. Location continued to be the No. 1 appeal, followed closely by convenient course scheduling, faculty and friendly staff.[72]

A 1996 survey by Arthur Andersen's Enterprise group indicated that one-fourth of 919 small businesses were concerned that a lack of qualified workers would hamper their corporate growth. The sentiment was echoed in north Houston by employers who specified that software knowledge, math skills, verbal and written communication ability and keyboarding were necessary to employee success.[73]

The college continued to address these employer needs with the expansion of programs at both Parkway and Carver. North Harris College and Aldine ISD were determined to prepare the work force through a solid, working partnership, first-class facilities and a quality curriculum.

As crews prepared to break ground for the new Carver Center, the stories of individual students continued to underscore the need for work force training and personal development. At age 32, Patricia Williams decided to attend college for the first time. Not surprisingly, she was intimidated. On her first day of class, she said, her knees were knocking and her stomach was doing flip-flops. She had second thoughts and said to herself, "You'll never make it. Your friends told you how difficult college can be. Don't go through with it. Turn back now before it's too late." Just as she was beginning to doubt her decision to start college, Williams she saw a familiar face at North Harris College's Carver Center. It was Carver High School principal Clarence Johnson, the same man who 14 years earlier had greeted her as she entered ninth grade at Carver High School. "That moment made the difference," Williams said. Suddenly, she knew she could succeed. She was determined not to become one of the failures that she had heard so much about.[74]

And Williams was succeeding against the odds. She was a high school drop-out at age 15 and pregnant at 16. She began the ninth grade for the second time at age 17 and graduated at age 20 from Nimitz High School. Somewhere in the midst of all that, she said, she grew up.[75]

By age 32, she was happily married, raising a family, working a full-time job, and attending college at North Harris College's Carver Center to make an even better life for her and her family— not to mention her community. In fact, Williams planned to obtain her associate's and bachelor's degrees in education so that she could open a youth center in her neighborhood, Acres Homes. "I want to give back something to this community that has given so much to me," she said.[76]

Not surprisingly, Williams won an essay contest at North Harris College, sharing her personal journey to a higher quality of life. The scholarship money she earned helped pay her tuition and allowed her to continue working toward her lifelong dream, opening that youth center. Williams said she believes that her dream would never even have been possible if it were not for the Carver Center and North Harris College because, she explained, "they have provided a college near my home, a campus with familiar faces and caring instructors, making the opportunity of a college education obtainable."

Williams' story demonstrated that the dream of NHMCCD trustees and administrators for more accessible learning in the Aldine community had approached reality. "North Harris College sends a positive message to the people in this community by making an education available to everyone," Williams said. "They have met me more than half way." Having a college campus near her home lowered her fears of returning to school after 14 years. Also, seeing familiar faces and being in a place she knew gave Williams the confidence she needed to jump right in.

Williams balanced her core college program with her family by attending school two nights a week, spending countless hours studying, and reserving weekends for her husband and 15-year-old daughter. "I see my family more than I originally anticipated because the Carver campus is so close to my home," she added. Williams was one of more than 154,000 north Houston students who had taken courses at North Harris College in the college's first 23 years—students who, like Williams, were searching for ways to improve their lives.[77]

"Our goal is to create a bridge for students to services and programs offered at the main campus. For 20 years, North Harris College has been delivering dreams to the people of north Houston," Dr. Shugart said. "With these new efforts, those dreams have come within reach of thousands more of our neighbors to the south."[78]

In fact, college officials estimated that the college's outreach would make education and training more accessible to 216,000 more residents.[79]

In late 1995, Dr. Sandy Shugart, North Harris College president, recognized trustee Randy Bates and Rep. Sylvester Turner for having "taken the lead to engage the community in town hall meetings to solicit input for the kind of programs they would like to see implemented at the Carver Center."[80] The real work had begun, and the process of building was soon to start.

On Jan. 20, 1996, the *Houston Chronicle* recommended the Carver Center ground-breaking ceremony in its "Weekend Things To Do" column, pointing out that "the new college satellite center is the result of a dynamic and innovative partnership between the college and Aldine ISD."[81]

Just three short years after the ribbon-cutting festivities at ACE Center, NHMCCD and AISD trustees again gathered at the high school, which had been renamed George Washington Carver Contemporary High School. This time the ceremony took place outside near the spot where Carver Center would begin to rise from the ground. The January 20th, 1996 ceremony was dedicated to the memory of stateswoman Barbara Jordan, who had passed away the week before and was being laid to rest that day.[82] In a cold, driving rain that didn't visibly dampen anyone's spirits, 167 people huddled under a heated tent for a sign unveiling that marked the upcoming ground-breaking for the $2.5 million North Harris College's George Washington Carver Center.[83]

College and school district board members shared red-and-white striped golf umbrellas as they yanked the covering off a brightly painted, red, white and blue sign heralding the fall 1996 arrival of the new facility. The Eisenhower High School Wind Ensemble provided a rousing musical accompaniment to the unveiling and the simultaneous release of 100 red-and-white helium balloons from behind the sign. Channel 11 captured the damp, yet moving moment for Houston-area viewers on the evening news.

This was a bright spot for college district employees, who that same evening received word that Cy-Fair residents had voted not to become part of the North Harris Montgomery Community College District, despite the fact that the Cy-Fair Chamber of Commerce and Independent School District both publicly had supported joining NHMCCD.[84]

The next day, the *Houston Chronicle* heralded "The victory on victory street." *North Freeway Leader* editor, Diane Hess, wrote: "It's not often that the phrase 'ground-breaking' can take on both meanings on the same project. But... that's exactly what will happen when construction begins on the new college satellite facility in Acres Homes. When ground is broken on North Harris College's Carver Center... it will signal the culmination of an innovative, ground-breaking partnership between NHC and Aldine Independent School District. It will also symbolize the dream of the Acres Homes Chamber of Commerce members to bring comprehensive higher education to the area." Acres Homes Chamber Chairman, Roy Douglas Malonson, told the *North Freeway Leader*, "We will finally have the opportunity in Acre Homes to receive a four-year degree. The community is very excited about it. From the chamber's point of view, we've put a lot of time into this."[85]

Through the college district's University Center partnership, which was being developed at the same time, north Houston residents were looking forward to easy access to not just an associate's degree, but also a bachelor's degree and, eventually, a master's degree through NHMCCD sites, including Carver Center.

The journey to bring quality education to Acres Homes was lengthy and sometimes divisive. "One of the major hurdles we were faced with is that our community is divided in half," Malonson told the *North Freeway Leader* in January 1996. A portion of Acres Homes belongs to Houston Community College System, while the rest belongs to the North Harris Montgomery Community College District, which affects taxing and tuition rates. "Whoever decided to divide the community did more harm than good."[86]

Although the Acres Homes community faced struggles in its quest for education, the innovative relationship between Aldine ISD and NHMCCD did not go unnoticed. In the Dec. 5, 1995 issue of *Northeast News*, editor Mike Keeney wrote: "Partnership between Texas high schools and colleges are rare; working partnerships make headlines. Aldine Independent School District and North Harris College share classrooms, guidance counselors, a seamless Tech Prep program and dual-credit courses." Sonny Donaldson, AISD superintendent, reported on the successful relationship, saying, it would "afford students a seamless transition from high school to the community college. The fact that a community college exists nearby also will encourage our students to continue their education. It may even attract some residents who need skills to qualify for jobs back in education."

Dr. Sandy Shugart explained that sharing goals had cemented the partnership. "Both institutions are deeply committed to the Aldine community. Both know that the level of education available to the community and the work force will have a great impact on the quality of life in the Aldine area. College classes offer the community more hope and high expectations that lead to high retention, higher graduation rates, higher percentages of college-bound students, higher college completion, higher skill levels, higher employment and ultimately higher incomes. The alternative is a downward spiral." The partnership also made good economic sense, reported Dr. Rosario Martinez: "In times of tight money, when two institutions can get together to collaborate on resources, they make it possible for students to get the most from scarce educational dollars."[87]

The new Carver Center was off to a great beginning. "I don't think we could have had a better start... than we had on Jan. 20, the day of the ground breaking," Chancellor Pickelman told a meeting of the Acres Homes Citizens Chamber of Commerce on Feb. 1, 1996. "It was a celebration of partnerships and of the commitment that we are here to serve all the residents of the community.... Economic development starts with a trained work force."[88]

By summer 1996, construction on North Harris College's Carver Center was well underway, providing 10 classrooms and three computer labs and course work in a host of majors, including computer technology, LVN nursing and CAD drafting.[89]

In addition to funneling students to the original campus, both college outreach centers will emphasize adult literacy and developmental classes, work force training, high tech courses and college-credit classes for university transfer. All Carver Center classrooms and labs were smart-wired for computer-aided instruction. And the new center's curriculum was designed to enhance Aldine ISD's magnet programs in engineering technology, electronic technology and art.

The Carver Center initiative underscores the partnership between AISD and the community college. Not only would the center operate in an AISD-financed building and continue to share the high school's wet labs, but the school district participated in planning meetings. The center's

## THE MISSION OF THE CARVER CENTER

*To provide educational programs and services for the Acres Homes and Aldine communities, including university-transfer course work, career-preparation programs and adult basic education*

*To create a bridge for students leading to North Harris College*

*To serve as the center for workforce and economic development programs in the Aldine community through a unique partnership with Aldine Independent School District*

*To enhance magnet programs at George Washington Carver High School in the arts, applied technology and engineering technology.*[91]

distance learning courses were open to high school juniors and seniors as well.

To complete "the seamless bridge" North Harris College and AISD envisioned, the next step would be to offer classes toward a bachelor's degree and eventually a graduate degree, which the college expects to be offered in the Aldine community through the new University Center partnership. With Aldine's Montessori schools, magnet schools, the community college and the university center in operation, Aldine children would enjoy first-class education from pre-school to a university or graduate degree close to home.[90]

To more effectively meet the educational needs of non-traditional students, the comprehensive learning center was designed to provide personalized tutoring and learning resources for both high school and college students. The lab offered open-entry assistance for language and math skill-building, tutorials for all educational programs, and academic and career assessment and placement.

Classrooms featured audio/visual technology. And labs included state-of-the-art computers and interactive technology. In addition to the Learning Center, there were labs for computer information systems, office administration, writing, mathematics, CAD drafting, multimedia and art. Always planning ahead, NHMCCD and AISD constructed a facility with a second-story option for future expansion.

The first classes started in the new Carver Center on August 26th, 1996. College administrators scheduled evening classes to begin the first week of fall semester, but planned day classes to start on a fast-track schedule September 23rd—in case of inevitable construction delays.

The grand-opening ceremony for the new facility was September 7th at 10:30 a.m. Rep. Sylvester Turner, who grew up in Acres Homes, offered the keynote address. The many individuals responsible for bring victory to Victory Street received a carved granite rock engraved with words from namesake George Washington Carver.

Clearly the Aldine initiative, just a dream five years before and now a creative, vibrant reality, was making a difference. Carver student Patricia Williams explained in an article in the May 1996 *Acres Home Citizens' News*: "The new Carver Center of North Harris College has meant for me the opportunity to attend college, an opportunity which would not otherwise been available. The Carver Center has provided me with a college near my home, which has made it physically and financially possible for me to attend college," she explained. "The kind and caring professors at Carver Center have make it possible for me to remain in college because they have made learning and performing difficult tasks seem much easier and enjoyable. ... the professors at Carver have made the difference between success and failure in college for me."[92]

The reality is, that despite what Thomas Wolfe said, you <u>can</u> come home again. The delivery of improved services to more of the Aldine community was part of North Harris College's homecoming. But it was just the beginning.

"This is where the rubber meets the road. The grassroots effort. If everyone is working together, business, the chambers, the colleges, the school districts, we make a difference," Dr. Nellie Thorogood explained. "And this is the future of services for colleges—more workforce development closer to where people work or where they live before they go to work." She concluded, "Now we look at Victory Street and it is paved. Not only that, that one street has education from pre-K to Montessori to elementary school through the middle school, the magnet high school and now the college's Carver Center. With the University Center, you'll be able to attend college from pre-K to graduate school on Victory Street. What an opportunity."[93]

What a difference.

*The Parkway Center of North Harris College.*

# NOTES

[1] North Harris College Fact Sheet, 1992.

[2] NHMCCD Office of Institutional Research 1992-1993; NHMCCD Catalog 1996-97.

[3] North Harris College Fact Sheet, 1995.

[4] North Harris College Fact Sheet, 1992.

[5] Interview with Dr. Sanford Shugart, 1996.

[6] Demographic data provided by Dr. Sanford Shugart and Professor Gary Clark, 1992-1993.

[7] Board of Trustees, Proposed Goals and Initiatives IV, 1991.

[8] Interviews with Dr. Sanford Shugart and Dr. Nellie Thorogood, 1996.

[9] Interview with Dr. Nellie Thorogood, 1996.

[10] Informative Report No. 2, Board Meeting, November 1992.

[11] "Aldine/N.Harris College partnership offers advantages to college, community," *Northeast News*, Dec. 5, 1995, p. 6.

[12] Informative Report No. 2, Board Meeting, November 1992.

[13] "NHC creates new Aldine Center to offer variety of college classes," Dec. 31, 1992.

[14] "Surveys show next decade's workforce requires technical training and literacy education: North Harris College brings college credit courses to neighborhoods to reach underserved populations," News Release, North Harris College Office of College Relations, December 1992.

[15] "North Harris College brings college credit courses to south [sic] the Aldine area," News Release, North Harris College Office of College Relations, December 1992.

[16] "Surveys show next decade's workforce requires technical training and literacy education: North Harris College brings college credit courses to neighborhoods to reach underserved populations," News Release, North Harris College Office of College Relations, December 1992.

[17] "Martinez will direct Aldine Center," *The North Freeway Leader*, March 4, 1993, p. 2.

[18] North Harris Montgomery Community College District Midyear Budget Appraisal, Fiscal Year 1992-93.

[19] "Surveys show next decade's workforce requires technical training and literacy education: North Harris College brings college credit courses to neighborhoods to reach underserved populations," News Release, December 1992.

[20] Interview with Dr. Nellie Thorogood, 1996.

[21] Interview with Dr. Nellie Thorogood, 1996

[22] "N. Harris College launches second satellite campus," *Houston Chronicle*, Nov. 15, 1995.

[23] "The Aldine Center seeks to serve community," News Release, North Harris College Office of College Relations, July 1993.

[24] "What North Harris College Means to Me," by Stephanie Carter, student essay, 1994.

[25] "The Aldine Center seeks to serve community," News Release, North Harris College Office of College Relations, July 1993, and "North Harris College outreach program boasts successes," News Release, North Harris College Office of College Relations, July 1993. See also "The family that studies together, stays together" *Northeast News*, April 25, 1995, p. 4.

[26] Informative Report No. 2, Board Meeting, March 1993.

[27] Aldine Center Agenda, Fall 1993.

[28] "North Harris College's Aldine Center supports children," News Release, North Harris College, Office of External Affairs, May 1993.

[29] "Aldine Center to offer summer camps," *The North Freeway Leader*, June 3, 1993, p. 9.

[30] "Aldine Center to offer summer camps to disadvantage [sic] area youth," *Northeast News*, May 11, 1993, p.3.

[31] "Sponsors needed for Aldine Center summer youth camp," *Northeast News*, April 12, 1994.

[32] "Sponsors needed for Aldine Center Summer Youth Camp," News Release, North Harris College Office of College Relations, April 1994.

[33] "Aldine Center to offer summer camps," *Northeast News*, June 15, 1993.

[34] "College, school district host summer youth camp," *Houston Chronicle*, July 20, 1994.

[35] Ibid.

[36] "Computer camp helps youth get headstart," *Houston Chronicle*, Aug. 24, 1994

[37] Ibid.

[38] "Aldine Center youth camp teaches at-risk students some technological survival skills," *The North Freeway Leader*, Aug. 11, 1994, p. 6.

[39] "Grant will help Carver Center students with child care services," *Houston Chronicle*, Feb. 28, 1996.

[40] "Carver Center offers child care scholarship," *Northeast News*, Feb. 20, 1996, p. 12.

[41] Marketing outreach plan, Aldine Outreach Initiative, March 1995.

[42] Interview with Dr. Nellie Thorogood, 1996.

[43] North Harris College Fact Sheet 1993.

[44] "Interview with Sandy Shugart," by Alan Hall, *The Advocate*, Newsletter of the NHMCCD Employee Federation, May/June 1996.

[45] Ibid.

[46] Aldine Center enrollment report, Dr. Rosario Martinez, fall 1993, and "North Harris College's Aldine Center enrollment flourishes," News Release, North Harris College Office of College Relations, October 1993.

[47] "It's not too late to start college at NHC's Aldine Center satellite sites," News Release, North Harris College Office of College Relations, January 1994.

[48] *Aldine Center Agenda*, Spring 1994.

[49] "North Harris College breaks ground on second satellite campus to better serve Aldine community," News Release, North Harris College Office of External Affairs, December 1995.

[50] "Partnership award: Acres Homes Citizens Chamber honors N. Harris College official," *Houston Chronicle*, April 19, 1995.

[51] "North Harris College - Aldine Center at Carver High School: College within your reach," *The Leader*, May 18, 1995.

[52] "North Harris College opens satellite center for outreach," *Greater Greenspoint Reporter*, May 1995, p. 10. See also "Expansion: N. Harris College plans new Greenspoint education center," *Houston Chronicle*, April 19, 1995, zone 2, p. 7.

[53] "Parkway Center Grand-Opening Media Kit," News Release, North Harris College, Office of College Relations, May 1995, and "North Harris College's new Parkway Center brings learning closer to home," News Release, North Harris College, Office of College Relations, May 1995.

[54] Ibid.

[55] "North Harris College - Parkway Center to provide workforce training for busy adults," News Release, North Harris College Office of College Relations, May 1995.

[56] Ibid.

[57] Ibid.

[58] Financial Reports and Consideration No. 2 (Action Item 8), Board Meeting, August 1995.

[59] "North Harris College opens satellite center for outreach," *The Greater Greenspoint Reporter*, May 1995, p. 10.

[60] Parkway Center Fall 1996 Schedule Dustcover.

[61] 1995-1997 Districtwide Advertising and Recruitment Campaign, "Your Star is Within Reach."

[62] *North Harris College Report*, July 1995 Board Meeting, Dr. Bill Richards.

[63] "Fall semester at Parkway Center begins on Aug. 26," *Northeast News*, Aug. 22 1995, p. 17.

[64] "Students taking advantage of seminars," *Northeast News*, March 19, 1996, and "Parkway Center gets ready for its initial fall semester," *The North Freeway Leader*, Aug. 24, 1995. See also "Fall semester at Parkway Center begins on Aug. 26," *Northeast News*, Aug. 22, 1995, p. 17, and "NHC Parkway Center celebrates anniversary," May 23, 1996, p. 7.

[65] Parkway Center Fall 1996 Schedule Dustcover.

[66] Building and Grounds Reports No. 2, February 1996 Board Meeting.

[67] Financial Reports and Considerations No. 3 (Action Item 4) November 1995 Board Meeting: "Consideration of Approval of an Interlocal Agreement with Aldine Independent School District to Lease Facilities for Carver Center."

[68] *Building and Grounds Reports No. 2*, May 1996 Board Meeting.

[69] "Parkway Center celebrates 1st anniversary," *Northeast News*, June 11, 1996.

[70] "Fall semester at Parkway Center begins on Aug. 26," *Northeast News*, Aug. 22 1995, p. 17.

[71] "Parkway Center celebrates 1st anniversary," *Northeast News*, June 11, 1996.

[72] Ibid.

[73] "North Harris College - Parkway Center's work force training offers job skills for new workers," News Release, North Harris College Office of External Affairs, January 1996.

[74] "North Harris College - Carver Center helps student achieve her dream," News Release, North Harris College Office of External Affairs, January 1996.

[75] Ibid.

[76] "Former student Patricia Williams recalls experiences as freshman at Carver High School; return as college student highlights value," *Acres Home Citizens' News*, May 1996 (p. 2).

[77] "North Harris College - Carver Center helps student achieve her dream," News Release, North Harris College Office of External Affairs, January 1996.

[78] "N. Harris College launches second satellite campus," *Houston Chronicle*, November 15, 1995.

[79] "North Harris College - Carver Center helps student achieve her dream," News Release, North Harris College Office of External Affairs, January 1996.

[80] Dr. Sanford Shugart, North Harris College report, NHMCCD Board Meeting, November 1995.

[81] "Weekend things to do : North Harris College to break ground for new Carver Center," *Houston Chronicle*, Jan. 20, 1996.

[82] George Washington Carver Center Sign Raising Program, Jan. 20, 1996.

[83] Dr. Sanford Shugart, North Harris College report, February 1996 Board meeting.

[84] Martha Newsome, Faculty Senate report, February 1996 Board meeting.

[85] "Work to start on Carver Center," *North Freeway Leader*, Jan. 4, 1996

[86] Ibid.

[87] "Aldine/N.Harris College partnership offers advantages to college, community," *Northeast News*, Dec. 5, 1995, p. 6.

[88] "College official touts new Carver Center," *Houston Chronicle*, Feb. 14, 1996.

[89] Building and Grounds Reports No. 2, May 1996 Board Meeting.

[90] "North Harris College - Carver Center helps student achieve her dream," News Release, North Harris College Office of External Affairs, January 1996.

[91] Mission of the George Washington Carver Center, January 1996.

[92] "Former student Patricia Williams recalls experiences as freshman at Carver High School; return as college student highlights value," *Acres Home Citizens' News*, May 1996 (p. 2).

[93] Interview with Dr. Nellie Thorogood, 1996.

The University Center
North Harris Montgomery Community College District

RWS Architects Incorporated

# THE UNIVERSITY CENTER

by Kathie Scobee Fulgham and Nellie Thorogood

## A JUMP START ON THE NEXT 25 YEARS

If the first 25 years for North Harris Montgomery Community College District were marked with unrivaled growth, groundbreaking educational development and sustained community involvement, the second 25 years will be marked with an explosion of technologically advanced and enhanced education that will begin rumbling in north Houston, then reverberate far beyond the boundaries of a college campus... or even many college campuses. Welcome to the future.

*The University Center in
The Woodlands, Texas establishes
a new frontier in higher education.*

*Imagine a place where ...*
- *Learning knows no boundaries*
  Universities grow far beyond their campuses to convene and collaborate in order to provide students with unduplicated bachelor's and master's degrees, continuous learning opportunities and coordinated student services.

- *Learning is a highway with many points of entry*
  Some students are at the beginning of a well mapped out journey, with their freshman and sophomore-level courses complete and a degree plan in place; some arrive with a shoe box

*Kathie Scobee Fulgham is the former District Director of Public Information.*
*Dr. Nellie Thorogood is the Vice Chancellor for External Affairs and The University Center.*

full of transcripts and need help finding out where they are and which direction to go to achieve their goals; some yearn for a promotion or career change to advance them on their journey, but lack the needed education or skills to be competitive; and some need to get to their educational destination but are concerned about all the potential pit-stops of an existing job or family situation that make it inconvenient or unaffordable to attain their goals.

- *Learning is a lifelong endeavor*
  From short-term intensive training to post graduate courses and degrees and professional development, The University Center will be accessible to businesses and individuals to upgrade and keep their job skills current and vibrant.

- *Learning is an ever-evolving process*
  Interactive technologies will extend teaching and learning beyond chalkboards and classrooms, and students will learn telecommunications skills they take back to the local and even global workforce.

- *Learning means good business*
  Collaboration with business and industry creates an alliance of public and private members for common developments, technology transfer, joint training efforts, friendly "tryout" locations, and intellectual dialogue for continuous business competitiveness and productivity improvement.

Such will be the daily events at The University Center.

The college district has accomplished this enormous task by forming partnerships with six major universities, along with interested research centers, chambers of commerce, businesses, and industries. Together, this unlikely partnership has collaborated in dreaming, planning, and implementing its fresh, creative ideas of higher education goals for its service area.

Not only is The University Center a technologically advanced facility, its scope extends to other university campuses and NHMCCD's four

community colleges through interactive means—a 'virtual' campus, if you can imagine it. Students will be able to earn bachelor's and master's degrees from six area universities—all without leaving home.

The University Center, which is adjacent to Montgomery College, is the result of a partnership between the North Harris Montgomery Community College District, six universities and The Woodlands Corporation.

The impact the facility will have on area residents and businesses is already being predicted by government officials, educators, business leaders and students. Those benefits include convenient access, lower costs for students who won't have to travel long distances or stay in dormitories, efficient use of resources and facilities and the fueling of work force development.

"The potential of The University Center is almost unlimited," says Congressman Kevin Brady of The Woodlands. "The University Center is the wave of the future in delivering affordable higher education to communities. The state legislature has signaled that it can't afford to continue to put an emphasis on bricks and mortar. They want universities and colleges to expand by working smarter. This is an innovative model, I think, for Texas communities that want higher-level education."[1]

The University Center will serve more than 8,000 credit students from NHMCCD's four campuses and a service area of more than 1,100 square miles and 1.2 million residents. Nearly 188,000 of those residents have some college but have not completed a bachelor's degree.

"The University Center is setting the standard for the entire country. In these times of quickly changing economies, technologies and social awareness, the movement toward meeting the higher educational needs of more citizens within each community has never been more relevant," remarks Dr. John Pickelman, NHMCCD chancellor. "Gone is the view that college and university education is only for young adults during four consecutive years. New realities show us that college education and other formal training must recur during a person's entire life—lifelong learning. We now know that colleges and universities must provide additional opportunities that do not deny the traditions of higher education, but build upon them by reaching out to meet the educational needs of people who are location-bound by jobs, families and finances."[2]

The University Center is a seamless educational journey for community college students. They begin the freshman and sophomore leg of their college journey at one of the four NHMCCD colleges or at one of the several off-campus locations. As students transition into their upper level courses at The University Center, they already have a degree plan working, goals established, and a plethora of programs offering choices from any of six universities. All this without having to move or commute great distances.

"The University Center is the 'ultimate' with regard to access to higher education," says Dr. Nellie Thorogood, NHMCCD vice chancellor for external affairs. "Students will be able to enroll in a bachelor's or master's program, then choose several credit and non-credit courses from any of the six universities—all within easy reach from the community in which they live. It's better than an educational home-shopping network—it provides a multi-level education continuum for individuals..."[3]

Thorogood explains that the traditional mission for community colleges was to give students their freshman and sophomore-level coursework, then prepare them to transfer to four-year universities in order to earn a bachelor's degree. The University Center carries that mission to the highest order without ever leaving the community.

"Accomplishing The University Center's mission is a lot like building a car," explains Thorogood. When a giant General Motors-type company builds a car, it makes parts of the car in different places and sends the parts off to Detroit to be built into a finished Cadillac, truck or Corvette. Community colleges have been traditionally responsible for building the engines. They get the student "engines" running, then they send them off to be built into a whole car. At their respective universities, the "engines" get together with the other "parts" they need to become a car and have a successful career, complete with bachelor's degree. The University Center provides NHMCCD the opportunity to become the "Detroit" of education. The engine gets built by NHMCCD, and The University Center helps assemble the car

University Seals of the six University Center partners.

— all at one location. The graduated students, degree in hand, are "revved up" for their future.[4]

It's convenient. It's cost effective. It makes sense. And it was no accident.

## WANTING, WILLING AND WAITING

It all began 25 years ago, according to George P. Mitchell, chairman and CEO of Mitchell Energy & Development Corp. In addition to the incredible demographic growth in The Woodlands, there was an explosion of knowledge-based industries in the area: the Research Forest, now home to more than 32 technology-based corporations, the Houston Advanced Research Center (HARC), 300 Ph.D.s, and 800 additional area companies.

Mitchell and other community leaders wanted upper-level higher education to be more accessible to north Houston residents and industries for continuing education and job retraining. In 1968, the Texas Higher Education Coordinating Board recommended that the University of Houston establish two additional campuses in the metropolitan Houston area. It seemed a logical idea for the University of Houston to build a campus in The Woodlands akin to its southern Clear Lake campus, which is practically in NASA's backyard.

*Above left: Dr. John E. Pickelman, Chancellor of NHMCCD (left) and Elmer Beckendorf, Board member (right), receive a check from George P. Mitchell, chairman and CEO of Mitchell Energy & Development Corp.*

*Bottom right: Buckets and shovels for the Groundbreaking ceremony of The University Center, The Woodlands, Texas.*

Mitchell offered a 200-acre gift of prime land and a half million dollars to plan The Woodlands campus in 1972, but when University of Houston completed its Clear Lake campus and its University of Houston-Downtown campus, it was concluded by the Coordinating Board that the University of Houston campuses amply covered the northern and southern regions of Houston.

Mitchell and the University of Houston persisted. The University of Houston opened a center in The Woodlands in 1980 which operated there until 1988, when it moved to the Greenspoint area. The University of Houston's North Houston Institute eventually shared space with NHMCCD.

In 1984, the Coordinating Board was again approached about a University of Houston campus in The Woodlands. A bill passed in the state legislature that outlined a plan to build a $250,000 campus with state funds. Former Gov. Mark White vetoed the bill, partly because some state institutions were under threat of closing at the time due to decreases in enrollment.

Ever hopeful of building a full-service college campus in The Woodlands, Mitchell and other Woodlands community leaders in 1986 began taking a serious look at NHMCCD as a higher education option. Already braced with phenomenal success and three growing colleges: North Harris, Kingwood, and Tomball, NHMCCD was poised and positioned for north Houston. Community leaders appealed to Conroe Independent School District voters for approval of an annexation order so that a fourth campus could be built in Conroe.

In the mid-1980s, the annexation election passed in The Woodlands but failed in Conroe. Far from being discouraged, the annexation coalition better organized itself and created a group strengthened by participation from the Woodlands and Conroe chambers of commerce. In 1991, the annexation election passed. Mitchell sold NHMCCD 90 acres of land and gifted the college district with an additional 10 acres for Montgomery College. His 25-year dream of higher education in The Woodlands would become a reality.

Pickelman began his tenure with the college district in 1991 and picked up the torch carried by his predecessor, Dr. Joe Airola, George Mitchell, and others. "Frequently I was approached by residents throughout our district who recognized the need in our area for bachelor's and master's degree programs, and suggested that NHMCCD should expand to offer bachelor's degrees. The often-heard theme was, 'When will you grow up and be a four-year university?' Pickelman explains.[5]

"My response then, as it is today, is that maintaining the mission of NHMCCD as a comprehensive community college is absolutely critical to the social and economic development of our community. With 20 percent of the population having bachelor's degrees or higher, and with the projection that 70 percent of all skilled professional jobs will require training and education beyond high school, but not yet require a bachelor's or master's degrees, it was not difficult for us to conclude that we are more than sufficiently challenged in meeting the educational and training needs of the remaining 80 percent of our population. But the need for upper level higher education in our area persisted. We are more than one million people and 1,100 square miles, and we have no easy access to bachelor's or master's degrees," adds Pickelman.

"We believe that North Harris Montgomery Community College District is a catalyst in promoting a seamless educational journey and for nurturing the intellectual and cultural life of the community."[6]

A new chancellor, a clear vision and a new college for Montgomery County.

With construction and associate's degrees well underway for the new Montgomery College, efforts and enthusiasm never waned from developing new bachelor's and master's degree opportunities in The Woodlands.

Four years ago, Montgomery College president Bill Law, Thorogood, Pickelman and Dr. David Gottlieb, formerly with UH and current director of the Cynthia Woods Mitchell Pavilion, began studying the handful of university-type centers across the nation and brainstorming ideas. The abstract ideas jelled into The University Center, a public/private partnership where students could earn full bachelor's degrees, master's degrees, and continuing professional studies from many universities.

The University Center would be the first of its kind in Texas.

Law, Thorogood and Pickelman then went a-courtin'. Proposals and videotapes in hand, the group called on state university presidents and system chancellors and Dr. Kenneth Ashworth, commissioner of the Coordinating Board. And it wasn't always an easy sale, remarks Mitchell, who consistently served as the group's cheerleader.

"At first, the universities were concerned with turf protection, but they gradually started coming around," says Mitchell. John and Nellie have driven this thing. They know the bureaucratic language. They've kept The University Center alive."[7]

"It turned out that just about everybody wanted to dance, although several universities wanted to get a closer look at their partners and their dancing style before they committed," says Thorogood.[8]

"Working with six universities on a project is a little like herding cats," jokes Pickelman. "And Nellie is the chief cat-herder—armed with a luggage carrier filled with degree plan proposals and countless charts and graphs illustrating a seamless educational journey from our community colleges to the six universities. She is a tireless worker, and she rarely takes 'no' for an answer. The glass is always half full with Nellie."[9]

Thorogood credits much of the success of the project to an attitude strongly held by everyone involved with The University Center: "We have never given anybody a chance to say it won't work," she says. "We are constantly solving the problems and developing the opportunities."[10]

Early in 1994, the Texas Higher Education Coordinating Board approved The University Center. Then the tedious task began for developing degree plans for 50 unduplicated degrees, common student support services, library cooperation and distance education methods.

And it all started coming together. University partners currently include: Prairie View A&M University, Sam Houston State University, Texas A&M University, Texas Southern University,

Top left: William P. Hobby, Jr.,
Chancellor of the University of
Houston system, and former Lt.
Governor of Texas, takes the lead in
the groundbreaking ceremony.

Bottom left: Dr. Nellie Thorogood, vice
chancellor of external affairs; Dr. John
Pickelman, NHMCCD Chancellor;
and Randy Bates, member of the
NHMCCD Board of Trustees; present
gift to George Mitchell.

University of Houston, and University of
Houston-Downtown.

George Mitchell's gift of 10 acres and $2 million from The Woodlands Corporation provided the private funding for The University Center facility, NHMCCD voters provided the remaining $9 million when they approved a bond referendum in December 1995 to support the remaining construction and telecommunications hub.

In June 1997, Woodlands resident Gail Evans was named executive director and dean of The University Center by NHMCCD trustees. Evans serves as chief operations officer in charge of programs, student services, and activities.

"In addition to her vast experience in the world of academia, Gail's strength is in her commitment to students," says Thorogood. "She has already demonstrated a continuing and consistent commitment to help students achieve their personal goals by creating an environment that supports learning, but also includes flexible education delivery systems to accommodate their complex lives.

"She understands that students' education doesn't stop at the classroom door," Thorogood continues. "That's what The University Center is all about: innovation in education. Gail is an innovator of the first order."

## DEGREE PLANS

One of the first major decisions made for The University Center was the designation of unduplicated degrees to be offered by the universities. Initially, partner universities will offer 26 bachelor's and 24 master's degree programs at The University Center. Additionally, the bachelor of applied arts and sciences degree will open opportunities for 31 NHMCCD associate of applied arts and sciences degrees to articulate for the bachelor's degree. This creates many new opportunities for NHMCCD graduates who obtained their A.A.S. degrees, have been employed in their profession, and now have the opportunity to achieve a bachelor's degree and continue their lifelong learning journey.

NHMCCD colleges will provide the freshman and sophomore courses for the bachelor's degrees utilizing seamless, articulated A.A., A.S., and A.A.S. degrees as the link from the community college to the university.

## THE COMMON GOALS FOR THE COMMON GOOD

On June 13, 1996, 12 buckets emblazoned with the logos from all six universities and the NHMCCD campuses were filled with soil from the "home campuses" and were arranged at The University Center site.

In a new twist to the traditional shovel-dig at most groundbreaking ceremonies, administrators chose instead to break ground, then spread the soil from all the partner university buckets in a symbolic gesture of educational commitment and unity.

Thorogood explains that the idea of the "ground-sharing" was that future students would actually walk on the "grounds" of their university when they stepped foot on The University Center grounds.

The ceremony was completed by Rev. W.D. Broadway, Interfaith of The Woodlands, who blessed The University Center grounds and sprinkled the soil with holy water.

Randy Bates, chairman of the NHMCCD Board of Trustees, said: "From Acres Homes to The Woodlands, from Tomball to Lake Houston, from New Caney to Greenspoint and Humble to Conroe, The University Center is the long await-ed connection to bachelor's and to master's degrees. We believe this investment in commu-nity development and people's lives is what North Harris Montgomery Community College District is all about. The progress of the people is what we are about."[11]

Dr. John Pickelman, chancellor of North Harris Montgomery Community College District explained: "This ceremony is not so much about the symbolism of breaking ground and the subsequent production of brick and mortar, as it is about serving people and the partnerships that have been forged to meet the needs of the people."[12]

Dr. Nellie Thorogood, vice chancellor for external affairs said: "Today we gather to capture the richness and quality of the universities, community college, private sector and the com-munity to "ground break" new partnerships, a new facility, and new technologies. We believe the common goals and common ground shared indeed will produce individual and community successes over many lifetimes. We believe that this will connect us to the future and indeed improve higher education for the common good of our region and our communities."[13]

Former Lt. Governor William P. Hobby, Jr. added: "The state of Texas is embarking on a new adventure in higher education. This is a new breed. This is the wave of the future. This is the most economical way of delivering higher edu-cation. And we are honored to be a part of it."[14]

George P. Mitchell, chairman and CEO of Mitchell Energy & Development Corporation, was instrumental in the development of The University Center concept. "The University Center is the educational capstone for our com-munity. The dream is finally being realized, and higher education will be within reach for citi-zens of all ages, from all walks of life."[15]

## BRICKS AND MORTAR... AND MORE

"The University Center facility will be like a beautiful higher education shopping mall," describes Dr. Duane Hansen, project developer for The University Center.[16]

Hansen, a retired senior vice president from Miami Dade Community College, was looking forward to spending some time with his "grand-babies" in his golden years, but, "This new baby— this University Center—called to me. I just could-ndn't resist," says Hansen, who has responsibility for planning the facility, working with the archi-tects, the contractors and with the university part-ners to orchestrate the blending the instructional

*The University Center in progress.*

*Construction of The University Center.*

programs with the building specifications.

"Although it will be very close to the Montgomery College campus, The University Center will have an identity all its own," says Hansen. He describes the three-story, 78,000-square-foot building as very open, with an abundance of glass, glass blocks and a majestic three-story entryway. But the beauty doesn't end in just the aesthetic sense, although it is "aesthetically amazing," he adds.

The University Center facility will be filled with "smart stations," locations where students can plug in their own computers or check e-mail, engage Internet or hook into the interactive library at any of the facility's many open computers.

Primarily, the facility will be interactive classrooms, seminar and conference rooms, group and individual study areas, computer rooms and lecture halls. The learning resource area will provide electronic access to services and reference materials at the libraries of each of the partner universities, local public libraries, and the Jones Library at the Texas Medical Center. Hansen says students will also have access to Montgomery College's library and Extended Learning Center.

Hansen likens The University Center to a shopping mall because of its focus on satisfying the customer. "Why do people go to malls? They don't want to run around town to do their shopping. They want to get all their shopping done in one location. The same is true for students attending The University Center: Students want to have a choice of universities and program offerings at a one-stop, multi-shop place."

And like a shopping mall, Hansen says The University Center will cater to a broad range of people. "You'll see a broader mix of people at the center. We'll certainly have a large number of the traditional college students in their early 20s, but we'll also have a lot of adult students completing their bachelor's degrees and master's degrees or re-directing their careers, in addition

to corporate students who are part of the executive MBA programs."

He further explains that, not only will The University Center focus on tailoring its offerings to individual needs, but also to industry needs. "Industry needs to have relevant education offered at the times and places convenient for employees."

"The heart and soul of The University Center will be at the facility, but the arms, legs and everything else are at the colleges and universities," continues Thorogood. "Educational programs will come to students in person at the facility or electronically or interactively."[17]

The facility includes classrooms, seminar rooms, and laboratories to support the delivery of bachelor's, master's and professional development training offered through The University Center. The only specialized laboratories in the facility are those designed for the Texas A&M University Electronic and Telecommunications Engineering Technology Program.

## TELECOMMUNICATIONS HUB AND INTERACTIVE TECHNOLOGY

The University Center is committed to maximizing the use of information technology, interactive delivery systems and telecommunications for delivery of:

- Instruction
- Laboratory simulation and observation
- Library and learning resources support
- Interconnected student support
- Database approach to common application process (utilizing the national standards for higher education common applications electronic data transfer)
- Transcript analysis and common data elements for report generation

This is accomplished through a telecommunications "hub" approach that will be interactive among the universities and The University Center, with The University Center interconnecting to all four NHMCCD colleges and their centers.

The facility also includes a state-of-the-art technology training center, which will serve secondary and higher education faculty and staff, as well as industry trainers, by integrating technology and distance learning techniques.

RWS Architects, Inc., is the project architect for The University Center. Tellepsen Corporation is the general contractor.

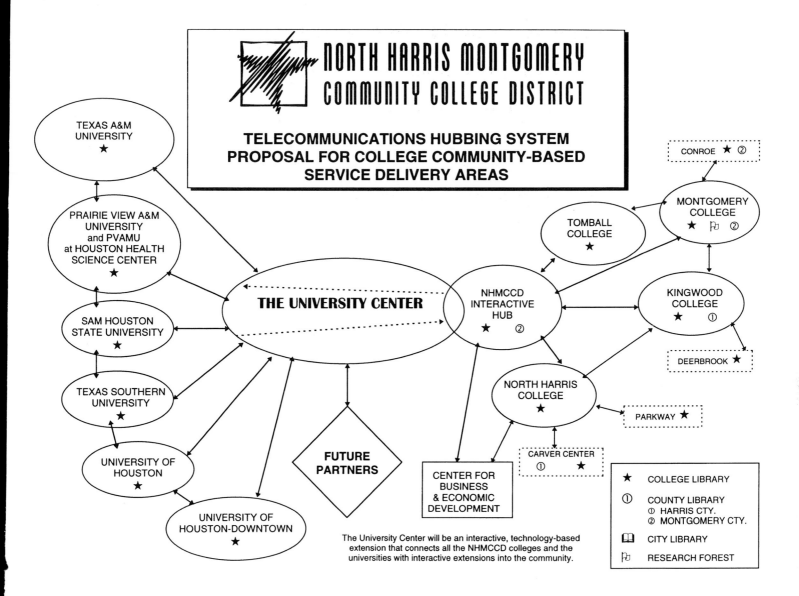

## NORTH HARRIS MONTGOMERY COMMUNITY COLLEGE DISTRICT

### TELECOMMUNICATIONS HUBBING SYSTEM PROPOSAL FOR COLLEGE COMMUNITY-BASED SERVICE DELIVERY AREAS

TEXAS A&M UNIVERSITY ★

PRAIRIE VIEW A&M UNIVERSITY and PVAMU at HOUSTON HEALTH SCIENCE CENTER ★

SAM HOUSTON STATE UNIVERSITY ★

TEXAS SOUTHERN UNIVERSITY ★

UNIVERSITY OF HOUSTON ★

UNIVERSITY OF HOUSTON-DOWNTOWN ★

THE UNIVERSITY CENTER

FUTURE PARTNERS

CENTER FOR BUSINESS & ECONOMIC DEVELOPMENT

NHMCCD INTERACTIVE HUB ★ ②

TOMBALL COLLEGE ★

MONTGOMERY COLLEGE ★ Pʋ ②

CONROE ★ ②

KINGWOOD COLLEGE ★ ①

DEERBROOK ★

NORTH HARRIS COLLEGE ★

CARVER CENTER ① ★

PARKWAY ★

★ COLLEGE LIBRARY
① COUNTY LIBRARY
  ① HARRIS CTY.
  ② MONTGOMERY CTY.
📖 CITY LIBRARY
Pʋ RESEARCH FOREST

The University Center will be an interactive, technology-based extension that connects all the NHMCCD colleges and the universities with interactive extensions into the community.

## BUSINESS PARTNERSHIPS

"A reason many people in this area don't complete their bachelor's degrees is because there is no outlet in the area," says Lee Murdy, vice president of client services for Kingwood-based Administaff. "I think having a bachelor's degree is more important today than it was five to 10 years ago. The competition is greater today than it used to be."[18]

There are three categories of people who will especially benefit from The University Center, says Dr. Nellie Thorogood. "One group is students who have completed their associate's degrees but, because of family and work commitments, have not been able to finish their bachelor's degrees," she says. "The second group is the students who have some college and want to finish. I encounter these people almost daily. I saw one at a service station the other night. He said, 'I

wanted to finish my bachelor's degree, but I didn't get to.' I said, 'Have we got a deal for you.'"

A third group, she says, is composed of professionals in such fields as nursing and engineering technology. Offering these degrees will also spur economic development, Thorogood believes.

Congressman Kevin Brady believes that The University Center partners will be more responsive than traditional four-year institutions in meeting the technical training needs of area employers. "NHMCCD is very aggressive in identifying what employers need and what types of skills their employees will need in the future," he says. "That relationship between businesses and the NHMCCD and The University Center partners translates to a very responsive higher education center."[19]

The University Center will be an important factor for both current and relocating businesses

*Telecommunications Hub.*

*Above: RWS Architects Bruce Wallace and John Robertson with Dr. Nellie Thorogood and Duane Hansen (left).*

*Opposite: Dr. Gail Evans, dean and executive director, and Dr. Nellie Thorogood, vice chancellor of external affairs, anticipate the grand opening of The University Center.*

PHOTO: HOUSTON CHRONICLE.

in the area, says Heather Montgomery, president of the North Houston-Greenspoint Chamber of Commerce.

"Education is where it's at," she says. "As businesses move into the area, they will recognize that their employees can receive an expanded education. With the growth in technology, more people will need bachelor's degrees."[20]

## WHERE WILL THE UNIVERSITY CENTER TAKE THE COMMUNITY AND EDUCATION IN THE FUTURE?

The University Center will fill in the education gap in the north Houston region with adult literacy to general academic, workforce development training, bachelor's degrees to research and development at HARC. Dr. Thorogood states:

"If the communities and businesses in the north will capture and use those components for new resources, local and regional economies will thrive. It provides full-scope higher education."[21]

The University Center is the culmination of a new strategy that will link businesses to universities and community colleges to produce a highly-trained workforce for the future. It's not only a culmination of many strategies and dreams—The University Center is a brilliant and enduring commitment to higher education in the Gulf Coast region of Texas.

## INTERACTIVE FUTURES

The founders of The University Center believe that "virtual" classrooms with interactive real-time telecommunications will connect us to the future by extending learning far beyond a classroom environment into neighborhoods, the workplace and entire communities.

Possible future projects include:

- *Doctoral degree offerings*
- *Additional partner universities joining The University Center*
- *Alliances with businesses.* Currently, an industry and education alliance is proposed for the purpose of information sharing, intellectual dialogue and discovery, technology transfer, education, training, supplier network connections, and strategic direction setting regarding interactive technologies and applications for industry, education, training (and retraining), research, organizational development and problem solving within the greater Houston area and the Gulf Coast. Alliance membership will be by annual subscription and provide a number of direct services and interaction among alliance members.
- *Possibility for individuals will be "virtually" unlimited.* The "shoe box full of transcripts" individuals; the "briefcase full of in-house training" professionals; and the "lunch-box full of certificates" employees will be able to continuously learn at home, the office and in the field, and perhaps even on off-shore platforms.

"Individuals and businesses will have a bright future at The University Center," says Thorogood. "This dream is a plan put to action to make a new interactive future for many generations into the 21st century."[22] The University Center opened in January 1998.

A Work in Progress...

# NOTES

[1] NHMCCD, *Maxim*, Summer 1996, p. 1.

[2] Dr. John Pickelman, interview by Kathie Scobee Fulgham, 1996.

[3] Dr. Nellie Thorogood, interview by Kathie Scobee Fulgham, 1996.

[4] Ibid.

[5] Pickleman, interview by Kathie Scobee Fulgham, 1996.

[6] Ibid.

[7] George Mitchell, interview by Kathie S. Fulgham, 1996.

[8] Thorogood, interview by Kathie S. Fulgham, 1996.

[9] Pickelman, interview by Kathie S. Fulgham, 1996.

[10] Thorogood, interview by Kathie S. Fulgham, 1996.

[11] Groundbreaking ceremony, June 13, 1996.

[12] Ibid.

[13] Ibid.

[14] Ibid.

[15] Ibid.

[16] Dr. Duane Hansen, interview by Kathie S. Fulgham, 1996.

[17] Thorogood, interview by Kathie Scobee Fulgham, 1996.

[18] *Maxim*, Summer 1996, p. 1.

[19] Ibid.

[20] Ibid, p.2.

[21] Thorogood, interview by Kathie S. Fulgham, 1996.

[22] Ibid.

# BIBLIOGRAPHY

## Documents and Collections

Aldine Independent School District. "Aldine, A Future with a Plan," Promotional pamphlet, 1973. North Harris College archives.

Aldine Independent School District. Archives and historical collection.

Bush, George W. Governor, State of Texas. "Community Colleges, The Oil of the Twenty-First Century," Dedication speech, Montgomery College, 1995.

Greater Houston Community Junior College Commission, Local Survey Report: A Comprehensive Survey in Support of Application to Establish a Public Junior College. July 15, 1968.

Harris County, County Clerk's Office, Archives. Deed search on select 19th and 20th century maps and deeds pertaining to local communities (Aldine, Westfield, Spring, Humble) in northern Harris county, and North Harris College land. Houston, Texas.

Harris County, Department of Education. Annual Report. L.L. Pugh, County School Superintendent, "Report of Harris County Schools for Year ending August 31, 1910."

Houston Metropolitan Research Center, Houston Public Library- Archives. Schleuter photograph collection.

Houston North Association, *Minutes*, 3 vols., 1962-1975. North Harris College archives.

Houston North Association, "North Houston's Urban Pioneers: The Houston North Association 1962-1984." North Harris College archives.

Humble Museum, Archives. Humble, Texas.

Humble Museum, "The Humble, Texas Area,"pamphlet, (no date).

Klein, Texas Historical Foundation, Photographs- Robinson collection. Spring, Texas.

Klein Independent School District, Letter from Edwin Theiss, President of the Board of Trustees, to E.M. Wells, Citizen's Committee, Union Junior College (North Harris County College), April 11,1972.

Koetter, Tharp & Cowell (KTC) Architects. Letter to E.M. Wells, President of the Board of Trustees, North Harris County College, April 11, 1972.

Koetter, Tharp & Cowell (KTC) Architects. Report. Site Evaluation for North Harris County Junior College, 1972. North Harris College archives.

Lee College, Letter from Raymond Cleveland, President of Lee College, to E.M. Wells, Chairman of North Harris County College Steering Committee, July 21, 1972. E.M. Wells private collection.

North Harris College, Learning Resource Center. Archival photographs.

North Harris College, Learning Resource Center. News Releases, 4 vols., compiled by Karen Kincheloe, 1974-1984.

North Harris College, NHCC History, Student History Project, collection of interviews, 1975.

North Harris County Junior College Committee (Steering Committee), Local Survey Report: A Comprehensive Survey in Support of Application to Establish a Public Junior College. July 21, 1972.

North Harris County Junior College Committee (Steering Committee), *Minutes*. 1971.

North Harris County Junior College Committee (Steering Committee), "Our Next Big Step," campaign brochure, 1971. North Harris College archives.

North Harris County Junior College Committee (Steering Committee), "Public Hearing on the Proposed North Harris County Junior College District," June 20, 1972.

North Harris Montgomery Community College District, Board of Trustees, *Minutes*, 1972-1997.

North Harris Montgomery Community College District, District Office. Building Contract with North Harris County Junior College and Fleetwood Construction Company, January 11, 1974.

North Harris Montgomery Community College District, District Office. Deed- North Harris County College, 1973.

Pickelman, John E., Chancellor. North Harris Montgomery Community College District. "Message from the Chancellor," *Maxim*, Vol. 4, No.3, 1996.

Pickelman, John E., Chancellor. North Harris Montgomery Community College District. Vision Statement, 1996.

Robertson, E.C. "Aldine in Midwinter, As Portrayed by Kodak,"(promotional pamphlet on Aldine), February 1909. Aldine ISD.

Robertson, E.C. "All Doubts Dispelled by the Doubters Themselves,"(promotional pamphlet on Aldine), 1909. Aldine ISD.

Spring Independent School District, Local History archives.

Texas Education Agency, *Texas School Law Bulletin*. Austin, Texas,1994.

Texas Forestry Museum, Lufkin, Texas. Sawmill Database- Northern Harris County and Montgomery County.

Thorne, W.W., Superintendent of Aldine ISD. Letter addressed to Members of the North Harris County Junior College Steering Committee, July 25, 1972.

Thorne, W.W., President of North Harris County College, Letter to Louie Welch, Mayor of Houston, March 1, 1973.

Tomball Independent School District, School Board, Special Minutes, 1982.

United States Government. President's Commission on Higher Education (Truman's Commission), *For American Democracy, A Report of the President's Commission on Higher Education*, Vols. 1-6. New York: Harper & Brothers, 1947.

## Newspapers

*Conroe Courier.*

*Houston Chronicle.*

*Houston Post.*

*The Humble News-Messenger.*

*Humble Observer.*

*The News.*

*The North Freeway Leader.*

*The Northeast Sentinel.*

*North Harris College, The Paper.*

*North Harris County News.*

*Tomball (Texas) Potpourri Newspaper.*

## Articles

Maxwell, Zach. "The Story of his Dreams." *Ellipsis*, NHMCCD, Fall 1994.

Rhinehart, Marilyn D. "Country to City: North Harris County College and the Changing Scene in Gulf Coast East Texas." *Houston Review*, 1982.

Smith, Kathleen Bland. "Crossroads in Texas," found in Roger Yarrington, ed., *Junior Colleges, Fifty States, Fifty Years*. American Association of Junior Colleges, Washington, D.C., 1969.

## Unpublished Papers, Memoirs

Clark, B.F., Principal. "The History of Southwell, The Spring School For Black Students," report, (no date). Spring ISD archives.

Grandy, William Harley. "A History of Montgomery County, Texas." Master's Thesis, University of Houston, 1952.

Severance, Diana. "Klein, Texas," Klein, Texas Historical Foundation, 1994. Peter Wunderlich collection of letters, May 6, 1853 and April 13,1857.

Tullos, Gladys Hildebrandt. "A German Family Contributes to the Development of Spring, My Family Heritage," memoir. Spring ISD, 1986.

## Interviews

Joe Airola, interviewed by Link Hullar. Houston, Texas, 1996; interviewed by William D. Law, Jr., 1996; interviewed by Theresa McGinley. Houston, Texas, 1996.

Ed Albracht, interviewed by Rebecca Tate. Tomball, Texas, 1996.

Richard Almstedt, correspondance with Theresa McGinley, 1996.

Rose Austin, interviewed by Link Hullar. Houston, Texas, 1996.

H.E. Barrett, San Jacinto River Authority, interviewed by Theresa McGinley. Conroe, Texas, 1996.

Marie Bayard, interviewed by Theresa McGinley. The Woodlands, Texas, 1996.

Arthur Bayer, interviewed by Theresa McGinley. Houston, Texas, 1996.

Elmer Beckendorf, interviewed by Theresa McGinley. Houston, Texas, 1997; interviewed by Rebecca Tate. Rose Hill, Texas, 1996.

Debbie Bell, interviewed by Douglas Boyd. Tomball, Texas, 1996.

Diane Blanco, interviewed by Dean Wolfe. Houston, Texas, 1996.

Rep. Kevin Brady, interviewed by William D. Law, Jr., The Woodlands, Texas, 1996.

Joyce Brown, correspondance with Theresa McGinley. Coldspring, Texas, 1997.

Linda Bryan, interviewed by Rebecca Tate. Tomball, Texas, 1996.

Lester Burks, interviewed by Theresa McGinley. Houston, Texas, 1996.

Francette Carnahan, interviewed by Rebecca Tate. Tomball, Texas, 1996.

Charles Chance, correspondance with Theresa McGinley, 1996.

B.F. Clark, interviewed by Theresa McGinley. Spring, Texas, 1997.

Gary Clark, interviewed by Theresa McGinley. Houston, Texas, 1996.

Bob Colt, interviewed by Link Hullar. Kingwood, Texas, 1996.

W.E. Crozier, interviewed by Theresa McGinley. Houston, Texas, 1996.

Steve Davis, interviewed by Link Hullar. Kingwood, Texas, 1996.

Mark Dial, interviewed by Douglas Boyd. Tomball, Texas, 1996.

Roger Galatas, interviewed by William D. Law, Jr., 1996.

Charles Gillis, interviewed by Dean Wolfe, 1994.

David Gottlieb, interviewed by William D. Law, Jr., 1996.

Rick Grimes, interviewed by Rebecca Tate. Tomball, Texas, 1996.

Steve Haberman, interviewed by Rebecca Tate. Tomball, Texas, 1996.

Duane Hansen, interviewed by Kathie Scobee Fulgham. Houston, Texas, 1996.

Hap Harrington, interviewed by Douglas Boyd. Tomball, Texas, 1996.

Dan Hauser, interviewed by William D. Law, Jr., 1996.

Steve Head, interviewed by Link Hullar. Kingwood, Texas, 1996.

Carolyn Hohl, interviewed by Rebecca Tate. Tomball, Texas, 1996.

Diane Holland, interviewed by Douglas Boyd. Tomball, Texas, 1996.

Joseph Kaough, interviewed by Theresa McGinley. Houston, Texas, 1996.

Karen Kincheloe, interviewed by Theresa McGinley. Houston, Texas, 1996.

Linda King, interviewed by Dean Wolfe, 1996.

Marilyn Theiss Kron, interviewed by Theresa McGinley. Houston, Texas, 1996.

Roy Lazenby, interviewed by Theresa McGinley. Tomball, Texas, 1996; interviewed by Rebecca Tate. Tomball, Texas, 1996.

Joan Link, interviewed by Theresa McGinley. Houston, Texas, 1996.

Sandra Lloyd, interviewed by Rebecca Tate. Tomball, Texas, 1996.

Tom Lovell, interviewed by Rebecca Tate. Tomball, Texas, 1996.

Elizabeth Lunden, interviewed by Link Hullar. Kingwood, Texas, 1996.

Hulon Madeley, interviewed by Rebecca Tate. Tomball, Texas, 1996.

Chris Martin, interviewed by Dean Wolfe. Kingwood, Texas, 1996.

Mary Matteson, interviewed by William D. Law, Jr., 1996.

Joe McMillian, interviewed by Theresa McGinley. Houston, Texas, 1996.

Joyce McQueen, correspondance with Theresa McGinley. Houston, Texas, 1997.

Joseph Minton, interviewed by Link Hullar, 1996.

George Mitchell, interviewed by Kathie Scobee Fulgham. The Woodlands, Texas, 1996.

M.M. "Rusty" Morris, interviewed by Theresa McGinley. Houston, Texas, 1996.

Scott Nelson, interviewed by Link Hullar. Kingwood, Texas, 1996.

Louise Panzarella, interviewed by Theresa McGinley. Humble, Texas, 1996.

Katherine Persson, interviewed by Link Hullar. Kingwood, Texas, 1996.

Janice Peyton, interviewed by Douglas Boyd. The Woodlands, Texas, 1996.

Larry Phillips, correspondance with Theresa McGinley, 1996.

John E. Pickelman, interviewed by Kathie Scobee Fulgham. Houston, Texas, 1996.

Camille Pittman, interviewed by Rebecca Tate. Tomball, Texas, 1996.

Michael Richard, interviewed by Douglas Boyd. Tomball, Texas, 1996.

John M. Robinson, interviewed by Theresa McGinley. Houston, Texas, 1996-1997.

Joan Samuelson, interviewed by Link Hullar. Kingwood, Texas, 1996.

Arlene Schultz, interviewed by Theresa McGinley, 1996.

Betty Shafer, interviewed by Dean Wolfe, 1996.

Brian Shmaefsky, interviewed by Dean Wolfe, 1996.

Sanford Shugart, interviewed by Geraldine Gallagher. Houston, Texas, 1996.

Anna Stafford, interviewed by Douglas Boyd. Tomball, Texas, 1996.

Rebecca Tautenhahn Strack Stone, interviewed by Theresa McGinley. Rosehill, Texas, 1996.

Patsy Talbert, interviewed by Link Hullar, 1996.

W.W. Thorne, interviewed by Theresa McGinley. Houston, Texas, 1996.

Nellie Carr Thorogood, interviewed by Kathie Scobee Fulgham. Houston, Texas, 1996; interviewed by Geraldine Gallagher, 1996; interviewed by Link Hullar, 1996.

Lee Topham, interviewed by Link Hullar. Kingwood, Texas, 1996.

Lessie Upchurch, interviewed by Douglas Boyd. Tomball, Texas, 1996.

Bruce Wallace, interviewed by Douglas Boyd. Houston, Texas, 1996.

Candace Washburn, interviewed by Dean Wolfe. Kingwood, Texas, 1996.

E.M. Wells, interviewed by Theresa McGinley. Houston, Texas, 1996.

Penny Westerfeld, interviewed by Link Hullar. Kingwood, Texas, 1996.

Sondra Whitlow, interviewed by Dean Wolfe. Kingwood, Texas, 1996.

Bob Williams, interviewed by Theresa McGinley. Houston, Texas, 1996.

George Younger, interviewed by Rebecca Tate. Tomball, Texas, 1996.

Nockie Zizelmann, interviewed by Douglas Boyd, 1996.

## Books

American Association of University Women, North Harris County Branch, *The Heritage of North Harris County*, (n.p.), 1977.

American Cultures Class, Spring High School South, *Spring Lofts and Lore*. Houston, Texas: Armstrong Printing Co., 1977-78.

Brint, Steven and Jerome Karabel. *The Diverted Dream, Community Colleges and the Promise of Educational Opportunity in America, 1900-1985*. New York: Oxford University Press, 1989.

Cohen, Arthur M. and Florence B. Brawer. *The American Community College*. California: Jossey-Bass Publishers, 1989.

Fountain, Ben E. and Terrence A. Tollefson. *Community Colleges in the United States: Forty-Nine State Systems*. Washington, D.C.: American Association of Community and Junior Colleges, 1989.

Gleazer, Edmund. *This Is the Community College*. New York: Houghton Mifflin Co., 1968.

Harrington, Shirley Klein, ed., *A Tribute to Tomball: A Pictorial History of the Tomball Area* .n.p., 1982.

Johnston, Marguerite. Houston, *The Unknown City*, 1836-1946. College Station: Texas A & M University Press, 1991.

Jordan, Terry. *German Seed in Texas Soil, Immigrant Farmers in Nineteenth Century Texas*. Austin: University of Texas Press, 1966.

Landrith, Harold F. *Introduction to the Community Junior College*. Illinois: Interstate Printers and Publishers, 1971.

McComb, David. *Houston, A History*. Austin: University of Texas Press, 1981.

Montgomery, Robin. *The History of Montgomery County*. Austin: Jenkins Publishing Company, 1975.

Payne, Richard and Drexel Turner. *The Woodlands*. The Woodlands Corporation, 1995.

Phillippe, Kent, ed. *National Profile of Community Colleges: Trends and Statistics, 1995-1996*. American Association of Community Colleges, Washington, D.C., 1995.

Texas State Historical Association, *The Handbook of Texas*. Austin, Texas, 1952; *The New Handbook of Texas*, (6 vols.), Austin, 1996.

Upchurch, Lessie. *Welcome to Tomball, A History of Tomball, Texas*. Houston, Texas: D. Armstrong Co., Inc.,1976.

Whisenhunt, Donald W. *The Encyclopedia of Texas Colleges and Universities, An Historical Profile*. Austin, Texas: Eakin Press, 1986.

Wiggs, Jon Lee. *The Community College System in North Carolina: A Silver Anniversary History, 1963-1988*. Raleigh, North Carolina: North Carolina State Board of Community Colleges, 1989.

Works Progress Administration, *Houston, A History and Guide*. Anson Jones Press, 1942.